War in Greek Mythology

By the Same Author

Women in Ancient Rome (2013)
Roman Women: The Women Who Influenced Roman History (2015)
In Bed with the Romans (2015)
Wars and Battles of the Roman Republic (2015)
Roman Military Disasters* (2015)
In Bed with the Ancient Greeks (2016)
Ancient Greece in 100 Facts (2017)
Women in Ancient Greece (2017)
When in Rome…A Sourcebook for Daily Life in Ancient Rome (2017)
Women at War in the Classical World* (2017 and 2020 in Paperback)
How to be a Roman (2017)
Wars and Battles of Ancient Greece (2018)
Roman Record-Keeping & Communications (2018)
Emperors of Rome: The Monsters* (2018)
Rome: Republic into Empire – The Civil Wars of the First Century BCE* (2019)
The Romans in the North of England (2019)
Reportage from Ancient Greece and Rome (2019)
War in Roman Myth and Legend* (in press)
Marvels, Mysteries & Magic in the Ancient World (in press)

* Denotes titles in print with Pen & Sword Books

War in Greek Mythology

Paul Chrystal

Pen & Sword
MILITARY

First published in Great Britain in 2020 by
Pen & Sword Military
An imprint of
Pen & Sword Books Ltd
Yorkshire – Philadelphia

ISBN 978 1 52676 616 8

A CIP catalogue record for this book is
available from the British Library.

Typeset by Mac Style
Printed and bound in the UK by TJ International Ltd,
Padstow, Cornwall.

Pen & Sword Books Limited incorporates the imprints of Atlas,
Archaeology, Aviation, Discovery, Family History, Fiction, History,
Maritime, Military, Military Classics, Politics, Select, Transport,
True Crime, Air World, Frontline Publishing, Leo Cooper, Remember
When, Seaforth Publishing, The Praetorian Press, Wharncliffe
Local History, Wharncliffe Transport, Wharncliffe True Crime
and White Owl.

For a complete list of Pen & Sword titles please contact

PEN & SWORD BOOKS LIMITED
47 Church Street, Barnsley, South Yorkshire, S70 2AS, England
E-mail: enquiries@pen-and-sword.co.uk
Website: www.pen-and-sword.co.uk

Or

PEN AND SWORD BOOKS
1950 Lawrence Rd, Havertown, PA 19083, USA
E-mail: Uspen-and-sword@casematepublishers.com
Website: www.penandswordbooks.com

'*Greek myths, early Roman history, is configured around violence against women. And I think we need to get in there, get our hands dirty, face it, and see why and how it was.*'

Mary Beard

'*The higher Greek poetry did not make up fictitious plots; its business was to express the heroic saga, the myths.*'

Gilbert Murray

Front Cover Image: Triumphant Achilles: Achilles dragging the dead body of Hector in front of the gates of Troy. The original painting (1892) is a fresco on the upper level of the main hall of the Achilleion at Corfu, Greece.

Franz Matsch (1861–1942)
Photographer: User: Dr.K.

Contents

Acknowledgements

My thanks to Susan Deacy, Professor of Classics, University of Roehampton, London for permission to quote from her work on Greek myth and autism which has resulted in a project whose goal was to develop activities for autistic children focused around classical myth. This can be seen at https://www.facebook.com/search/top/?q=susan%20deacy&epa=SEARCH_BOX Please also have a look at http://myth-autism.blogspot.com/, Susan Deacy's blog on autism and the Greek myths.

About the Author

Paul Chrystal has Classics degrees from the Universities of Hull and Southampton. He then went into medical publishing for more than thirty years but now combines this with writing features for national newspapers and history magazines such as *Minerva Magazine*, *BBC History Magazine*, *Ancient History Magazine*, *Omnibus* and *Ad Familiares*. He has appeared regularly on BBC local radio on the BBC World Service and Radio 4's PM programme. He has been history advisor for a number of York tourist attractions and is the author of 100 or so books on a wide range of subjects, including many on ancient Greece and Rome, and specifically women, sexuality, war and conflict in those civilizations. He is a regular reviewer for and contributor to *Classics for All* and a contributor to the Classics section of OUP's *Oxford Bibliographies Online*. He is a prepublication referee for Yale University Press. He is the editor of *York Historian*, the journal of the Yorkshire Architectural & York Archaeological Society. Paul is also guest speaker for the prestigious Vassar College New York's London Programme in association with Goldsmith University. He lives near York and is married with three grown-up children.

York, May 2020
www.paulchrystal.com

Preface

This is the first of two books on war and conflict in Greek and Roman mythology and legend.

Even though war, and conflict generally, form a seminal part of Greek and Roman mythology and Roman legend, comparatively little has been written on the subject either in books or in scholarly articles. A search through the indexes of the most influential books on Greek mythology published in the late twentieth and early twenty-first centuries will reveal few entries for 'war' as a specific topos: Giants, Titans, Trojan heroes and Hercules are all there but it is only indirectly and tangentially that 'war' per se is treated. This is perhaps surprising because wars and battles in the mythologies and legends of both civilizations are freighted with symbolism and were laden with meaning and significance; historical, political, social and cultural. The gods and goddesses of war are prominent members of the pantheons of both Greece and Rome; in addition many other deities and heroes were by no means averse to belligerence and dabbled in conflict in one form or another. In Greece the Theban and Trojan Wars were of major significance culturally; for Rome the battles to secure its very foundations were similarly crucial.

These books then – the second is *War in Roman Mythology and Legend* – are an attempt to collect together the mythologies relating to war and conflict in Greece and Rome as depicted both in literature and the visual arts and to explain, where possible, their symbolism and significance.

The battles fought by and between Titans, Giants and Amazons, between centaurs and Lapiths, and by heroes like Heracles were pivotal in the annals of Greek civilization. The Trojan War itself had massive consequences for the troubled Greek houses of Atreus and Thebes and for the many heroes who battled relentlessly around the Mediterranean on their various ways home.

All of this is covered here in this first book which shows how conflict in mythology and legend resonated loudly as essential, even existentialist symbols in Greek culture and how they are represented in classical literature, philosophy, religion, feminism, art, statuary, ceramics, architecture, numismatics, etymology, astronomy and even vulcanology.

The book concludes with a survey of how Greek mythology and legend has been adapted, repurposed and rewritten and put to good use in modern culture and society, not just in retellings but in radical literary and theatrical interpretations, and indeed the use of Greek myths in the treatment of those on the autistic spectrum. To ensure the ongoing survival of these wonderful myths we need to harness, harvest and encourage, more than ever, the ingenuity and inventiveness of those who are striving to keep them dynamic, vigorous and relevant.

Chapter One

Introduction: Exploding Myth

Exploding myth

Myths and mythology provide some of the most exciting adventure stories in the literature and visual arts of many cultures and societies. Yet what exactly is a myth? The reader or researcher could be forgiven for thinking that there are as many theories on what constitutes a myth as there are myths. One of the most popular definitions is given by the Finnish folklorist Lauri Honko:

> Myth, a story of the gods, a religious account of the beginning of the world, the creation, fundamental events, the exemplary deeds of the gods as a result of which the world, nature and culture were created together with all parts thereof and given their order, which still obtains. A myth expresses and confirms society's religious values and norms, it provides a pattern of behavior to be imitated, testifies to the efficacy of ritual with its practical ends and establishes the sanctity of cult.

Alan Dundes defines myth as 'a sacred narrative explaining how the world and man came to be in their present form.' Dundes classified a sacred narrative as 'a story that serves to define the fundamental world view of a culture by explaining aspects of the natural world and delineating the psychological and social practices and ideals of a society.' To him, 'the critical adjective *sacred* distinguishes myth from other forms of narrative such as folktales, which are ordinarily secular and fictional.'[1] They are 'sacred' because knowledge and dissemination of them can be exclusive to priests, shamans or other religious officials. However, myths were never prescriptive or dogmatic: the Greek never turned to his or her mythology for guidance on how to behave or for his or her morals and ethics. Anthropologist Bruce Lincoln defines myth as 'ideology in narrative form'.[2]

2 War in Greek Mythology

Some would argue that the Greek myths and the various adventures, events, monsters and heroes they cover are the most dramatic and exciting of all mythologies. They give us sex, incest and bestiality; they celebrate hermaphrodism, heterosexual and homosexual love, family strife, domestic violence, infidelity, murder, rape, human sacrifice, fantastic creatures, hybrid forms, giants and monsters, bogeywomen, cannibalism, the supernatural, witches, witchcraft and magic; they glory in hate, fear, loathing, jealousy and revenge; they explain the origin of natural phenomena, places, palaces, names, cities and towns, cult sites, monuments, tribes, races and ritual; they are forever metamorphosing and transmogrifying; they blur gender identities and boundaries; they queer sexuality and they describe life after death and the hell for some and utopia for others; they invented the soap opera, film noir, the epic historical movie, fake news, scamming, grooming and stalking. They killed babies, murdered husbands and raped each other relentlessly. They also give us war, battles and conflict aplenty.

However, Greek myths are, of course, much more than exciting adventure, risqué stories. They were conceived, sung, acted out, narrated and written down for a crucial, fundamental purpose: to explain why things were as they were in the daily life of the ancient Greeks. Greek myths are, therefore, existentialist and seminal: they underpin and inform Greek society, Greek philosophy, politics and culture; they explain the origin of the Greek species and the Greek world; they are precisely why ancient Greece is ancient Greece.

Myths were for the Greeks the early history of their society and culture, conceived before the days of historiography as pioneered by Herodotus and then Thucydides, and doubtless by others whose work has not survived. Homer, Hesiod and the poets of the Epic Cycle between them fabricated and embroidered a pseudo-history of Greece which assumed a direct line of descent from the Heroic Age – the Late Bronze Age (ca.1400–1200 BCE) – as populated by heroes a mere three generations or so removed from the Olympian and chthonic (subterranean) gods. Before the myths were written down in the *Iliad* and *Odyssey*, and perhaps in other non-extant works, they were handed down from generation to generation, reshaped, revised and embellished in a thriving, dynamic oral tradition. The audiences and readers of Homer, Hesiod and the like were, then, shown to be direct descendants of the heroes of old; they and the myths that went with them were their history and heritage as delineated by this continuum. The mythologies expounded by the poets and the gods and heroes described therein explained the raison d'être of the Greek citizen and the Greek *poleis*: why this and why that, life and death, love and hate, war and peace.

It is precisely because Greek myths are so elemental to ancient Greek culture that they similarly define aspects of Western culture generally. A myth was first and foremost an entertainment, but it also served to eloquently explain why the *poleis* and obligations thereto were as they were; why women were kept inconspicuous and segregated from male society, where certain cities came from: for example, Thebes and the dragon, the origin of the Ionians (Ion) and Aeolians (Aeolus), why Sparta was Sparta and why Athens could lay claim to Aegina. Furthermore, myths left no doubt in the Greek mind about the necessary gulf between man and god, the supremacy of gods over mortals and the consequences of hubris in all its manifestations, not least when it involved sexual relations between men and women and gods, which all end in more than tears; ask Semele, whose transgressing affair reduced her to ashes. Just as importantly, myths provided an efficient vehicle for the explanation of the origin and workings of individual rituals.

Kirk defines Greek myths as

on the one hand good stories, on the other hand bearers of important messages about life in general, and life-within-society in particular... it is difficult for us, living as we do in an age of super literacy, but also dominated by the 'media' and by advertising, to envisage a way of life in which the only forms of mass communication (as distinct from practical communication between individuals) are ritual on the one hand, story-telling on the other. Yet it was from that kind of life that myths emerged and passed down through the tradition until they were finally recorded in writing by ethnologists, grammarians or missionaries...[and] gave myths their characteristic density and complexity, their imaginative depth and their universal appeal.

Kirk was writing in the social media-free days of the early 1970s; the growth and ubiquity of emailing, Googling, facebooking, tweeting, whatsapping and instagramming since then adds further poignancy to his comments in the early twenty-first century. Elsewhere, Kirk informs that

> there can be no doubt that the main Greek myths were formed before the spread of general literacy in the seventh century BC. Homer, Hesiod, Stesichorus and others provided connexions and a kind of consistency, but the central themes of divine emergence as well as of heroic adventure seem to be Mycenaean at least, and probably much earlier still.[3]

How do we know the myths?

There is a fine tradition of mythography over the centuries which at once illuminates classical mythology and simultaneously confuses it for us.

Homer, Hesiod and the Homeric Hymns

Interpolating myth into your work all started with the poets of the oral-poetic tradition – Minoan and Mycenaean singers – from the eighteenth century BCE which culminated in the myths relating to the heroes of the Trojan War and its aftermath; then Homer's *Iliad* and *Odyssey* from around the late eighth or early seventh century BCE, his mythology reaching far back in time to the days of the Trojan War itself around the thirteenth century BCE and beyond when the Seven Against Thebes, Heracles and Bellerophon stalked the world; near-contemporary Hesiod, with his *Theogony* and the *Works and Days*, followed by his accounts of the creation, the warlike Succession Myth, human ages, women – the source of human trials and tribulations – and the origin of sacrificial practices, wars and conflicts. He serves up more mythology in the *Shield of Heracles*.

According to Kirk:

> Much of the *Iliad* can be treated as legend (that is, the parts of it that describe the action before Troy in human and realistic terms) yet it

overlaps myth on the intervention of the supernatural (the gods). The *Iliad* as a whole can be classified as 'myth' in a very general sense.[4]

Myths can also found be in the thirty-three *Homeric Hymns* and in fragments of epic poems of the *Epic Cycle*: the war-themed *War of the Titans*, the *Little Iliad*, the *Sack of Ilium*, the *Cypria* and the *Aethiopis* are of particular relevance to us. The *Homeric Hymns* celebrate individual gods. They are 'Homeric' only in so far as they are composed in the same epic meter – the hexameter – as the *Iliad* and *Odyssey*, they use similar formulae and are written in the same dialect as the Homeric epics. We have Thucydides (3, 104) to thank for the enduring but erroneous attribution to Homer. Most of the hymns are seventh century BCE, although some may be Hellenistic and the hymn to the god of war Ares – one of the ones of most interest to us (the others are to Athena and Heracles) – may well be much later, added in because Ares was conspicuous by his absence in the original list of Olympians featured.

Sung by a rhapsode as a prelude to an epic recital, the purpose of the hymns would have been to subtly remind the audience of the ubiquity and power of the gods, and to clarify the relationship between the gods and mankind. Some of the hymns praise and glorify their gods and many of them conclude with a request for a blessing from the god they address, thus explaining why they are designated as hymns.

A number of the seventeen so-called Homeric epigrams feature myths, as do some of the poems collected together as 'Homerica': the *Batrachomyomachia* or the *Battle of the Frogs and Mice* is of special interest here, it being a parody of the *Iliad*. Aesop's (620–564 BCE) *Battle of the Weasel and the Mice* with an earlier version wrongly attributed to Homer and surviving in fragmentary form is not dissimilar. The 'Homerica' probably date from the second century BCE and the first century CE, and are representative of an ancient genre of 'Animal and Bird Epics', according to Martin L. West in his *Homeric Hymns. Homeric Apocrypha. Lives of Homer*, 2003, p.229, 'that may have had its ultimate roots in Egypt long before the *Iliad* and *Odyssey* arrived on the scene'.

Greek myths also appear in the Greek lyric poems of Mimnermus (mythical allusions to Jason in his *Nanno*, and Helios' nightly journey),

Stesichorus, fifth-century Pindar, Bacchylides who narrates myths involving Theseus, Heracles and Cerberus, and later in Theocritus and Bion, in the dramas of the tragedians and Aristophanes of the fifth century BCE. Stesichorus deals with many myths, including the hunt for the Calydonian bear, Heracles' robbing of the Geryon cattle, the sack of Troy and the revenge of Orestes. The *Idylls* of Theocritus contain myths relating to Heracles and the Dioskuroi. Herodotus (ca.484 BCE–ca.425 BCE) came along with some delightful mythology, tales and legends in his *History*. Pindar's oeuvre is replete with mythology, notably the *Seventh Olympian Ode* (about Helios), the *Ninth Pythian Ode* (Apollo and lion-wrestling Kyrene) and the *Sixth Olympian Ode* in which he describes the birth, exposure and rescue of the seer Iamos.

Greek myths, being full of the fabulous, fantastic and weird, soon began to attract a degree of scepticism, at least among the literate and educated classes. The doubts regarding veracity and plausibility of the myths were articulated initially by the pre-Socratic philosophers, starting with Xenophanes and Heraclitus of Ephesus from about 550 BCE, followed by the rationalists and historians. Rigorous thinking, scientific analysis, the search for robust proof, searching questions relating to the nature of god and exposure of the average Greek to a wider world through war and colonization all helped to sow the seeds of doubt. Theagenes of Rhegion added to the debate around 525 when he posited a theory that Homer never literally meant what he said. Homer was speaking allegorically and his myths could be deconstructed to reveal an underlying moral truth: the strife of the gods in Homer (*Iliad* 20) was actually the strife of the natural elements. In the third century Euhemerus of Sicily (translated by Ennius but now lost) took it a stage further when he answered the question 'What did the Greek myths do for us?' by stating that the Greek gods were originally human and mythical events were once historical.

The Sceptics: the rationalists

As mythologizing gradually elided into historiography, so prose-writers also made use of mythology. The pioneers were two mythographer-historians in the sixth century BCE: Akousilaos of Argos and Hecataeus of Miletus, both acknowledged as primary sources by Apollodorus.

Akousilaos described in prose the legendary history of Argos, his home town, and included numerous myths from the epic heritage. In the next century they were followed by historian Pherecydes of Athens, a completist who was aiming for comprehensiveness in his catalogue. These were succeeded by Hellanicus of Lesbos, a mythographer-historian who Apollodorus consulted particularly with regard to the Trojan War. Attempts at rationalistic interpretation, not least by a late-fourth century treatise, Palaephatus' *Peri Apiston (On Unbelievable Tales)*, add to our primary sources:

> Greek mythology comes to be seen as a record of past misunderstandings which could be reverse-engineered to show that these stories of fabulous monsters and other-worldly deeds derive in fact from prosaic events. The end result is a new version of the traditional story which preserves elements of the original while adhering to a stricter standard of possibility.[5]

To the rationalists we can add Heraclitus Paradoxographus, author of another *Peri Ariston, Of Unbelievable Stories*: this text is of particular interest because it exemplifies such a range of ancient ways of interpreting myth. Palaephatus' work comprises an introduction and fifty-two paragraphs on various Greek myths. The first forty-five share a common format: a brief introduction to a wondrous tale from Greek mythology, usually followed by an exclamation of disbelief ('This is absurd!' or 'This is not likely' or 'The true version is…'), and then a sequence of everyday occurrences which gave rise to the wonder-story through misunderstanding. The last seven are equally brief retellings of myth, without any rationalizing explanation.

Palaephatus' position is somewhere between those gullible people who believe everything that is said to them and those more subtle minds who consider that none of Greek mythology ever happened. He has two premises: that every story derives from some past event, and a principle of uniformity, that 'anything which existed in the past now exists and will exist hereafter.' So there must be some probable series of events behind all myth, but the 'poets and early historians' made them into wonderful tales to delight their audience. Palaephatus then claims to base what follows on personal research, travelling far and wide and asking older people what happened in days past.

A typical example of Palaephatus' method can be found in his handling of the Callisto myth:

> The story about Callisto is that while she was out hunting she turned into a bear. What I maintain is that she too during a hunt found her way into a grove of trees where a bear happened to be and she was devoured. Her hunting companions saw her going into the grove, but not coming out; they said that the girl turned into a bear (§14, tr. Stern).

The Sceptics: history and philosophy

By the time Thucydides was writing his *History of the Peloponnesian War* around 431 BCE, mythology was discredited as a record of events; Thucydides accepted that omitting 'the mythical element' made his work less entertaining, but all the more edifying for all that. While Plato was not averse to making up his own myths (notably eschatological as in the Myth of Er, *Republic* 10,614–10,621) under self-imposed conditions of propriety, he was definitely anti-myth, as was Aristotle (*Metaphysics* 2, 1000a9). There are two works attributed to Aristotle: *On Marvellous Things Heard* about foreign myths, and *Peplos* on the fate of warriors who fought at Troy. Both philosophers asserted that myths were not serious vehicles for serious thought and their moral content was dubious at best. Poets had by now lost much of their influence to prose writers in history and philosophy: the Hellenistic poets such as Callimachus and his contemporaries persisted with myth, but their work circulated to a much more exclusive audience; their main influence was to be on later Roman poets, not least Catullus in the late Republic and Ovid, in the early Principate.

Despite this powerfully endorsed criticism among Greek rationalists and philosophers, myths continued to thrive...

The Hellenistic Age (321–31 BCE)

The Hellenistic Age had seen the start of attempts by completists to catalogue and organize myths as culminating to a certain degree much later in Apollodorus. The aim was to adumbrate and explain mythical references in Greek and Roman literature. The various scholia were active in these endeavours up to the fifth century. Prominent among them is the collection of mythological scholia on Homer, initially published as a separate book in its own right. Eratosthenes' work on astral myths, *The Catasterisms* in the third century BCE, adds substantially to our knowledge of these obscure myths.

In the third century BCE we have the Hellenistic poets: Apollonius of Rhodes; Callimachus with his six hymns addressed to Artemis, Tiresias and the like; Pseudo-Eratosthenes; and Parthenius. Apollonius of Rhodes describes Jason, the Golden Fleece and the voyage of the *Argo*, a theme taken up by Valerius Flaccus 300 years later. Apart from the version in Pindar's *Fourth Pythian Ode* and the *Orphic Argonautica*, most of the early versions are lost. Parthenius gave us his *Erotica Pathemata* (*Sufferings for Love*), thirty-six obscure love myths. Anticipating Eratosthenes, Aratus (315–240 BCE) wrote an astronomical poem, the *Phenomena*, with some mythology. Lycophron (b. ca.320 BCE) is remembered for his *Alexandra*, a mythological puzzle poem in which Cassandra poses puzzles about the fall of Troy and the fate of veterans of Troy. Moschus in the second century BCE tells us how Zeus assumed the guise of a bull in order to rape Europa, in his *Europa*. Nicander of Colophon wrote the *Heteroioumena*, transformational myths, which influenced Ovid while Antoninus Liberalis wrote summaries.

Greek myth in Rome

In the Roman Empire we can call on Virgil (70 BCE–19 BCE), Ovid (43 BCE–18 CE), particularly in the *Metamorphoses*, *Tristia* and *Fasti*; and geographer Strabo (63 BCE–ca.24 CE) who coined the word 'mythography'. These were followed by Diodorus Siculus in the first century BCE with his valuable biography of Heracles. Conon wrote his *Diegesis*, fifty myths, mainly foundation myths, preserved for us by the Byzantine Photius; Plutarch (46 CE–120 CE), his *Life of Theseus* and Pausanias (ca.110 CE–ca.180 CE) the Greek traveller and geographer in his *Description of Greece*.

However, it was the true mythographers like Apollodorus who, with his *The Library of Apollodorus* or the *Bibliotheca of Pseudo-Apollodorus*,

produced a cutting-edge, state-of-the-art compendium of Greek myths
and heroic legends, in three books, dated to the first or second century
CE. Apollodorus leaves us some of the best surviving accounts of many
of the Greek myths, in the Hesiodic style as followed by Pherecydes and
Hellanicus. Concise it may be, but it embraces the colourful and exciting
world of Greek mythology from Creation to the Trojan War and its
diaspora and fallout, taking in metamorphoses, fabulous monsters and
all manner of feuding and conflict, disputatious, incestuous, zoophilic
and rapacious Olympians, chthonic and heavenly. Apollodorus was, in
part, responding to an educational need for an accessible encyclopedia
of myths to satisfy Romans whose standing and advancement in
the world, whose progress along the all-important *cursus honorum*,
depended in part on a ready familiarity and facility with Greek and
Roman mythology. The extensive knowledge of mythology in all its
minutiae became a school exercise standard despite the myth bores
and pedants it was no doubt creating. Some of the mythographers, of
course, made their myths up or added alternative versions in a bid to
'outmyth' each other.

Statius with his epic *Thebaid* and epic poet Valerius Flaccus with
his *Argonautica*, and tragedian-philosopher Seneca continued the
deployment and manipulation of myths, all in the first century CE. In
the early second century Lucian of Samasota parodied some of the
fantastic tales told by Homer in the *Odyssey* in his *A True Story*. Other
mythology satires include *The Lover of Lies* which pokes fun at people
who believe in the supernatural and features the oldest-known version
of *The Sorcerer's Apprentice*; Lucian penned numerous satires ridiculing
traditional stories about the gods including *Charon*, *The Dialogues of the
Gods*, *Icaromenippus*, *Zeus Rants*, *Zeus Catechized* and *The Parliament of
the Gods*. *Philosophies for Sale* and *The Banquet of Lapiths* and *Dialogues
of the Dead* target various earnest philosophical schools. Aelian (ca.172–
235 CE) compiled a prose anthology of animal stories comprising some
mythology.

Such was the rich and abundant literary heritage to which Apollodorus
had access for his primary source material, much of which, sadly, is either
lost to us or available only in fragmentary or epitome form.

Later mythologizing Greeks include Nonnus (a forty-eight book
prolix *Dionysiaca* giving everything you wanted to know about Dionysus

in India; Antoninus Liberalis; Ptolemy Chennus (Ptolemy the Quail) in his *Old History*, and Quintus Smyrnaeus. Quintus leaves us with a conservative account of the fallout from the Trojan War and the journeys home. Antoninus Liberalis authored an extant anthology of forty-nine transformation myths, the *Collection of Metamorphoses*; much of it is based on lost works by two Hellenistic authors: Nicander with five books of transformations, and Boio, author of a verbose and curious poem, the *Ornithogonia*, in which groups of people are transformed into birds. Prose writers who reference myths include historian Diodorus Siculus who included a history of Greece in myth in his standard history, novelists Petronius (*Satyricon*), Apuleius (*Metamorphoses*), Heliodorus (*Aethiopica*) and Phlegon of Tralles with his marvellous *Book of Marvels*. Less well-known are the *Fabulae* (catalogues of inventors, people suckled by animals and the like) and *Astronomica* by the Roman writer Pseudo-Hyginus, the *Imagines* of Philostratus the Elder and Philostratus the Younger, and the *Descriptions* of Callistratus.

It should be noted that these are just the works that are extant today; many other works featuring myths, for example Ovid's *Medea*, were written which have not survived but would have been available to successive Greek and Roman authors from the early first century CE.

There was also Fabius Planciades Fulgentius, the late fifth- to early sixth-century Latin writer whose *Mythologies* (*Mitologiarum libri III*) collated and offered moralistic interpretations of a multitude of myths; Byzantine Greek writers include Arnobius, Hesychius, the author of the *Suda*, John Tzetzes who made extensive use of Apollodorus, and Eustathius with more moralizing from a Christian perspective. Stephanus of Byzantium wrote his voluminous geographical lexicon, the *Ethnica*, full of mythical allusions. Tryphiodorus was the author of a short epic on the capture of Troy. As noted, in the ninth century Photius, a pre-eminent Byzantine scholar, thought Apollodorus very useful. Benedictine Pierre Bersuire (ca.1290–1362), took Ovid to new heights with his *Ovidius Moralizatus* and helped create a new *aetas Ovidiana*. Then there was the *Ovide Moralise*: a 72,000-word moralizing poem and one of the longest medieval texts featuring mythology. The preface promises '*la veritez seroit aperte*' ('the truth will out').

Mediaeval and Renaissance Greek myth

The anonymous medieval Mythographi Vaticani are the authors of three Latin mythographical texts found together in one manuscript (Vatican Regina. lat. 1401), an anthology of Christianized moral and theological interpretations of classical myths that remained influential to the end of the Middle Ages; and Renaissance scholar Natalis Comes, whose *Mythologiae* in ten volumes became a standard source for classical mythology in later Renaissance Europe.

The widespread popularity of pagan Greek mythology continued apace, even after the coming of Christianity. As noted, the Renaissance revived the poetry of Ovid which became a major influence on poets, dramatists, musicians and artists. From the early years, artists such as Leonardo da Vinci, Michelangelo, Titian, Rubens, Caravaggio, Raphael and Poussin right up to Picasso all portrayed the pagan myths alongside more conventional and politically correct Christian themes. Greek myth had a profound influence on medieval and Renaissance poets such as Petrarch, Boccaccio and Dante in Italy and on Chaucer in England.

Greek mythology inspired Shakespeare and Milton and through Shakespeare to Robert Bridges in the twentieth century. Racine and Corneille in France and Goethe in Germany resurrected Greek drama, reworking the ancient myths. In the eighteenth century the myths provided source material for the libretti for many of Handel's, Purcell's and Mozart's operas.

Romantic myth

Romanticism embraced Greek mythology and inspired contemporary English poets such as Tennyson, Keats, Byron and Shelley and painters Lord Leighton and Lawrence Alma-Tadema. Christoph Gluck, Richard Strauss, Jacques Offenbach and many others set Greek mythological themes to music. The nineteenth century saw a surge in the study of mythology in France, soon to be overtaken by Germany, led by Heyne. American authors of the nineteenth century, such as Thomas Bulfinch and Nathaniel Hawthorne, held the study of the classical myths in the highest regard. In the last century the mantle was taken on by Jean Anouilh, Jean Cocteau, Jean Giraudoux, Jean-Paul Sartre and Albert Camus in France,

Eugene O'Neill in America and T.S. Eliot in Britain and by novelists such as James Joyce and André Gide. The importance of ritual achieved prominence with the work of Sir James Frazer (1854–1941) and Walter Burkert.

Mythical images

Then there are the myriad representations of myths in the visual arts, from the Geometric period from the mid-seventh century BCE onward: gods, heroes, and mythic events and episodes start to feature in numerous vase paintings, mosaics, wall paintings, architecture, votive gifts and populate many other sundry artefacts. Battles depicted in art are familiar scenes throughout ancient Greece at every stage of the history, beginning with the Mycenaean culture of the early Bronze Age. Pottery of the seventh century BCE, for example, depicts scenes from the Trojan cycle as well as the labours and battles of Heracles; an Attic vase from 660 BCE shows Heracles slaying the centaur Nessos. Contemporaneous pottery depicts Heracles releasing Prometheus, Odysseus blinding Polyphemus and Perseus fleeing the surviving Gorgons after killing Medusa.

Throughout the rise of the *polis*, mythic war scenes in the arts extolled Greek culture and heightened a sense of nationalism and Greek pride. They appeared in many mediums, from the painted clay of pots to the huge stone pedimental sculptures of temples. It is significant that there is only one extant temple decoration that shows a historical battle rather than a mythological one: the Temple of Athena Nike on the Acropolis pictures the crucial defeat of the Persians on its pediments. Aside from this, pedimental sculptures for the most part illustrated myths and legends. Such legends include the battle of the Gods and the Giants, the Amazons and the Greeks, and the sack of Troy. However, the most recognizable and memorable of all these battles is undoubtedly the epic battle of the Lapiths and the Centaurs.

After the successful conclusion of the Persian Wars, things really took off culturally in and around Athens, and myths – particularly centauromachy and gigantomachy – took pride of place on major public buildings such as the Parthenon at Athens, the Temple of Zeus at Olympia and the Temple to Apollo at Delphi; all were adorned with larger-than-life sculptures representing famous and dramatic scenes from mythology. The battles also figured in the monumental wall painting in the Doric Theseum (the Temple of Hephaestus or Hephaisteion) in the Athens *agora*, and on the frieze of the *pronaos* which depicts a scene from the battle of Theseus with the Pallantides in the presence of gods, while the frieze of the *opisthodomos* shows the battle of Centaurs and Lapiths.

Mythical wars and battles, then, are extremely well-represented, indicating just how important a facet of life war was to the Greek in the numerous *poleis* and colonies. The temple of Artemis at Corcyra (600–580 BCE) shows the Gigantomachy, as does the temple of Athene Polias in Athens (550–525); the Treasury of Siphnians in Delphi portrays the Gigantomachy in its frieze; the temple to Apollo at Delphi another Gigantomachy on its pediment (520–510); the pediment of the temple of Apollo in Eretria shows Theseus and the Amazonomachy (510) and the Treasury of Megarians in Delphi yet another Gigantomachy (510–500) as well as an Amazonomachy and actions of Heracles; the west pediment at Olympia gives us Theseus and a centauromachy as does the huge bronze Athena by Phidias; Mikon the famous mural painter has his battle of the Amazons in the Stoa Poikile (significantly and symbolically right next to the famous painting of the battle of Marathon); in Aegina the temple of Aphaia shows Heracles fighting in the Trojan War on the east pediment; there is more battling in the temple of Apollo at Bassae in Arcadia – now in the British Museum – showing Achilles fighting Penthesilea on the ground. The fourth century brings us an Amazonomachy and centaurs on the metopes of the Tholos at Delphi; there is more Amazonomachy in the west pediment of the temple of Asclepius at Epidaurus and on one of the friezes of the Halicarnassus Mausoleum.

Interestingly, gigantomachy, and sex, are the two themes in which artists bring largish groups of gods together as first manifested on the early sixth-century Attic vases dedicated on the Acropolis and continued down to the Hellenistic age.

The Siphnian Treasury in Delphi provides an excellent example of how Greek myths were translated onto public buildings as a powerful, enduring and very visible medium for transmitting prestige, power and propaganda. It was one of a number of treasuries lining the 'Sacred Way', the processional route through the Sanctuary of Apollo, built to curry favour with the gods and boost the prestige of the donor *polis*. It probably dates from around 525 BCE.

The people of Siphnos grew rich from their silver and gold mines (Herodotus 3, 57) and used their income to erect the treasury, the first religious structure made entirely out of marble. The sculptural friezes are replete with various scenes from Greek mythology, particularly those related to the Trojan War. The eastern side shows the gods seated and watching the Greeks assault Troy just as if they were at an assembly, agonizing over the fate of the two sides. To the right is Athena as leader of the pro-Greek faction. To the left are seated the pro-Trojan gods: Apollo, Ares, Aphrodite and Artemis. In the middle sits almighty Zeus on his throne. The west side shows the Judgement of Paris, depicting three chariot groups (each attributed to Athena, Aphrodite and Hera). The north side displays the Gigantomachy. The reliefs would have been painted over with vivid shades of green, blue, red and gold to create a unique sense of polychromy.

Indeed, this is a good demonstration of how mythology was tied up inextricably with everyday Greek life and pedagogy, both formal and informal; the myths were there for all to see, and to read by the literate, observable by all strata of Greek society, by all demographics. Women told myths to each other while they were dutifully weaving and in their sewing groups (Euripides, *Ion* 196f); elderly men will have expatiated on them in their *leschai* (clubs), other, more agile, men in the gymnasia; schoolteachers surely included myths in their story time or as edifying explanations for all sorts of events and phenomena; mothers and nurses will have continued the age-old tradition of comforting myth-telling to their children in bedtime stories or, less cosily, by cautioning little boys and girls on the need for good behaviour lest the terrifying bogeywoman comes to get them and eat them up.

If we need any evidence of the power of myths and their ability to indelibly haunt lives, then witch-lite, the scary bogeywoman, provides it; she was just as malevolent and equally repulsive as any witch. Some of Greece's pre-eminent philosophers believed that 'of all wild things, the child is most unmanageable...the most unruly animal there is. That's why he has to be curbed by a great many bridles.' One of these bridles, apparently endorsed by flustered wet nurses, was the introduction of the bogeywoman into the impressionable imaginations of children in their charge. Bogeywomen often appeared as big bad wolf types; precursors of the one that terrified little Red Riding Hood. They ate naughty boys and girls alive and were never without a freshly-devoured child digesting in their stomach. In ancient Greece the queen of bogeywomen was Mormo – a horrifying donkey with the legs of a woman – variously a queen of the Lystraegones who had lost her own children and now vengefully murdered those of others, or a child-eating Corinthian. Another was Empusa, who appeared either as a cow, a donkey or beautiful woman; Empusa could be a beautiful, cannibalistic child-eater. Yet another was Gello, an evil female spirit and child-snatcher. The Romans equalled Mormo with Lamia: a sexy Libyan woman whose children by Zeus were murdered by Hera; like Mormo, she too was a cannibal and exacted revenge by murdering other women's babies, eating them alive.

Gendering Greek myth

How do we explain the prominent role played by female deities and Amazons in the canon of war-themed Greek mythology? In the real world, the man's world, Greek women were, by and large, kept down by men, very much excluded from society and even secluded, partitioned off, in their own homes. Their primary societal role was to work the wool, clean the house and provide an endless source of hoplites to fill the ranks of the *polis'* armies in their constant warring: serial childbirth for serial warfare. Indeed, Dowden asserts that 'Greek mythology is by and large a man's mythology, describing a world from a man's point of view.'[6] The nearest most women got to war (Spartan women were much more military-minded) was bidding farewell to father, husband or son as he left for another war, war widowhood, being besieged, raped, displaced or enslaved. Their role in ensuring and organizing the funeral rites of their menfolk is perhaps the only example of where the woman is given the dignity and respect she deserves in her execution of this vital but harrowing role.

From the time of the misogynist and violent rant against women by Hesiod, women were the cause of all evil: in myth Helen, Cassandra and Medea were all powerful women, trying to take control of their lives in the face of adamantine male domination, but because of the indomitability of men their lives and the lives of others around them, things ended badly for all of them, and countless others, no doubt, who tried similar assertiveness. The female war deities too – Hera, Athena, Artemis and Enyo, for example – while effective and influential in short episodes, ultimately succumb to the might of their male counterparts. Amazons, though highly respected as warriors and thus completely at odds with historical convention, were ultimately portrayed as symbols of barbarism, hailing from the end of the civilized world.

Lefkowitz (1985) argues for a more nuanced, charitable approach to the cavalier treatment of women by men in Greek myth but, when all things are considered, a woman it is who is blamed for the trauma and destruction caused by the Trojan War and its terrible aftermath. Helen is depicted as the *casus belli*, a status surely in part forced on her by the laddish behaviour of her abductor; whatever, she becomes a convenient scapegoat, almost, for the men's war that ensued. While Helen is the only character in the whole twenty-four book epic who has the epithet 'of Troy' to her name, Homer still only gives her twenty-four lines; the talking Trojan Horse utters more lines than her. Euripides salvages the situation to some degree by naming one of his (extant) plays *Helen*, with a dozen or so more having the name of a woman or women in the title.

Homer and the relatively more sympathetic Greek tragedians did war-affected women a huge service by giving them a voice, a chance to express a view and offer another way: Sophocles' Antigone is history's first conscientious objector; in Aristophanes' *Lysistrata*, the heroine leads a successful 'sex strike', forcing the men of Athens and Sparta to abandon a senseless war. Yet in the final analysis women were never going to win, goddesses and mortals alike.

The 'myth' word

The word 'myth' derives from ancient Greek μῦθος with the general meaning 'word, speech, narrative, fiction, myth, plot', as in Homer and other poets of the period. By the fifth century it had acquired the meaning of an entertaining if somewhat dubious tale. In Greek drama *mythos* referred to the myth, the narrative, the plot and the story of a play, taking in a whole range of meanings from undeniable falsehoods to stories with religious and symbolic significance.[7] When it eventually entered the English language and other European languages in the early nineteenth century, the word was used in a much less general sense and more as an academic term for 'a traditional story, typically involving supernatural beings or forces, which embodies and provides an explanation, aetiology, or justification for something such as the early history of a society, a religious belief or ritual, or a natural phenomenon.'[8] The Greek *mythologyía* was adopted into Late Latin as *mythologia* and features in Fulgentius' *Mythologiæ* – the explication of Greek and Roman stories about their gods – classical mythology. This Latin term entered Middle French as *mythologie* and then the English adopted the word 'mythology' in the fifteenth century, initially to denote 'the exposition of a myth or myths; the interpretation of fables; a book of such expositions.' The word is first attested in John Lydgate's *Troy Book* of about 1425.[9] The modern alternative meaning of myth as something that is simply not true although thought to be so (as in urban myth) is obviously not relevant in this study.

Mythos also described the primary source material of some Greek tragedy. According to Wiles the tragedians drew on Greek mythology, a body of 'traditional storylines' which concerned gods and heroes. It is often thought the ancient audiences had to endure spoilers all the time and were denied suspense because they knew all about the *mythos* underpinning a play and could predict the denouement. However, the Greek dramatists were no fools: they were under no obligation to faithfully reproduce traditional myths when adapting them for the stage.[10] Myths were repurposed and new versions were produced to maximize unpredictability, tension, pathos, catharsis and suspense.

Wiles goes on to explain that the traditional *mythos* was initially bound up in its oral tradition. While many Greeks were literate, there were in Greek culture no canonical editions, no sacred texts in which were published definitive or authoritative versions of myths. Instead there were numerous variants of myths in circulation. These were fair game for variants and adaptations into songs, dances, drama, poetry and visual art. Writers of myths and mythographers could freely refashion their source material for a new work, interpolating new names, interesting tangents and adapting as required to the specific needs of a new audience or in response to a different contemporary situation, something topical or a twist in the plot. For example, Homer and his near contemporaries sanitize the mythology which had seeped into his culture and society from the east by largely bowdlerizing the incest, sexual violence and rape and the mythical beasts which accompanied many a Greek myth in later versions. Homer focused much more on the heroic, the anthropomorphic and the initiatory, hubris and the undeniable fact that the gods dictated fate and were very much in charge. As Greek societies became more sophisticated and complicated, so these social dynamics and forces figured more in myths, with family tensions and the citizen's obligation to the *polis* replacing to some extent the heroic and the dynastic. Euripides' *Medea* is of Euripides' making: for him she is a bad parent who kills her children, while for others before him she was a good parent and looked after her children. Myths were the intellectual property of no one in ancient Greece. Even in the twentieth century, Graves' *Greek Myths* contains some Gravesian additions to jazz up some of the duller mythology.

Helen Morales sums up this fluidity, the dynamic nature of classical myths with '[Myth] is a continuous process of telling and retelling, of provoking and responding, of critiquing and revising. It is process, rather than an event. Or, to borrow Mary Beard's formulation, we should think of it as a verb, and not a noun.'[11]

Bruce Lincoln identifies the very different meanings of *mythos* and *logos* in Hesiod. In the *Theogeny* the Muses can both proclaim truths and tell plausible falsehoods; falsehoods which seem like real things. The verb used for telling lies is *legein*; the verbs for the telling of truths are *gerusasthai* and *mythesasthai*. In the *Works and Days*, Hesiod describes his dispute with his brother Perses and tells his readers that he will tell the truth to his brother by way of *mythesaimen*, another form of *mytheomai*.

Lincoln concludes, then, that Hesiod associated *mythos* with telling the truth and *logos* with telling lies and dissimulation. In the *Theogeny* Hesiod lists *logoi* among the offspring of Eris, the goddess of strife. Eris's children have a sinister air about them, personifying physical and verbal aspects of conflict.[12]

Greek myths, then, were essential and fundamental. They became an indispensable and inextricable fact of everyday Greek life on every level, insinuating themselves into all aspects of culture and civilization, in politics, education, philosophy, religion and ritual. They answered the need for a solution as to why things were as they were. The mythology of the Greeks explained for the Greeks the meaning of Greek life. A deep and extensive knowledge of Homer, for example, was considered by the Greeks to be the basis of their culture. Homer was the 'education of Greece' (Ἑλλάδος παίδευσις), and his poetry 'the Book'.[13]

Chapter Two

The Gods of War

Allcultures and societies have their gods or goddesses of war in much the same way as they had their gods of love, the sea, the sun, hunting and childbirth, their creation, chthonic and aetiological myths. Southern Arabia had Attar, Armenia had Vahagn, Cannaan had Anat and Celtic Britain had Andraste. All cultures and societies, that is, except the Chewong people of Malaysia, a peace-loving and non-violent community whose mythology is devoid of war and conflict. The Chewong, however, are very much the exception to the rule.

In ancient Greece war was pivotal and decisive in the mythical, Hesiodic creation of earth, reflecting as it does the central role that war and conflict played in historical ancient Greek life. The Titans, the Giants, the Centaurs and Lapiths, the monstrous Typhon all had a belligerent role to play in what was an ongoing battle, an 'oedipal struggle' as Dorothea Wender neatly describes it in her *Hesiod and Theognis* (1973, p.17), for world supremacy, a superhuman succession conflict finally won by Zeus. These war myths are collectively known as the Myth of Succession, which climaxes in Zeus and his fellow Olympians exercising supremacy. It is a bizarre journey, taking in family feuds to end all family feuds, castration, incest, rape, baby-swallowing, serial vomiting and general all-round violence and delinquency. In the event they provided Hesiod with a convenient template from which to explain how Zeus got to be top god, the Olympian family tree, justification for incessant war in the Greek world and how women via goddesses such as Athena and Hera in the Trojan War, and Titanesses, had a role to play in the world, despite the misogynistic invective he heaped on women after Pandora's infelicity and the suppression and seclusion of women in real-world Greek society.

Hesiod, however, did not make this up. He had, unknowingly no doubt, precedents from earlier civilizations to the east. A Hurro-Hittite cuneiform text of the thirteenth century BCE and the Babylonian *Enûma*

Eliš (the *Hymn of Creation* in which we have a battle between gods focused on the supremacy of Marduk of Babylon who supplanted Enlil of Nippurand in his treatment of the children of Tiamet), both trod the same ground and infiltrated Greece at some indeterminate point via Crete (where Zeus grew up as an infant) and Delos (where the stone that masqueraded as the baby god was on display). The Hurrian text reveals the sequence of events that led to the accession of their equivalent to Zeus; Anu (= Ouranos) led a coup which deposed Alalu and reigned for nine years, after which Kumarbi deposed him and seized power after dragging down a fleeing Anu and biting off and swallowing his testicles. Anu, however, brought bad news, warning Kumarbi that he had just become impregnated by three terrible gods; Kumarbi attempted to spit them out. The Storm-god (principal God of the Hurrians and the Hittites = Zeus), however, was still in his stomach and then emerged to displace Kumarbi.

The *Enûma Eliš* was known to the Hittites by 1200 BCE and to the Hurrians and Phoenicians, having originated in Sumeria. Interestingly, the Creation myth is not confined to nearby eastern civilizations: child-swallowing and the like crop up in mythologies all over the ancient world at one time or another: for example, the Pandora myth has a parallel with an Inca myth far closer to anything percolating westwards from the near east. The crucial carving-up of the world between Hades, Poseidon and Zeus (*Iliad* 15, 187–193) originates in the Akkadian epic *Atrahasis*.

How did this near eastern influence come to be? While the Greeks are descendants of Indo-Europeans who migrated into what became Greece via the Balkan Peninsula around the last quarter of the third millennium BCE, it is more likely that the mythology came directly from near eastern neighbours such as the Phoenicians, Hittites and Babylonians. Around the end of the first century a certain Philo of Byblos was a firm advocate of the belief that Hesiod's theogenic myths were taken from a then extant Phoenician version and adapted to suit the mythic needs of Greeks: 'Thus Hesiod and the celebrated poets of the epic cycle fabricated their own theogenies, gigantomachies, titanomachies and castrations, and in popularizing these they beat truth (FGrH 790F 2 ~240).'

The Greeks had to re-learn how to write at the end of their Dark Ages; a process facilitated by trading relations with the Phoenicians who had their own alphabetic language and script. The Greeks adopted and adapted this into a simple alphabetical system with twenty-four or so characters. It was the first alphabetic script to offer distinct letters for vowels as well as consonants and is the ancestor of the Latin and Cyrillic scripts. Here is Herodotus' account (5, 58) written in the 450s BCE which describes the Phoenician origin of the Greek alphabet and writing:

> The Phoenicians who came with Cadmus…introduced into Greece, after their settlement in the country, a number of accomplishments, of which the most important was writing, an art till then, I think, unknown to the Greeks. At first they used the same characters as all the other Phoenicians, but as time went on, and they changed their language, they also changed the shape of their letters. At that period most of the Greeks in the neighbourhood were Ionians; they were taught these letters by the Phoenicians and adopted them, with a few alterations, for their own use, continuing to refer to them as the Phoenician characters…. In the temple of Ismenian Apollo at Theba in Boeotia I have myself seen cauldrons with inscriptions cut on them in Cadmean characters – most of them not very different from the Ionian.

It is not too much of a leap from adopting and adapting something as fundamental as writing to the assimilation of some of the more fundamental myths of the Phoenicians.

War and the Greeks

The Romans have a well-known and deserved reputation as serial warmongers. It is less well-known that the Greeks were equally bellicose. Greece, or rather the *poleis*, the Greek city states, has a history of endless battling and warring, be it focused on Athens, Sparta or in the colonies. For much of the time, somewhere an army of Greeks was doing battle with a foreign army or, much more likely, with another Greek army. Greece's wars and battles extend from Mycenaean conflicts through the wars with Persia to the end of the Peloponnesian War in 404 BCE, Alexander and the Macedonian power struggles, down to the conquest by the Romans. Wars and battles defined these years; war was the norm. Indeed, as Yvon Garlan (*War in the Ancient World*, 1982) has said, 'peace was understood…simply as the absence of war.' To Heraclitus 'War is the father of all things' (DK 22 B 53). In the words of W.K. Pritchett (*The Greek State at War*, 5 vols, 1971–91), the fabric of Greek society was made out of war 'on a par with earthquakes, droughts, destructive storms and slavery'. War explains the dominance of the male citizen warrior, the relegation of women to a subservient and secluded non-political life, and the ongoing celebration of military glory in Greek literature. To Aristotle, militarism and social and political status were inseparable (*Politics* 4 1927 B 10–24).

As Finley points out: ' Athens…was at war on average more than two years out of every three between the Persian wars and the defeat… at Chaeronea in 338 BC, and…it never enjoyed ten consecutive years of peace in all that period.' Thucydides tells us that early Greek wars were largely squabbles over territory;[1] one of the first, he says, was the Lelantine War between Chalkis and Eretrea in Euboea which took place between ca.710 and 650 BCE. The war was triggered by a dispute over the much-coveted fertile Lelantine Plain; the conflict spread and sucked in a number of other city states; according to Thucydides it was the only war to take place in Greece between the time of the Trojan War (around 1300 BCE) and the Persian Wars (499 BCE–449 BCE) in which multiple allied cities rather than single ones were involved. The Persian Wars themselves in which the cities of Greece eventually repulsed the Persians is famous for its battles of Marathon, Thermopylae, Salamis and Plataea. The war was pivotal in Greek history, leading to the Athens-led Delian League and a huge expansion of Athenian influence, and the establishment of Athenian democracy.

Ancient Greece, of course, was never one single identifiable civilization or nation state in the way that, say, Rome was; rather, Ancient Greece comprised a number of independent city states and societies which existed more or less independently at different times. So we have, for example, the Minoan civilization on Crete and, on the mainland or on islands nearby Sparta, Mycenae, Athens, Crete and Macedonia, all exerting power and influence and often only really coming together to do battle, trade or forge alliances. Add to this the various Greek colonies scattered around the Mediterranean and the Black Sea and there is a very complex picture, geographically, militarily, politically, economically and socially: ancient Greece was anything but homogenous; the ancient Greeks were never one people.

The Athenians, Spartans and other city states, and the Macedonians all engaged in warfare at one time or another. The city state (*polis*) has its origin in the Mycenaean Greeks who, based around Athens, established twelve fortified cities in the tenth century along the Aegean coast, looking to Athens as their centre. These were supplanted by barbaric invaders from the north, the Dorians, who captured the cities, grabbed the lands and enslaved the inhabitants.

In Crete, political rights in the period 850–750 BCE were granted only to those rich enough to bear arms, thus forging a society in which allegiance to the state far outweighed any domestic obligations. Military service began at age 17 with strict discipline, athletics, military exercises, hunting and mock battles. By the age of 19, cadets were assigned to a mess for which the fees were paid out of public funds. Marriage was permitted but wives lived separately and family life was kept to a minimum. Later migrations to the Greek mainland saw the exportation of this way of life, notably to Sparta where we can recognize many aspects of the Cretan military lifestyle and where the distinction between the franchised warrior and the serf devoid of rights was at its most pronounced.

Despite the absence of geographic, political or social cohesion, all of this did coalesce, to a large extent, in a catalogue of ever-changing, fluid and flexible mythologies which had war and battle among its major influential characteristics. The Greeks did little in life without the sanction of the gods; doing battle was no exception and military divination was an extremely and obligatory serious affair, ignored at one's peril. *Hiera* were sacrificial rites carried out before the army moved out of camp. Armies on the move were always accompanied by a *mantis* (seer) and a flock of sheep ready for sacrifice. The rites of bloodletting, or *sphagia*, were called upon and evident at every critical juncture: crossing a river, invading a border, striking camp, starting the battle. Often, the sacrifices were preceded by a meal washed down with generous amounts of alcohol; this meal might be the soldiers' last, the alcohol delivering courage and abandon in battle.[2]

The sacrifices, and the reverence shown to deities generally, were necessary to get a god on your side to protect you and, with a bit of luck, lead you to victory. The sacrifices were the crucial media through which god and man communicated; the ritual slaughtering of a bird or beast pre-battle signified the impending death of the enemy and acted as a substitute for the death of one's comrades. The procedure involved slitting the victim's throat (*sphazein*) and observing how the blood gushed out and how the victim fell. If all was well, then the enemy was engaged. Examples include Xenophon *Lac. Pol* 13, 8; Plutarch *Lyc.* 22; and Thucydides 6, 69, 2.

After the battle, the Greek soldier was careful to give more thanks. Military success in the field was attributable to divine favour, but the obeisance did not end there: sanctuaries and monuments were set up while booty, captured weapons and armour were heaped on the beneficent deity. In Athens an annual burial ceremony commemorated the fallen and the funeral oration linked their sacrifice to the collective achievement of the *polis*. The sheer importance of war can also be seen, obliquely, in the anti-war sentiment it stimulated. Herodotus was an early critic: 'No one is so foolish as to prefer war to peace, in which, instead of sons burying their fathers, fathers bury their sons' (1, 87, 4); Thucydides had war down as 'a violent teacher' (3, 82, 2), while the dramatists combined in a chorus of disapproval. Aristophanes' *Lysistrata* from 411 BCE is one of the most eloquent in its account of a woman's astonishing plan to end the Peloponnesian War between Greek city states by refusing to have sex with their men.

So the extensive Greek pantheon has no shortage of gods involving themselves in the time-honoured Greek activity of serial warfare and in lending his or her lowly mortals with insurance, confidence and a dose of high-octane morale. They provided for every conceivable military decision and outcome.

The Trojan War divided the Olympians: some, like Hera, Athena and Poseidon, supported the Greeks, while others backed the Trojans. This may account for the attempted coup against Zeus by Hera, Athena and Poseidon which Homer describes in the *Iliad* (1, 396–405). The prompt action of Thetis thwarted this revolt when she called up 100-handed Briareos from the sea to persuade them to think better of their plan.

Apollo and Ares are constant warmongers, but Greek goddesses also play a significant role in the prosecution of war among mortals. Aphrodite, Artemis, Enyo, Athena, Hera and Thetis all share a major responsibility for aspects of warfare. Victory too, Nike, was a female goddess.

Aphrodite

However, despite the pre-eminence of female divinities, the father of the gods himself, Zeus, had some patronizing advice for Aphrodite (*Iliad* 5, 330–430) when she emerged injured from the battlefield, wounded by Diomedes: war is not for you, my child, you stick to the marriage bed, Ares and Athena will look after military affairs. She would have known how Andromache felt when she was similarly patronized by Hector on the walls of Troy. This apart, Aphrodite is known for her protective role of sailors in sea battles and she was worshipped as an armed war goddess at Cythera and Sparta and as Nikephoros, the bringer of Victory, at Argos. Her romantic, adulterous relationship with Ares is another indicator of her martial predilections.

Apollo

As with other deities involved in war and conflict, Apollo has a number of other unrelated responsibilities; in the case of Apollo he could count in his portfolio music, poetry, the arts, oracles, archery, herds and flocks, diseases, healing, light, sun, knowledge and the protection of the young. Despite these peaceful and civilized duties, Apollo also exhibited a decidedly bellicose side: he slew the giant Tityos and was heavily involved in the Trojan War in which he sided with the Trojans.

Apollo sprang into action when Tityos assaulted Leto, his mother, as she was travelling to the shrine of Delphi. Apollo slew the giant with a volley of arrows and the blade of his golden sword. However, Apollo's retribution did not end there: as further punishment Tityos was staked to the ground in the underworld where two vultures fed on his ever-regenerating liver. Odysseus gives us the gruesome detail in his *nekyia*:

I saw Tityos also, son of the mighty goddess Gaia (Earth); he lay on the ground, his bulk stretched out over nine plethra [900ft]. Two vultures, one on each side of him, sat and kept plucking at his liver, reaching down to the very bowels; Tityos could not beat them off with his hands. And this was because he had once assaulted a mistress of Zeus himself, the far-famed Leto, as she walked towards Pytho through the lovely spaces of Panopeus. (Homer, *Odyssey* 11, 576ff.)

The *katabasis* of Aeneas rejuvenates the story:

Tityus too, the nursling of Tellus Gaia who mothers all, was to be seen [in Tartarus], his body pegged out over a full nine acres, a huge vulture with hooked beak gnawing for ever his replenishing liver, the guts that are rich in torment, pecking away for its food, burrowing deep through the body it lives in, and giving no rest to the always-replenishing organs. (Virgil, *Aeneid* 6, 595ff (trans. adapted from Day-Lewis).)

Apollo's affiliation to the Trojans was triggered by the appropriation by Agamemnon of Chryseis, the daughter of Apollo's priest Chryses. To demonstrate his anger at this and to seek redress, Apollo fired arrows tipped with plague spores into the Greek encampment. He demanded the girl be returned, and although the Greeks complied, this only made matters much worse by incurring the wrath of Achilles when Briseis, Achilles' war booty, replaced Chryseis in Agamemnon's bed.

On his father's bidding Apollo assumed the aegis from Zeus and entered the fray that was the Trojan War, instilling terror in the Greeks with his hallmark war cry, pushing them back and slaughtering many. He is described as 'the rouser of armies' because he rallied the Trojans when they needed it most.

Apollo intervened when Diomedes injured Aeneas: Aphrodite tried to rescue the Trojan but Diomedes injured her too; Apollo enveloped Aeneas in a cloud to protect him, repelling Diomedes' assaults on him and warning him not to attack a god. Aeneas was then taken to Pergamos, a sacred spot in Troy, where he was healed.

After the death of Sarpedon, a son of Zeus, Apollo rescued the corpse from the battlefield in line with his father's wishes and, having cleaned it up, gave it to Hypnos and Thanatos. Apollo had also persuaded Athena to stop the war for that day, to give the warriors some respite.

Apollo favoured Trojan Hector who, according to some, was the god's own son by Hecuba. When Hector was injured, Apollo healed him and encouraged him to resume the fight. During an ill-fated duel with Achilles, Apollo hid Hector in a cloud of mist and saved him. When Hector was slain, Apollo protected his corpse from Achilles' attempt at mutilation by creating yet another magical cloud around the corpse.

When Patroclus tried to break into Troy he was prevented from doing so by Apollo. Apollo urged Hector to attack Patroclus, making it easy by stripping the armour off Patroclus and breaking his weapons. Patroclus was eventually slain by Hector.

Apollo's anger towards Achilles can be traced back to two murders perpetrated by Achilles. First Achilles had murdered his son Tenes before the war began, and then brutally assassinated another son, Troilus, in his own temple.

Apollo was responsible for Achilles' death when he guided an arrow shot by Paris into Achilles' vulnerable heel. Some versions have it that Apollo himself killed Achilles when he disguised himself as Paris.

Ares

Ares is *the* Greek god of war, one of the top-ranking Twelve Olympians, the son of Zeus and Hera. He represents the savage, unrestrained and more brutal and bloody aspects of war in contrast to his sister, Athena, whose martial side was altogether more subtle and intelligent. Ares, on the other hand, is the personification of brute force and strength, delighting in the tumult of battle, the fog of war and its horrors. Amid the din and roar of battle he slaughters men and devastates towns, dealing out strife and depredation.

These are typical of the endorsements and descriptions Ares earned for himself:

Ares, manslaughtering (*brotoloigos*), blood-stained (*miaiphonos*), stormer of strong walls (*teikhesipletes*). (Homer, *Iliad* 5, 27ff (trans. Lattimore).)

Hera has reared a violent son [Ares] whom she has borne to Zeus, an irascible god, hard to control, and with no respect for others. He shot travellers with deadly arrows, and ruthless hacked...with hooked spears...he rejoiced and laughed...evil...scent of blood. (Aeschylus, Fragment 282 (from *Papyri Oxyrhynchus*) (trans. Lloyd-Jones).)

Ares insatiable in battle, blazing like the light of burning fire in his armour and standing in his chariots, and his running horses trampled and dented the ground with their hooves.... And all the grove and the altar...were lit up by the dread god, Ares, himself and his armour, and the shining from his eyes was like fire...man-slaughtering Ares screaming aloud, courses all over the sacred grove. (Hesiod, *Shield of Heracles* 56ff (trans. Evelyn-White).)

Seven warriors, fierce regiment-commanders, slaughtered a bull over a black shield [before the commencement of battle], and then touching the bull's gore with their hands they swore an oath by Ares, by Enyo, and by Phobos (Rout) who delights in blood, that either they will level the city and sack the Kadmeans' town by force, or will in death smear this soil with their blood. (Aeschylus, *Seven Against Thebes*, 41ff.)

The wanton lord of war, insatiate of battle-cry, Ares, who reaps a human harvest in alien fields, destroy[s] this Pelasgian land by fire. (Aeschylus, *Suppliant Women*, 630ff.)

Ares speeds to gory strife, wroth with foes, his heart is maddened, and his frown is grim, and his eyes flash flame around him, and his face is clothed with glory of beauty terror-bent, as on he rushes and the very gods quake. (Quintus Smyrnaeus, *Fall of Troy* 7, 400ff.)

In addition, Homer uses Ares as a personification of or synonym for 'war' thirteen times in the *Iliad*, and once in the *Odyssey*; Aeschylus seven times (five in the *Seven Against Thebes*).

Casualties of war were frequently described as being slain by Ares and the blood of the dead was said to glut the god. Ares appears as a personification of various weapons and armour – spear, sword and arrow – for example, Homer uses this device ten times in the *Iliad*. More military metaphor comes with Homer's use of *therapontes* of Ares as the god of war; a term applied to warriors (*Iliad* 2, 110; 6, 67; 15, 733; 1978) to denote an attendant or ritual substitute. When a warrior is killed in the field, he dies for Ares by assuming the exact identity of Ares at the moment of death. Post-mortem the casualty qualifies for membership of that exclusive club of cult heroes who now serve as a sacred attendant of Ares.

Rose calls Ares (*The Routledge Handbook of Greek Mythology*, p.168) swashbuckler, butcher, berserker.

Ares was also the god of civil disturbance, riots, rebellions and insurgencies. More surprisingly, on the plus side he was also a guardian of civil order and was the patron of ancient police forces and armed guards.

> These shall incur as much disgrace as the man who disobeys the officers of Ares [i.e. the city wardens or police of Athens]. (Plato, *Laws* 670b (trans. Lamb).)
>
> Ares...ally of Themis (civil order), stern governor of the rebellious. (*Homeric Hymn 8 to Ares* (trans. Evelyn-White).)

Here is the full hymn; a veritable soldier's *curriculum vitae*:

> Ares, of prodigious strength, chariot-rider, golden-helmeted, strong in heart, shield-bearer, Saviour of cities, harnessed in bronze, strong arm, tireless, mighty spear thrower, O defence of Olympus, father of warlike Victory, ally of Themis, stern governor of the rebellious, leader of righteous men, sceptred King of manliness, you who whirl your fiery sphere among the planets in their sevenfold courses through the aether wherein your blazing steeds ever bear you above the third firmament of heaven; hear me, helper of men, giver of dauntless youth! Throw down a beneficent ray from above on my life, and strength of war, so that I can expel bitter cowardice from my mind and quash the deceitful impulses of my soul. Restrain also the keen fury of my heart which provokes me to tread the ways of blood-curdling strife. Rather, O blessed one, give me boldness to abide within the harmless laws of peace, avoiding strife and hatred and the violent fiends of death. (*Homeric Hymn 8 to Ares*; trans. adapted from Evelyn White.)

Ares was never very popular – either on Olympus or on earth – and his worship and cult was rarely enthusiastically or frequently observed. His atrocities and brutishness make him hated by the other gods and by his own parents. (*Iliad* 5, 889–909). He is surrounded by the personifications of all the dreadful phenomena and effects of war (*Iliad* 4, 440ff; 15, 119ff).

Ares therefore presented the Greeks with something of a dilemma: although he offered the bravery and mettle to win in war, he was regarded as a dangerous and unpredictable force for the bad, surrounded by his equally dreadful sons Phobos (Fear) and Deimos (Terror) and his lover, or sister, Enyo (Discord) on his war chariot.[3] All were born to him by Aphrodite, his mistress.[4] Other comrades, equally odious and redolent with the overtones of conflict, are Kydoimos, the demon of the din of battle; the Makhai ('Battles'); the 'Hysminai' ('Acts of manslaughter'); Polemos, a minor spirit of war and Polemos's daughter, and Alala, the goddess or personification of the Greek war-cry, which Ares uses as his own war-cry. Just as belligerent was Adrestia, 'she who cannot be escaped', venerated as a goddess of revolt, just retribution and the balancing of good and evil. As such she was often associated with Nemesis, who herself had the epithet Adrestia or Adrasteia.

It was because of their reluctance to give too much kudos or credit to such a bloodthirsty brute that, as we shall see, the Greeks often portrayed Ares as something of a misfit or failure. Saturnine Ares brought with him an air of doom, gloom, atrocity and militarism; let us also not forget that he was on the losing side at the end of the Trojan War, while Athena is often to be found in Greek art as holding Nike (Victory) in her hand, a champion of the victorious Greeks. He was also a bit of a buffoon in his love affairs and numerous offspring, and was often the subject of humiliation.

Diomedes, assisted by Athena, wounded him and in his fall he roared like 9,000 or 10,000 other warriors together (*Iliad* 5, 855ff). Athena opposed Ares, and threw him on the ground by hurling a huge stone at him (*Iliad* 20, 69; 21403). The gigantic Aloadae had likewise conquered and chained him.

Atlas had the misfortune to come up against Heracles. Apollodorus tells of one particularly monstrous son of Atlas, Cycnus of Macedonia, who was intent on building a palace from the skulls and the bones of travellers. Heracles slaughtered this odious monstrosity, which naturally angered Ares, who the hero wounded in a fight.

Hesiod's *Shield of Heracles* provides the detail:

[Heracles addresses Kyknos, the son of Ares:] Even before now, I claim, he [Ares] has at one time had experience of my spear, upon that time when, above sandy Pylos, he stood up against me, raging hard in fury for battle, and three times, under the stabling of my spear on his shield, he was knocked down upon the ground, and the fourth time, I thrust with all my rage at his thigh and split a great hole in his body, and headlong into the dust he tumbled then, under my spearing. And there he might have been disgraced among the gods, if he had gone down under my hands and left the bloody spoils to me. (Hesiod, *Shield of Heracles*, 357ff (trans. Evelyn-White).)

Stesichorus confirms the story: 'Kyknos, son of Ares, lived in the pass of Thessalia and beheaded strangers who came along in order to build a temple to Phobos (Panic) [son of Ares] from the skulls.' (Stesichorus, *Fragment* 207 (from Scholiast on Pindar) (trans. Campbell, Vol. Greek Lyric III).)

There is more Ares-related human sacrifice in Libya: 'After the sack of Troy Diomedes was cast upon on the Libyan coast where Lykos was king, whose custom it was to sacrifice strangers to his father Ares.... So says Juba in the third book of his Libyan History.' (Pseudo-Plutarch, *Greek and Roman Parallel Stories* 23 (trans. Babbitt).)

Pausanias records that local inhabitants of Therapne in Sparta recognized Thero, 'feral, savage', as a nurse of Ares:[5] 'A road from the city [of Sparta] leads [across the River Eurotas] to Therapne.... Of all the objects along this road the oldest is a sanctuary of Ares.... They name him Theritas, the feral savage, after Thero, who is said to have been the nurse of Ares.' (Pausanias, *Description of Greece* 3, 19, 7.)

In the *Iliad* we learn that there was no love lost between him and his father Zeus, who rebukes him cruelly when he returns from the fray nursing a wound:

Then glowering at him Zeus who gathers the clouds said to him:
'Don't sit there next to me whining, you two-faced liar. I detest you
more than all the gods on Olympus. To be always quarrelling is what
you love, wars and battles.... And yet I will not see you in pain for
very long, since you are my child, and it was to me that your mother
gave birth to you. But if you had been born of some other god and
proved to be just as bad, then you would have been dropped beneath
the gods of the bright sky a long time ago.'[6]

Furthermore, Ares had the misfortune to be said to have originated
from Thrace; the Greeks considered the Thracians to be barbaric and
essentially belligerent. Their bellicose nature led them to associate and
identify themselves with Ares and, along with Scythia, to establish the
principal seats of his worship.[7] In Scythia he was worshipped in the
form of a sword, by which not only horses and cattle but men also were
sacrificed. Herodotus described the Thracians (who inhabited what is now
roughly modern Bulgaria, Romania, the European part of Turkey and
northern Greece) as the most populous nation of all – after the Indians –
and said that they would be the most powerful of all nations if they were
not fighting each other so much. Ancient writers were hard put to decide
which of the Thracian tribes was the most valiant; they were employed as
mercenaries by all the great Mediterranean civilizations. Thrace had the
potential to field huge numbers of troops, and the Greeks and Romans
lived in fear of a dark Thracian cloud descending from the north,
devastating civilization in the Balkans. The Thracian way of warfare
had a huge influence on Classical Greek and Hellenistic warfare. Small
wonder that they freighted Ares with these Thracian characteristics.
After Thrace was conquered by the Romans, the Thracians provided a
ready source of robust auxiliaries for the Roman army.

This late sixth-century BCE funerary inscription from Attica illustrates
the fatal effect Ares was wont to inflict: 'Stay and mourn at the tomb
of dead Kroisos whom raging Ares destroyed one day, fighting in the
foremost ranks.'[8]

Not surprisingly, though, Ares was held in high regard in Sparta, that
most militaristic and war-disciplined of all the Greek states. The Spartans
are said to have made human sacrifices to him from among prisoners of
war.

Ares is well-named, etymologically associated as he is with the Greek word ἀϱή (arē), the Ionic form of the Doric ἀϱά (ara): 'bane, ruin, curse, imprecation'.

Because of his reputation, Ares seems to have been thought ill-suited to be represented in works of art: indeed, there are no artistic representations of Ares before Alcamenes, who appears to have created the ideal of Ares. Alcamenes of Lemnos and Athens flourished in the second half of the fifth century BCE, a younger contemporary of Phidias. Pausanias (*Description of Greece* 1, 8, 4) refers to a statue of Ares by Alcamenes that was erected on the Athenian agora, which some have associated, tenuously, with the Ares Borghese. There are few Greek monuments now extant with representations of the god, although he appears on coins, reliefs and jewellery. Ares does feature on the Parthenon frieze amid a group of Olympians and on the great frieze of the altar at Pergamum.

Ares was celebrated in two hymns, both of which celebrate his prowess in battle. We have already seen the *Homeric Hymn 8*; then there is the *Orphic Hymn 65 to Ares*:

> To Ares.... Magnanimous, unconquered, boisterous Ares, rejoicing in darts and in bloody wars; fierce and untamed, whose mighty power can make the strongest walls shake from their very fiundations: man killing king, defiled with gore, happy with war's dreadful and tumultuous roar. Human blood, and swords, and spears delight you, and the dire ruin of mad savage fight. Stay furious contests, and avenging strife, whose works with woe embitter human life; to lovely Kyrpis [Aphrodite] and to Lyaios [Dionysus] yield, exchange arms for the labours of the field; encourage peace, to gentle works inclined, and give abundance, with benignant mind. (*Orphic Hymn 65 to Ares* (trans. adapted from Taylor).)

He is never consistently partisan but sometimes assists the one and sometimes the other side, just as he feels; whence Zeus calls him ἀλλοπόσαλλος, *alloposallos*, 'most hated'.[9] He is even believed to have had a hand in the carnage wreaked by plagues and epidemics. (Sophocles *Oed. Tyr.* 185.). He had promised Athena and Hera that he would fight for the Achaeans but Aphrodite persuaded him to back the Trojans.[10]

At one point Athene, Ares' sister, asked Zeus to allow her to drive Ares away from the battlefield, which Zeus permitted; Athena encouraged Diomedes to attack Ares: Diomedes lunged at Ares with his spear, with Athena driving it home, and Ares' cries made Achaeans and Trojans alike tremble; Ares fled to Mount Olympus, forcing the Trojans to retreat.[11]

When Hera mentioned to Zeus that Ares' son Ascalaphus had been killed, Ares overheard and wanted to join the fight on the side of the Achaeans, disregarding Zeus' order that no Olympic god should enter the fray, but Athena stopped him. Later, when Zeus allowed gods to resume fighting in the war, Ares was the first to act, attacking Athena to avenge himself for his previous injury. As we have seen, Athena overpowered Ares by striking him with a boulder.[12]

Ares was active in the war against the Titans, the Titanomachy:

[Ares] brought low such another [giant], Ekhidna's son, the gods' enemy, spitting the horrible poison of hideous Ekhidna [the serpent-Nymphe]. He had two shapes together, and in the forest he shook the twisting coils of his mother's spine. Kronos used this huge creature to confront the thunderbolt [of Zeus], hissing war with the snaky soles of his feet; when he raised his hands above the circle of the breast and fought against your Zeus, and lifting his high head, covered it with masses of cloud in the paths of the sky. Then if the birds came wandering into his tangled hair, he often swept them together into his capacious throat for a dinner. This masterpiece your brother Ares killed. (Nonnus, *Dionysiaca* 18, 274ff (trans. Rouse).)

Nonnus mentions him again in a characteristic role: 'Ares, destroyer of the Titanes, his father's champion, who lifts a proud neck in heaven, still holding that shield ever soaked with gore.'

Ares has the dubious honour of being the first god or mortal to be tried for murder and has thus left his mark on the annals of ancient Athenian legal history. He killed Poseidon's son Halirrhothios for raping his own daughter, Alcippes. He was tried before a jury of twelve gods and acquitted; the trial took place on a hill to the west of the Acropolis which we know as the Areopagus, the venue for all subsequent murder trials.

The Giants Otos and Ephialtes had to contend with Ares in the Gigantomachy:

Poseidon mated with her [Iphimedeia] and fathered two sons, Otos and Ephialtes, who were known as Aloadai. Each year these lads grew two feet in width and six feet in length. When they were nine years old and measured eighteen feet across by fifty-four feet tall, they decided to fight the gods. So they set Mount Ossa on top of Mount Olympos, and then placed Mount Pelion on top of Ossa, threatening by means of these mountains to climb up to the sky. (Pseudo-Apollodorus, *Bibliotheca* 1, 53 (trans. Aldrich).)

The goddess Dione tells her daughter Aphrodite how two chthonic giants, the Aloadae, Otus and Ephialtes, made an assault on Olympus during which they bound Ares ignominiously in chains and left him languishing in a bronze urn, where he remained for thirteen months, a lunar year. 'And that would have been the end of Ares and his appetite for war, if the beautiful Eriboea, the young giants' stepmother, had not told Hermes what they had done,' she related.[13]

Nonnus does not spare Ares' humiliation: 'Ares...was shackled tight inglorious in earthly fetters in a jar, where Ephialtes had hidden him. Nor did heavenly Zeus help him.' (Nonnus, *Dionysiaca* 31, 41ff (trans. Rouse).)

Ares was held bawling and screaming and howling in the urn until Hermes rescued him, while Artemis tricked the Aloadae into slaying each other. In Nonnus' *Dionysiaca* Ares also killed Ekhidnades, the giant son of Echidna, and a great enemy of the gods.[14]

Ares slew the Giant Mimas: 'Aeetes [King of Kolkhis] put on his breast the stiff cuirass which Ares had given him after slaying Mimas with his own hands in the field of Phlegra.' (Apollonius Rhodius, *Argonautica* 3, 1227ff (trans. Rieu).)

Antoninus Liberalis records how Atlas was pursued by Typhon:

Typhon felt an urge to usurp the rule of Zeus and not one of the gods could withstand him as he attacked [Olympos]. In panic they fled to Aigyptos all except Athena and Zeus, who alone were left. Typhon hunted after them, on their track. When they fled they had changed themselves in anticipation into animal forms. Apollon became a hawk [Horus], Hermes an ibis [Thoth], Ares became a fish, the lepidotus [i.e. the Egyptian god Onuris whose sacred fish was the lepidotus]. (Antoninus Liberalis, *Metamorphoses* 28 (trans. Celoria).)

Artemis

Artemis was principally goddess of the hunt, the wilderness, wild animals, the moon, childbirth and chastity. In the Trojan War Artemis, as with her mother Leto and twin brother Apollo, who was widely worshipped at Troy, was on the side of the Trojans. Apollo was the patron god of Troy and Artemis herself was widely worshipped in historical western Anatolia. In the *Iliad* we read that Artemis came to blows with Hera when the divine allies of the Greeks and Trojans fought each other. Hera hit Artemis on the ears with her own quiver, causing the arrows to fall out. As Artemis fled crying to Zeus, Leto gathered up the bow and arrows.

While the Greeks were sailing to Troy, Artemis becalmed the sea and put the task force on hold until an oracle decreed that they could win the goddess's heart by sacrificing Iphigenia, Agamemnon's daughter. Agamemnon, leader of men, had once promised the goddess he would sacrifice the dearest thing to him, which was Iphigenia, but he reneged on that promise. Artemis saved Iphigenia because of the girl's bravery.

The Spartans would routinely sacrifice to Artemis as one of their patron goddesses before starting a new military campaign.

We hear of the belligerence of Artemis on a number of occasions, first against the giants Otos and Ephialtes:

[During the assault on Olympus] Ephialtes paid amorous attention to Hera, as did Otos to Artemis. Artemis finished off the Aloadai in Naxos by means of a trick: in the likeness of a deer she darted between them, and in their desire to hit the animal they speared each other. (Pseudo-Apollodorus, *Bibliotheca* 1, 53 (trans. Aldrich).)

Other writers, however, say that they [the Gigantes Otos and Ephialtes] were invulnerable sons of Poseidon and Iphimede. When they wished to assault Artemis, she could not resist their strength, and Apollo sent a deer between them. Driven mad by anger in trying to kill it with javelins, they killed each other. In the Land of the Dead they are said to suffer this punishment: they are bound by serpents to a column, back to back. Between them is a screech-owl [a bird which was believed to drink blood], sitting on the column to which they are bound. (Pseudo-Hyginus, *Fabulae* 28 (trans. Grant).)

The giant Tityos also felt the wrath of Artemis:

> Tityos by Artemis was hunted down with darts from her unconquerable quiver suddenly sped [for attempting to rape her mother], so that a man may learn to touch only those loves that are within his power. (Pindar, *Pythian Ode* 4, ep.4 (trans. Conway).)
>
> Tityos saw Leto when she came to Pytho and in a fit of passion tried to embrace her. But she called out to her children [Apollo and Artemis], who shot him dead with arrows. He is being punished even in death, for vultures feast on his heart in Hades' realm. (Pseudo-Apollodorus, *Bibliotheca* 1, 22 (trans. Aldrich).)

Her petulant warmongering is vividly described in the *Iliad*:

> The Kouretes and the steadfast Aitolians were fighting and slaughtering one another about the city of Kalydon, the Aitolians in lovely Kalydon's defence, the Kouretes furious to storm and sack it in war. For Artemis golden-throned (*khrysothronos*) had driven this evil upon them, angered that Oineus had not given the pride of the orchards to her, first fruits; the rest of the gods were given due sacrifice, but alone to this daughter of great Zeus he had given nothing. He had forgotten, or had not thought, in his hard delusion, and in wrath at his whole mighty line the Lady of Arrows (*iokheaira*) sent upon them the fierce wild Boar with the shining teeth, who after the way of his kind did much evil to the orchards of Oineus. For he ripped up whole tall trees from the ground and scattered them headlong roots and all, even to the very flowers of the orchard. The son of Oineus killed this boar, Meleagros, assembling together many hunting men out of numerous cities with their hounds; since the Boar might not have been killed by a few men, so huge was he, and had put many men on the sad fire for burning. But the goddess again made a great stir of anger and crying battle, over the head of the boar and the bristling boar's hide, between Kouretes [an Aitolian tribe] and the high-hearted Aitolians. (Homer, *Iliad* 9, 530ff (trans. Lattimore).)

Also by Pseudo-Apollodorus:

When Oineus [king of Kalydon] was offering his annual sacrifice of the first fruits of the land to all the gods, he overlooked Artemis. The wrathful goddess let loose a great and powerful wild boar, which made the earth unsowable and destroyed herds and people that encountered it. In order to get rid of this boar, Oineus called together all the best men of Hellas and proclaimed the skin as a trophy to the man who could slay it [and it was slain by the heroes of the Kalydonian Boar Hunt]. (Pseudo-Apollodorus, *Bibliotheca* 1, 66 (trans. Aldrich).)

Athena

Athena is something of a paradox: her divine portfolio included responsibilities for wisdom, inspiration, enlightenment, law and justice, mathematics, the arts, crafts and skill; all peaceful, all constructive and civilizing. She was, moreover, patroness of weaving, that badge of the ideal Greek wife, mother and homemaker. However, she was also goddess of military strategy, military intelligence, town defence and the art of leadership; altogether a more analytical, nuanced and cerebral skill set than that exhibited by the unrestrained and violent Ares. Conflict and war were last options for Athena, deployed only when all diplomacy had failed. Athena was only interested in helping those fighting for a just cause. As such she was held in much higher esteem by the Greeks than was the brutish Ares.

Here is how the *Homeric Hymn to Athena* encapsulates her military nature and activity:

Of Pallas Athene, guardian of the city, I begin to sing. Dread is she, and with Ares she loves deeds of war, the sack of cities and the shouting and the battle. It is she who saves the people as they go out to war and come back. Hail, goddess, and give us good fortune with happiness! (*Homeric Hymn 11, to Athena*, translated by Hugh G. Evelyn-White (1914).)

So, she was an active guardian of cities, her inclination towards battle is evident in the cult of Athena Victory (Nike) and she is often portrayed as fully-armed wielding her terrible aegis. She is also an inveterate helper of heroes, as can be seen in her association with Heracles on several metopes on the Temple of Zeus at Olympia.

Athena takes credit, as Athena Hippeia, for inventing the war chariot and developing the art of horse-taming, and was patroness of the metals used to manufacture the weapons of war, thus adding to the bellicose flavour in her *curriculum vitae*. Her horse-taming skills were put to good use when she helped Bellerophon bridle Pegasus. Warships were a favourite of Athena's and account for the unusual presence of a regatta at the Panathenaia. She supervised the building of the *Argo*, the mythical prototype for the pentekonter [Greek galley], later to become the war galley in historical times. Indeed, when Athena was born from Zeus' head, not only was she already fully grown, but she emerged wearing a full suit of armour. As Athena Promachos she was Athena 'who fights from the front', leading troops into battle.

The Giants had the misfortune to come up against Athena, as Apollodorus narrates:

> There was an oracle among the gods that they themselves would not be able to destroy any of the Gigantes, but would finish them off only with the help of some mortal ally.... With Athena's help he [Zeus] called for Heracles to be his ally. Heracles first sent an arrow at Alkyoneus, who by falling to the earth recovered somewhat. Athena advised Heracles to drag him outside of Pallene, which he did, and Alkyoneus then died.... [During the battle of the gods and giants:] As Enkelados was fleeing, Athena threw the island of Sicily at him. She stripped off the skin of Pallas and used it to protect her own body during the battle. (Pseudo-Apollodorus, *Bibliotheca* 1, 35 (trans. Aldrich).)

Pausanias, *Description of Greece* 8, 47, 1 (trans. Jones) confirms her involvement: '[Athena] had the surname of Hippia. According to their account, when the battle of the gods and Gigantes took place the goddess drove the chariot and horses against Enkelados.'

As does Quintus Smyrnaeus: 'As in the old time Pallas heaved on high Sikelia (Sicily), and on huge Enkelados dashed down the isle, which burns with the burning yet of that immortal Gigante, as he breathes fire underground.' (Quintus Smyrnaeus, *Fall of Troy* 14, 632ff.)

Also Pseudo-Hyginus:

> Some also say this [constellation Draco] dragon was thrown at Minerva [Athena] by the Giants, when she fought them. Minerva, however, snatched its twisted form and threw it to the stars, and fixed it at the very pole of heaven. And so to this day it appears with twisted body, as if recently transported to the stars. (Pseudo-Hyginus, *Astronomica* 2, 3 (trans. Grant).)

While the Suidas explains, Suidas s.v. Pallas: 'Pallas: A great virgin. It is an epithet of Athena; from brandishing (pallein) the spear, or from having killed Pallas, one of the Gigantes.'

This is Athena's battle against the giant Typhon:

> Typhon was the son of Ge (the Earth), a deity monstrous because of his strength, and of outlandish appearance. There grew out of him numerous heads and hands and wings, while from his thighs came huge coils of snakes. He emitted all kinds of roars and nothing could resist his might. Typhon felt an urge to usurp the rule of Zeus and not one of the gods could withstand him as he attacked. In panic they fled to Egypt, all except Athena and Zeus, who alone were left. Typhon hunted after them, on their track. When they fled they had changed themselves in anticipation into animal forms. (Antoninus Liberalis, *Metamorphoses* 28 (trans. Celoria).)
>
> Typhoeus, boasting that already the kingdom of the sky and already the stars were won, felt aggrieved that Dionysos in the van [of a chariot] and Pallas, foremost of the gods, and a maiden's snakes [Athena's aegis] confronted him. (Valerius Flaccus, *Argonautica* 4, 235ff (trans. Mozley).)

The Titans also came up against Athena, among others:

After Hera saw that Epaphus, born of a concubine, ruled such a great kingdom, she saw to it that he should be killed while hunting, and encouraged the Titans to drive Zeus from the kingdom and restore it to Kronos. When they tried to mount to heaven, Zeus with the help of Athena, Apollo, Artemis, cast them headlong into Tartarus. On Atlas, who had been their leader, he put the vault of the sky; even now he is said to hold up the sky on his shoulders. (Pseudo-Hyginus, *Fabulae* 150 (trans. Grant).)

Athena's role in the Trojan War was significant. Along with Helen and her two co-contestants in the judgement of Paris – Aphrodite and Hera – she was a *casus belli*, offering Paris fame and glory in battle, but Paris was seduced by the prospect of marrying the most beautiful woman on earth – Helen – as offered by Aphrodite. Paris awarded Aphrodite the fateful apple, thereby enraging the other two goddesses who sided with the Greeks in the war. Athena proceeded to give measured advice and encouragement to the Greeks, especially to Achilles; she saved Menelaos from the arrow of Pandaros, and diverted the spear of Diomedes to injure Ares. In Books 5 and 6 of the *Iliad*, Athena helps the hero Diomedes.

Quintus Smyrnaeus tells of the conflict with the Amazon Penthesilieia:

Slumber mist-like overveiled her eyes like sweet dew dropping round. From heaven's blue slid down the might of a deceitful dream at Pallas Athena's hest, that so the warrior-maid might see it, and become a curse to Troy and to herself, when strained her soul to meet the whirlwind of the battle. In this wise Tritogeneia Athena, the subtle-souled, contrived: stood o'er the maiden's head that baleful dream in likeness of her father Ares, kindling her fearlessly front to front to meet in fight fleet-foot Achilles. And she heard the voice, and all her heart exulted, for she weened that she should on that dawning day achieve a mighty deed in battle's deadly toil. Ah, fool, who trusted for her sorrow a dream out of the sunless land, such as beguiles full oft the travail-burdened tribes of men, whispering mocking lies in sleeping ears, and to the battle's travail lured her then! (Quintus Smyrnaeus, *Fall of Troy* 1, 154ff (trans. Way).)

Loud clashed their [Achilles and Ajax's] glorious armour: in their souls a battle-fury like the War-god's wrath maddened; such might was breathed into these twain by Atrytone Athena, Shaker of the Shield, as on they pressed.

When the Mysian prince Eurypylos arrived at Troy as an ally of the Trojans, Athena returned to support the Greeks on the battlefield:

By their towers screened, did the trembling Danaans abide Telephos' mighty son [Eurypylos, who had driven them back to their ships]. Yea, he had burnt the ships, and all that host had he destroyed, had not Athena at the last inspired the Argive men with courage. Ceaselessly from the high rampart hurled they at the foe with bitter-biting darts, and slew them fast. (Quintus Smyrnaeus, *Fall of Troy* 7, 150ff (trans. Way).)

That desperate battle-travail Pallas saw [when Eurypylos laid siege to the Greek encampment], and left the halls of Heaven incense-sweet, and flew o'er mountain-crests: her hurrying feet touched not the earth, borne by the air divine in form of cloud-wreaths, swifter than the wind. She came to Troy, she stayed her feet upon Sigeion's windyness, she looked forth thence over the ringing battle of dauntless men, and gave the Greeks glory. Achilles' son [Neoptolemos] beyond the rest was filled with valour and strength which win renown for men in whom they meet. (Quintus Smyrnaeus, *Fall of Troy* 7, 620ff.)

Athena was there at the end of the war, to see Troy finished off (Quintus Smyrnaeus, *Fall of Troy* 11, 300ff): 'Then did the Argive might prevail at last by stern decree of Pallas; for she came into the heart of battle, hot to help the Greeks to lay waste Priam's glorious town.'

She was also the brains behind the Trojan Horse stratagem:

Next [in the Epic Cycle] comes the *Little Iliad* in four books by Leskhes of Mitylene: its contents are as follows.... The Trojans are now closely besieged, and Epeios, by Athena's instruction, builds the wooden horse. (Lesches or Cinaethon, *The Little Iliad Fragment* 1 (from Proclus, *Chrestomathia* 2).)

Fashion we [the Greeks] the Horse by Epeios' hands, who in the woodwright's craft is chiefest far of Argives, for Athena taught his lore. (Quintus Smyrnaeus, *Fall of Troy* 12, 84ff.)

In art Athena is often shown dressed in armour in the fashion of a male soldier wearing a Corinthian helmet; her shield bears at its centre the aegis, a goatskin shield, with the head of the gorgon (*gorgoneion*) in the middle and snakes around the edge. The *gorgoneion* was an apotropaic amulet showing the Medusa head, used most famously by Athena and Zeus as a protective pendant. As Athena Promachos, she wields a spear. The mighty bronze Athena Promachos statue fashioned by Pheidias from the Persian spoils at the Battle of Marathon showed Athena standing with her shield resting upright against her leg, and a spear in her right hand; it towered between the Propylaea and the Parthenon on the Acropolis, a highly visible, powerful symbol of a woman of war.

Early Christian writers, such as Clement of Alexandria and Firmicus, slurred Athena as the epitome of all the things loathsome about paganism, condemning her as 'immodest and immoral'. During the Middle Ages, however, many attributes of Athena were appropriated for the Virgin Mary who, in the fourth century, was often depicted wearing the *gorgoneion*. Some saw the Virgin Mary as a warrior maiden, much like Athena Parthenos; one astonishing anecdote tells that the Virgin Mary once appeared on the walls of Constantinople when it was under siege by the Avars, clutching a spear and urging the people to fight.

During the Renaissance, Athena assumed the mantle of patron of the arts and human endeavour; in Sandro Botticelli's painting 'Pallas and the Centaur' Athena is the personification of chastity; she is shown grasping the forelock of a centaur, who represents lust. Andrea Mantegna's 1502 painting 'Minerva Expelling the Vices from the Garden of Virtue' uses Athena as the personification of Graeco-Roman learning expelling the vices of medievalism from the garden of modern scholarship. Athena is also depicted as the personification of wisdom in Bartholomeus Spranger's 1591 painting 'The Triumph of Wisdom or Minerva Victorious over Ignorance'.

During the sixteenth and seventeenth centuries, Athena became a symbol for female rulers. In his *A Revelation of the True Minerva* (1582),

Thomas Blennerhassett portrays Queen Elizabeth I as a 'new Minerva' and 'the greatest goddesse nowe on earth'. A series of paintings by Rubens depict Athena as Marie de Medici's patron and mentor; the German sculptor Jean-Pierre-Antoine Tassaert depicted Catherine II of Russia as Athena in a marble bust in 1774. During the French Revolution, statues of pagan gods were torn down throughout France, but statues of Athena survived, transformed into the personification of freedom and the republic, while a statue of the goddess stood in the centre of the Place de la Revolution in Paris.

An imposing statue of Athena stands in front of the Austrian Parliament Building in Vienna, while depictions of Athena have influenced other symbols of Western freedom, including the Statue of Liberty in New York and Boadicea in London.

Enyo

Enyo was goddess of war and calamitous destruction, partner of the war god Ares. She is also his sister Eris, and daughter of Zeus and Hera.[15] She is the mother of the war god Enyalius, god of soldiers and warriors, by Ares.[16] The wholesale destruction of cities was Enyo's speciality; she is 'supreme in war'[17] and a frequent fighter alongside Ares.[18] '[The] goddesses, who range in order the ranks of men in fighting, [are] Athene [Athena] and Enyo, sacker of cities.' (Homer, *Iliad* 5, 333ff (trans. Lattimore).)

She was particularly active during the fall of Troy, where she handed down terror and carnage along with her dreadful stablemates Eris ('Strife'), Phobos ('Fear') and Deimos ('Dread'), the latter two being sons of Ares. Eris and the two sons of Ares are depicted on Achilles' shield.

Enyo was implicated in the Seven Against Thebes: 'Enyo, afire with torch fresh-charged and other serpents, was restoring the fight. They yearn for battle, as though they had but lately borne the opening shock of combat hand to hand, and every sword still shone bright and clear.' (Statius, *Thebaid* 8, 655ff (trans. Mozley).)

Also in Dionysius' war with the Indians: '[The Indian War of Dionysos:] Battle stirring Ares in mortal shape, with Enyo by his side...has armed himself against Dionysos at Hera's bidding and supports the Indian king

[Deriades]. (Nonnus, *Dionysiaca* 33, 55ff.) 'When Enyo elected not to take sides in the battle between Zeus and the monster Typhon, it was because this decision would extend the duration of the conflict, so much so did she delight in war.' 'Eris ('Strife') was Typhon's partner in the mêlée , Nike ('Victory') led Zeus into battle…impartial Enyo held equal balance between the two sides, between Zeus and Typhon, while the thunderbolts with booming shots danced like dancers in the sky.'[19]

Enyo was one of the three Graiae: three grotesque-looking sisters who shared one eye and one tooth between them.[20] Aeschylus describes them best in a horrid vignette:

The Gorgonean plains of Kisthene where the daughters of Phorkys dwell, ancient maids (*dênaiai korai*), three in number, shaped like swans (*kyknomorphoi*), possessing one eye amongst them and a single tooth; neither does the sun beam down on them, never the nightly moon. And near them are their three-winged sisters, the serpent-haired Gorgons, hated by mankind: no mortal will look at them and live to tell the tale.[21]

According to Pausanias a statue of Enyo, made by the sons of Praxiteles, stood in the temple of Ares at Athens.[22]

Here are just a few examples of how Enyo has been described in Greek and Latin literature:

Homer, *Iliad* 5, 590ff: 'And with him followed the Trojan battalions in their strength; and Ares led them with the goddess Enyo, she carrying with her the turmoil of shameless hatred.'

Aeschylus, *Seven Against Thebes* 41ff (trans. Weir Smyth): 'The leaders of the army of the Seven Against Thebes: Seven warriors, fierce regiment-commanders, slaughtered a bull over a black shield [before the commencement of battle], and then touching the bull's gore with their hands they swore an oath by Ares, by Enyo, and by Phobos (Rout) who delights in blood, that either they will level the city and sack the Cadmeans' town by force, or will in death smear this soil with their blood.'

Callimachus, *Hymn 4 to Delos* 275ff: 'On you [the island of Delos] treads not Enyo nor Hades nor the horses of Ares [i.e. Delos was free of war].'

Quintus Smyrnaeus, *Fall of Troy* 5, 25ff: 'And there were man-devouring wars, and all horrors of fight…. Phobos was there, and Deimos and ghastly Enyo with limbs all gore-bespattered hideously, and deadly Eris (Strife).'

Quintus Smyrnaeus, *Fall of Troy* 8, 286ff: 'Stalked through the midst [of the battle] deadly Enyo, her shoulders and her hands blood-splashed, while fearful sweat streamed from her limbs. Revelling in equal fight, she aided none, lest Thetis' or Ares' (the War-God's) wrath be stirred.'

Quintus Smyrnaeus, *Fall of Troy* 8, 424ff: 'Many of them [soldiers battling at Troy] dyed the earth red: aye waxed the havoc of death as friends and foes were stricken. O'er the strife shouted for glee Enyo, sister of Ares (War).'

Quintus Smyrnaeus, *Fall of Troy* 11, 151ff: 'The black Keres (Fates) joyed to see their conflict [the Greeks and the Trojans], Ares laughed, Enyo yelled horribly. With corpses earth was heaped, with torrent blood was streaming: Eris gloated over the slain.'

Quintus Smyrnaeus, *Fall of Troy* 13, 85ff: 'The Greek army enters Troy: In deadly mood then charged they on the foe. Ares and fell Enyo maddened there: blood ran in torrents.'

Tryphiodorus, *Sack of Ilium* 560ff (trans. Mair); Tryphiodorus was a Greek poet of the fifth century CE: 'Enyo, revelling in the drunkenness of unmixed blood, danced all night throughout the city of Troy, like a hurricane, turbulent with the waves of the surging war. And therewithal Eris lifted her head high as heaven and stirred up the Argives; since even bloody Ares, late but even so, came and brought to the Danaans the changeful victory in war.'

According to Nonnus, *Dionysiaca* 7, 7ff, the mad world all around him is all Enyo's fault: 'Lord Zeus! behold yourself the sorrows of a despairing world! Do you not see that Enyo has made the whole earth mad, mowing season by season her harvest of quick-perishing youth?'

Hera

Hera, wife-sister to Zeus, is the goddess of women, marriage, family, weddings and childbirth, of the sky and heavens. She is the daughter of the Titans Cronus and Rhea and rules over Mount Olympus as queen of the gods. Not unnaturally, Hera has a jealous and vengeful attitude towards Zeus' numerous lovers and illegitimate offspring, as well as against all mortals who cross her.

In the Gigantomachy, Apollodorus tells us how 'Porphyrion rushed against Heracles and also Hera. Zeus instilled him with a passion for Hera, and when he tore her gown and wanted to rape her, she called for help, whereat Zeus hit him with a thunderbolt and Heracles slew him with an arrow.'

We have already seen how Ephialtes came on to Hera, as did Otos to Artemis when these giants attempted to take Olympus.

Hera played a major part in the Trojan War and in its description by Homer in the *Iliad*; she loathed the Trojans with a vengeance after Paris decided that Aphrodite, and not her, was the most beautiful goddess; accordingly, she spent the next ten years doing her best to disadvantage the Trojan forces and supporting the Greeks during the war. She persuaded Athena to side with the Greeks and in Book 5, conspires with Athena to harm Ares, who was seen by Diomedes assisting the Trojans (Homer, *Iliad* 5, 711ff).

Now as the goddess Hera of the white arms perceived how the Argives were perishing in the strong encounter [with the Trojans], immediately she spoke to Pallas Athene her winged words: 'For shame, now, Atrytone, daughter of Zeus of the aigis: nothing then meant the word we promised to Menelaos, to go home after sacking the strong-walled city of Ilion, if we are to let cursed Ares be so furious. Come then, let us rather think of our own stark courage.'

So she spoke, nor did the goddess grey-eyed Athene disobey her....
[The two travelled to Troy in Hera's chariot.]

Now these two walked forward in little steps like shivering doves, in their eagerness to stand by the men of Argos, after they had come to the place where the most and the bravest stood close huddled about...there standing the goddess of the white arms, Hera, shouted, likening herself to high-hearted, bronze-voiced Stentor, who could cry out in as great a voice as fifty other men: 'Shame, you Argives, poor nonentities splendid to look on. In those days when brilliant Achilles came into the fighting, never would the Trojans venture beyond the Dardanian gates, so much did they dread the heavy spear of that man. Now they fight by the hollow ships and far from the city.' So she spoke, and stirred the spirit and strength in each man.

Hera, Ares' mother, saw this and asked Zeus, Ares' father and her husband, for permission to drive Ares from the battlefield. Hera encouraged Diomedes to attack Ares. When he threw his spear at the god, Athena drove the spear into Ares' body; he bellowed in pain and fled to Mount Olympus, forcing the Trojans to fall back.

Book 8 sees Hera attempting to enlist Poseidon's support for the Greeks, but he refuses on the grounds that he was unwilling to cross Zeus. In Book 14 Hera schemes to deceive Zeus after he had decreed that the gods were not to interfere in the mortals' Trojan War. Hera seduces Zeus, aided by Aphrodite, and tricks him into a deep sleep so that the gods could interfere without fear of Zeus. Hera's machinations continue in Book 21 when she orders Hephaestus to prevent the river from harming Achilles. Hephaestus sets the battlefield on fire; the river implores Hera to stop the attack with the promise to help the Trojans.

Hera was also active in the Indian Wars of Dionysos; Artemis confronted Hera in battle and was defeated:

Against Hera came highland Artemis as champion for hillranging Dionysos, and rounded her bow straight. Hera as ready for conflict seized one of the clouds of Zeus, and compressed it across her shoulders where she held it as a shield proof against all; and Artemis shot arrow after arrow moving through the airy vault in vain against that mark, until her quiver was empty, and the cloud still unbroken she covered thick with arrows all over. It was the very image of a flight of cranes moving in the air and circling one after another in the figure of a wreath: the arrows were stuck in the dark cloud, but the veil was untorn and the wounds without blood. Then Hera picked up a rough missile of the air, a frozen mass of hail, circled it and struck Artemis with the jagged mass. The sharp stony lump broke the curves of the bow. But the consort of Zeus did not stop the fight there, but struck Artemis flat on the skin of the breast, and Artemis smitten by the weapon of ice emptied her quiver upon the ground. (Nonnus, *Dionysiaca* 36, 28ff (trans. Rouse).)

Thetis

Thetis was a Nereid, but our interest in her is as the divine mother of Achilles and the actions of the son she influenced in the Trojan War. The wedding of Thetis and the Greek hero Peleus led to the birth of their child Achilles. Achilles, in Book 1 (400f) of the *Iliad* describes Thetis as a warlike goddess when she defended Zeus in an attempted coup by three Olympians, namely Hera, Poseidon, and Pallas Athene, by installing the terrifying Giant 'monster of the hundred arms whom the gods call Briareus' as a guard. She was, of course, implicated in the Trojan War since it was her wedding to which Eris was not invited which led to the fateful Judgement of Paris and the Trojan War itself.

Thetis plays a major and significant role advising Achilles during the conflict, for example: 'Thetis warned Achilles not to be the first to disembark from the ships [at Troy], because the first to land was going to be the first to die.' (Pseudo-Apollodorus, *Bibliotheca* E3, 29.)

More particularly in the spat with Agamemnon over Briseis (Homer, *Iliad* 1,348 and 495ff):

Many times stretching forth his hands he called on his mother [Thetis]: 'Since, my mother, you bore me to be man with a short life, therefore Zeus of the loud thunder on Olympos should grant me honour at least. But now he has given me not even a little. Now the son of Atreus, powerful Agamemnon has dishonoured me, since he has taken away my prize [Briseis] and kept it.'

So he spoke in tears and the lady his mother heard him as she sat in the depths of the sea at the side of her aged father, and lightly she emerged like a mist from the grey water. She came and sat beside him as he wept, and stroked him with her hand and called him by name and spoke to him: 'Why then, child, do you lament? What sorrow has come to your heart now? Tell me, do not hide it in your mind, and thus we shall both know.'

Later, after the death of Patroclus, she advises patience and caution to which Achilles adheres, even when urged by Hera, via Iris, to rejoin the fray (Homer, *Iliad* 18, 34–96). Thetis is also instrumental in having a splendid suit of armour made for Achilles by Hephaestus – greaves, shield, helmet and breastplate – armour which helps him to slay Hector. She was there for him when he was utterly demoralized by the loss of Briseis, the love of his life. She was there for him when he frets about the decomposition of Patroclus' body and embalms the corpse with preserving ambrose and nectar. She was there for him when he risked annoying the gods by retaining Hector's corpse, intending to mutilate it, only releasing it when Thetis, on the bidding of the gods, advises him to do so.

Other Greek gods of war

Enyo, Athena, Hera and Thetis were not the only female divinities associated with war. As in many other aspects of ancient Greek life, a whole host of goddesses and female spirits were on hand to oversee and patronize the minutiae of war and conflict. They include the following.

Alala, spirit of the war cry from the onomatopoeic ἀλαλή (*alalē*) and the verb ἀλαλάζω (*alalazō*), 'to raise the war-cry', reputed to be from the eerie sound made by owls. Pindar references her: 'Listen! O Alala, daughter of Polemos! Prelude of spears! To whom soldiers are sacrificed for their city's sake in the holy sacrifice of death.'[23] She is the daughter of Polemos and niece to Enyo; her uncle was Ares.

The Androktasiai were the female spirits of battlefield slaughter; Hesiod in the *Theogony* gives their mother as Eris (Strife), and some fairly unsavoury siblings as Ponos (Hardship), Lethe (Forgetfulness), Limos (Starvation), Algae (Pains), Hysminai (Battles), Makhai (Wars), Phonoi (Murders), Neikea (Quarrels), Pseudea (Lies), Logoi (Tales), Amphillogiai (Disputes), Dysnomia (Anarchy), Ate (Ruin) and Horkos (Oath).

Bia was the spirit of force and violent compulsion. She and her sister and brothers Nike, Kratos (Strength) and Zelos (Rivalry), were constant companions of Zeus, an honour accorded after they helped Zeus in the war against the Titans.[24]

Erida was twin sister of Ares and goddess of hatred and bloodlust.

Eris, goddess of discord, chaos and strife, notably in battle; one of two goddesses of that name, the other being much more benign than ours, whom Homer in Book 4 of the *Iliad* describes as

> Strife whose wrath is relentless, is the sister and companion of murdering Ares, she who is only a little thing at first, but then grows until she strides the earth with her head striking heaven. She then hurles down bitterness equally between both sides as she walks through the slaughter making men's pain heavier. She also has a son whom she named Strife.

The Hysminai were female spirits of fighting and combat descended from Eris. Quintus Smyrnaeus described them vividly in his *Fall of Troy*:[25] 'Around them hovered the relentless Fates; beside them Battle incarnate pressed forward yelling, and from their limbs streamed blood and sweat.'

The Keres were female spirits of violent or cruel death, including death in battle, death by accident, murder or ravaging disease. They are characterized as dark beings with gnashing teeth and claws and with a thirst for human blood, hovering over the battlefield in search of dying and wounded men. A description of the Keres is on the *Shield of Heracles*:[26]

> The black Dooms – gnashing their white teeth, grim-eyed, fierce, bloody, terrifying – fought over the dying men: they were all longing

to drink dark blood. As soon as they caught a man who had fallen or one newly wounded, one of them clasped her great claws around him and his soul went down to Hades, to cold Tartarus. And when they had sated their hearts with human blood, they would toss that one behind them and rush back again into the battle and the tumult.

There may be a link between the Keres and various Celtic battlefield deities and the Norse Valkyries.[27] **The Makhai** were spirits of fighting and combat, sons or daughters of Eris.[28] **Nike** was a goddess who personified victory and was the divine charioteer, flying round battlefields rewarding the victors with glory and fame in the shape of a wreath of laurel leaves. She was awarded her elevation to Olympia for her assistance in the war against the Titans. **Otrera**, wife of Ares, was goddess of violence and chaos, mother of the Amazons, daughter of Eurus, the east wind. **Palioxis** was the spirit of flight and retreat from battle, while **Proioxis** was the spirit of battlefield pursuit.[29]

Homados and **Cerdomus**: Homados was the personification of battle-noise, the din of battle, similar to Cerdomus. Cerdomus was also the personification of the din of battle, confusion, uproar and the general fog of battle.

Chapter Three

Titanomachy: War of the Titans – Who Shall Rule the World?

Hesiod gives us our first extant attempt to give order to the gods of ancient Greece. He begins his *Theogeny* with Chaos, an ancient black hole. Chaos, the first Greek deity, was a goddess who gave birth to 'Gaia, the broad-breasted' and 'Eros, the fairest of the deathless gods.' Chaos also gave birth to Erebos and dark Night who mated and produced Ether and Day. Then Night created Doom, Fate, Death, Sleep, Dreams, Nemesis and all the other chthonic entities that dwell in the darkness haunting mankind. From an immaculate conception of sorts, Gaia gave birth to Uranus, the sky. Uranus married his mother, Gaia, enveloping her: they gave birth to the three Cyclopes, the three Hecatoncheires and twelve pre-Olympian Titans. The latter comprised six males – Coeus, Crius, Cronus, Hyperion, Iapetus and Oceanus – and six females – Mnemosyne, Phoebe, Rhea, Theia, Themis and Tethys. They in turn produced more Titans: Hyperion's children Helios, Selene and Eos; Coeus' children Leto and Asteria; Iapetus' sons Atlas, Prometheus, Epimetheus and Menoetius; Oceanus' daughter Metis; and Crius' sons Astraeus, Pallas and Perses.

According to Hesiod, Cronus coveted the power of his father, Uranus, the then ruler of the universe. Uranus alienated Cronus's mother, Gaia, when he imprisoned her youngest children, the hundred-handed Hecatoncheires and one-eyed Cyclopes, in gloomy Tartarus as they were born, blocking their exit by endless sexual intercourse with Gaia. He did this for no better reason than he found them repulsive to look at: *horribile visu*. A piqued Gaia responded by first inventing adamant: a magical mythical mineral of extreme hardness (at the top end of Mohs' scale) and then fashioned a huge sickle with it. She summoned Cronus and his brothers to persuade one of them to castrate Uranus. Only Cronus was willing to take on the ghastly deed, so Gaia gave him the sickle and set him up in ambush.

When Uranus met with Gaia, intending to have sex with her, Cronus attacked him with the adamantine sickle, castrating him and then casting his testicles into the sea. From the blood that spilled out and fell on the earth came such belligerent and disputatious characters as the Furies and the armed-to-the-teeth Giants, along with the Meliae (ash tree) nymphs. In the sea the testicles produced a white foam from which the goddess Aphrodite emerged. [Gaia] received the bloody drops that gushed forth, and as the seasons moved round she bore…the great Giants.

Cronus, now the supreme pre-Olympian god, released and then re-incarcerated the Hecatoncheires and the Cyclopes in gloomy Tartarus and set the chthonic dragon Campe to guard them. Cronus and his sister Rhea assumed the throne of the world as king and queen, producing Hestia, Demeter, Hera, Hades, Poseidon and Zeus. This was the Golden Age, in which things were so good that there was no need for laws or regulations; everyone did what was right, and there was neither bad nor immorality. After the Golden Age, things went slowly downhill for us all and have continued doing so ever since.

Cronus then received some decidedly unwelcome news when he learned from Gaia and Uranus that he was destined to be killed by his own son, just as he himself had overthrown his father. So every time Rhea gave birth, he simply ate the baby. Rhea, understandably, was somewhat upset by her husband's serial cannibalism and apparent filicide. By the time the sixth child, Zeus, was born Rhea had had enough and so she devised a plan to save him and to eventually win retribution on Cronus for his heinous acts against father, sons and daughters.

Rhea had secretly given birth to Zeus in Crete, delivering Cronus a stone wrapped in blankets: the Omphalos Stone. Believing it to be his son, Cronus, as was typical, swallowed the stone. All the while Rhea kept Zeus hidden in a cave on Mount Ida where he was raised by a goat named Amalthea on a diet of local honey, while a company of Kouretes, armoured male dancers, shouted and clapped their hands to make enough din to mask the baby's cries from Cronus. Another version sees Zeus raised by the nymph Adamanthea, who hid Zeus by dangling him by a rope from a tree so that he was suspended 'twixt earth, the sea, and the sky', all of which were ruled by his father, Cronus.

Once he had grown up, Zeus took revenge against Cronus; he met a cunning Titaness named Metis who assured Zeus that there was still an opportunity to save his siblings. She gave him an emetic supplied by Gaia which he in turn administered to Cronus to make him disgorge the contents of his stomach. This he did in order of consumption: first out was the stone, which was set down at Pytho under Mount Parnassus as a warning to mortal men, followed by his two brothers and three sisters. The stone was followed by his two brothers and three sisters: Poseidon, Hades, Hestia, Hera and Demeter.

Zeus then released more allies against Cronus: the Hecatoncheires, revived after their long underworld imprisonment by nourishing nectar and ambrosia, and the Cyclopes who forged for him his trademark thunderbolts, Poseidon's trident and Hades' helmet of darkness; they used these weapons later to break the deadlock and defeat the Titans in a ten-year-long war of attrition we call the Titanomachy. The Titanic stronghold was on Mount Othrys; the Olympian on Olympus. Zeus and his brothers and sisters, with the help of the Hecatoncheires and Cyclopes, eventually overthrew Cronus and the Titans. After the war, many of the Titans were confined in Tartarus. However, Oceanus, Helios, Atlas, Prometheus, Epimetheus and Menoetius escaped chthonic incarceration after the Titanomachy. Gaia bore the monster Typhon to claim revenge for the imprisoned Titans.

Zeus too was obliged to partake in some frantic deglutition when he heard that Metis, his first wife and personification of sly wisdom, would give birth to a god greater than he. Making full use of the precedents set by Cronus, Zeus wasted no time in swallowing her whole, unaware that she was pregnant with Athena. Athena then made a sensational entry into the world when she burst out of Zeus's head, all kitted out for battle.

The Hecatoncheires or 'Hundred-Handed Ones' are also called the Centimanes; they were three giants of prodigious strength and ferocity that surpassed all of the Titans, who they helped to overthrow. Their name derives from the Greek ἑκατόν (*hekaton*, 'hundred') and χείρ (*cheir*, 'hand'), 'each of them having a hundred hands and fifty heads.' The Hundred-Handed Ones are 'giants' of great storms and hurricanes.

They were Briareos (Βριάρεως), 'strong', also called Aegaeon (Αἰγαίων); an alternative myth casts Briareos as summoned to Olympus by Thetis to save Zeus from an attempted coup by Hera; Kottos (Κόττος), 'strike, punch' and Gyges (Γύγης) or Gyes (Γύης), possibly 'limb' or 'curved'.

During the war against the Titans their *modus operandi* involved hurling rocks as big as mountains at the titanic stronghold on Mount Othrys, 100 at a time, and overwhelming the Titans. Hesiod graphically describes the cataclysmic battle between Zeus with his screaming thunderbolts, the Hundred-Handed Ones with their 300-boulder final salvo and the Titans as shaking creation to its very core. Hesiod (*Theogony* 624, 639, 714, 734–35) reports that the three Hecatoncheires fittingly became the guards of the gates of Tartarus whence the defeated Titans had been despatched for their opposition to the Olympian order; Tartarus was as far from earth as earth is from heaven, that is the space through which a bronze anvil would plummet in ten days.

The *Titanomachy* (Τιτανομαχία) is a lost epic poem which deals with the ten-year war against the Titans. It is attributed to the legendary blind Thracian bard Thamyris and mentioned in an essay *On Music* that was once attributed to Plutarch. The *Titanomachy* was traditionally ascribed to Eumelus of Corinth (eighth century BCE), a semi-legendary bard of the Bacchiad ruling family in archaic Corinth. The *Titanomachy* was divided into at least two books. The battle of the Olympians and Titans was preceded by some sort of theogony.

The Cyclops were a primordial race of giants, each with a single eye in the centre of his forehead. The word cyclops literally means 'round- or circle-eyed'. In the *Theogony* the cyclops – Brontes (Βρόντης, 'thunderer'), Steropes (Στερόπης, 'lightning') and Arges (Ἄργης, 'brightness') – were the primordial sons of Uranus and Gaia and brothers of the Hecatoncheires and the Titans. This made them blood-related to the Titans and Olympian gods and goddesses.[1] Homer locates them in a faraway, lawless and anarchic place.

They eventually became synonyms for brute strength and power, and their name was associated with monumental buildings and blacksmithery, often pictured working at their forge. The most celebrated Cyclops is, of course, Polyphemus in Book 9 of the *Odyssey* who captures Odysseus, eats some of his men live and raw and inadvertently and drunkenly allows the hero to escape slung under a sheep. Theocritus paints a very different picture of a Polyphemus infatuated with the nymph Galatea and failing in his attempt to woo her.[2] In manufacturing the thunderbolts of Zeus in gratitude for releasing them from Tartarus, the three Cyclops worked as a team: Arges contributed gleaming brightness, Brontes added booming thunder, and Steropes brought flashing lightning. The Greeks still tell the story today of the blinding of the one-eyed Polyphemus.

According to Callimachus,[3] they were Hephaestus' assistants at the Olympian forge. The Cyclops were credited for building the 'cyclopean' fortifications at Tiryns and Mycenae in the Peloponnese. The tremendous noises from volcanic explosions were attributed to the Cyclops.[4]

Euripides' only extant comedy is his *Cyclops*, which was written in 408 BCE and is the only complete satyr play of ancient Greece that is extant. It is set near the volcanic Mount Etna, and the cyclops is portrayed as a cave-dwelling, violent, cannibalistic, oafish character, similar to Homer's Polyphemus. Euripides' version may have been influenced by the comic handling of the cyclops found in Cratinus' play *Odysseus*, one of the many plays that are known to have lampooned Homer's cyclops story.

At 20,426 lines in forty-eight books, Nonnus' *Dionysiaca*, composed in the fourth or fifth century BCE, is the longest surviving poem from antiquity. It describes a war that occurred between Dionysus' troops and those of the Indian king Deriades. In Book 28 the Cyclops join forces with Dionysian troops, and prove to be great warriors, crushing most of the Indian king's troops.

Orphism leaves us with an alternative myth. The Titans destroyed the infant Dionysus as he sat playing with his toys; an enraged Zeus blasted them with a well-aimed thunderbolt and reduced the Titans to soot. This soot was to be a constituent in the physical make-up of mankind, imbuing us with an irrepressible tendency to crime, destroying the Dionysus within us as we repeat the crimes of the Titans.

Pallas

Of the sixty or so Titans and Titanesses, the one that interests us most is Pallas. He was the Titan god of battle, of the spring campaign season and the art of war. He was the father of Nike (Victory), Zelos (Rivalry), Kratos (Cratus, Strength) and Bia (Power) by Styx (Hatred), children who sided with Zeus during the Titan War. Pallas's name is derived from the Greek *pallô*, meaning 'to brandish (a spear)'. He is often confused with the Giant of the same name. According to John Tzetzes, his was the skin Athena peeled off to make her famous shield or aegis.

Chapter Four

Gigantomachy: War of the Giants –
Another Battle for the Cosmos

The hundred Giants, or Gigantes, embodied prodigious strength and aggression; they are best known for the Gigantomachy (*Gigantomachia*), the crucial battle they fought, urged on by Gaia, with the Olympian gods. Zeus and the Olympians were intent on overthrowing the old order as represented by the Gigantes. According to Homer, they were a gigantic and savage race of men, led by Eurymedon and living in the far west on the island of Thrinacia, but they were wiped out by Eurymedon for their insolence towards the gods. (Homer *Odyssey* 7, 59, 206, 10, 120; cf. Pausanias 8, 29, 2). Homer saw the Gigantes, like the Phaeacians, Cyclopes and Laestrygones, as a race of Autochthones (indigenous inhabitants of a place or aborigines), who, with the exception of the Phaeacians, the gods destroyed for their hubris and insolence, but neither he nor Hesiod mention anything about the war of the gods with the Gigantes.

> Homer, *Odyssey* 10.119ff: 'They [the Laistrygones] came thronging up in multitudes, looking not like men but like the lawless Giants.'
>
> Homer, *Odyssey* 7, 200ff (trans. Shewring): '[King Alkinoos (Alcinous) of the Phaiekes (Phaeacians) addresses his people:] 'In the past they [the gods] have always appeared undisguised among us at our offering of noble hecatombs; they have feasted beside us, they have sat at the same table. And if one of us comes upon them as he travels alone, then too they have never as yet made concealment, because we are close of kin to themselves, just like those of the Cyclopes race or the savage people of the Gigantes.'

As we have seen, Hesiod tells us that the Giants were divine beings, the offspring of Gaia (Earth), born from the blood drops spilt when

Uranus was castrated by his Titan son Cronus.[1] The most notorious were Enkelados who was buried by Athena beneath Mount Etna, Polybotes who was crushed by an island hurled by Poseidon, and Porphyrion who was killed by Zeus and Heracles when he attempted to rape Hera.

Like the brutish and much-disliked Ares, the Gigantes have strong associations with the primitive tribes of Thrace, whose barbaric culture stood in stark contrast with the finer aspects of Greek civilization. According to some, the Thracians were born from the blood or ashes of the vanquished Giants.

The Giants are often confused with other antagonists of the Olympians, particularly the Titans but also the huge monster Typhon, the offspring of Gaia and Tartarus, whom Zeus vanquished with his thunderbolt, and those big, mighty and aggressive brothers Otus and Ephialtes, who piled Mounts Pelion (the two great mountains of Magnesia) on top of Ossa in order to scale the heavens and attack the Olympians. To confuse matters further, Hyginus includes the names of three Titans – Coeus, Iapetus and Astraeus – along with Typhon and the Aloadae in his list of Giants, and Ovid conflates the Gigantomachy with the later siege of Olympus by the Aloadae.[2] The defeated Giants were said to be buried under volcanoes and to be the trigger for volcanic eruptions and earthquakes, especially in southern Italy from the plains of Campania to the active volcanoes Etna and Vesuvius.

There is little consistency in the literature regarding the origins of the Giants. The three references to the Gigantes in Homer's *Odyssey* have Giants among the ancestors of the Phaiakians, a race of men encountered by Odysseus, their ruler Alcinous being the son of Nausithous, who was the son of Poseidon and Periboea, the daughter of the Giant king Eurymedon. Secondly, Alcinous says that the Phaiakians, like the Cyclopes and the Giants, are 'closely related' to the gods; and finally, Odysseus describes the Laestrygonians as more like Giants than men. Pausanias, the second-century CE geographer, took these lines to mean that, for Homer, the Giants were a race of mortal men.[3]

The sixth to fifth century BCE Bacchylides calls the Giants 'sons of the Earth'. 'Gegeneis' ('earthborn') became a common epithet of the Giants. Hyginus has the Giants as the offspring of Gaia and Tartarus.[4]

How were the Giants described? What sort of picture do we get of them? Homer describes the Giant king Eurymedon as 'great-hearted' (μεγαλήτορος) and his people as 'insolent' (ὑπερθύμοισι) and 'reckless' (ἀτάσθαλος).⁵ Hesiod calls the Giants 'strong' (κρατερῶν) and 'great' (μεγάλους);⁶ the *Theogony* also has the Giants born 'with gleaming armour, with long spears in their hands'.

Other early sources characterize the Giants by their excesses. Pindar describes the excessive violence of the Giant Porphyrion;⁷ Bacchylides calls the Giants arrogant, saying that they were destroyed by 'Hybris' (hubris personified).⁸ In the earlier seventh century BCE Alcman had already characterized the Giants as hubristic, with the phrases 'vengeance of the gods' and 'they suffered unforgettable punishments for the evil they did', referring to the Gigantomachy.⁹

Diodorus Siculus notes that it was not just the Olympian gods who were the targets of the Giants; the whole race of men attracted their unwanted attentions too:

Diodorus Siculus, Library of History 5. 71. 4 (trans. Oldfather): 'The Giants were punished by Zeus because they had treated the rest of mankind in a lawless fashion and, confiding in their bodily superiority and strength, had enslaved their neighbours, and because they were also disobeying the rules of justice which he was laying down and were raising up war against those whom all mankind considered to be gods because of the benefactions they were conferring upon men generally.'

Homer's comparison of the Giants to the Laestrygonians suggests similarities between the two races. The Laestrygonians 'hurled…rocks huge as a man could lift'; their king's (Antiphates') wife is described as being as big as a mountain.

Gigantes are often depicted as man-sized hoplites and human in form:

Pseudo-Apollodorus, *Bibliotheca* 1. 34 (trans. Aldrich): 'These creatures [Gigantes (Giants)] were unsurpassed in the size of their bodies and unconquerable by virtue of their power. They were frightening in appearance, with long hair that swept down from their heads and chins, and serpent-scales covering their lower limbs.'

Valerius Flaccus, *Argonautica* 2. 16ff (trans. Mozley): 'The monstrous forms of Earth's children (Terrigenum)…the Gigantum (Giants), whom in compassion their mother [Gaia, the Earth] clothed with rocks, trees, crags and piled up to heaven new-shaped as mountains.'

After ca.380 BCE, though, the Gigantes sport snakes for legs:

Nonnus, *Dionysiaca* 25. 206ff: '[Gigantes (Giants)] the snaky sons of Gaia (the Earth)…with huge serpents flowing over their shoulders equally on both sides much bigger than the Inakhian snake… went hissing restlessly about among the stars of heaven.' [i.e. Their serpentine legs coil downward and then upward over their shoulders.]

Over the years, the Giants lost more and more of their human characteristics, becoming instead more monstrous and even more 'gigantic'. According to Apollodorus the Giants were big and strong, they looked fearsome with long hair and beards and scaly feet.[10] Ovid has them 'snake-footed' with a 'hundred arms'[11] and Nonnus described them as 'serpent-haired'.[12]

The Hesiodic Catalogue of Women (or the *Ehoiai*) is an encyclopedia of heroic mythology (the women in the title are heroines), just as the *Theogony* presents a systematic account of the Greek pantheon. It refers to Heracles having slain 'presumptuous Giants' and elsewhere refers to the Gigantomachy when Zeus produces Heracles to be 'a protector against ruin for gods and men'.[13]

If Hesiod, when he says that the Muses sing of the Giants, and the sixth-century BCE poet Xenophanes singles out the Gigantomachy as a subject to be avoided at table, then there may well have been (a lost) epic poem, a *Gigantomachia*.[14] The Apollonius scholia refers to a 'Gigantomachia' in which the Titan Cronus (as a horse) sires the centaur Chiron by mating with Philyra (the daughter of two Titans). Other possible sources include Alcman and the sixth-century Ibycus.

Pindar provides one of our earliest sources for the battle between the Giants and the Olympians. He locates it 'on the plain of Phlegra' and has the seer Tiresias foretell Heracles killing Giants 'beneath [his] rushing arrows'. He calls Heracles 'you who slew the Giants', and has Porphyrion, whom he calls 'the king of the Giants', being overcome by the bow of Apollo.[15] Euripides' *Heracles* has its hero shooting Giants with arrows, and his *Ion* has the chorus describe seeing a depiction of the Gigantomachy on the late sixth-century Temple of Apollo at Delphi, with Athena fighting the Giant Enceladus with her 'gorgon shield', Zeus burning the Giant Mimas with his 'mighty thunderbolt, blazing at both ends', and Dionysus killing an unnamed Giant with his 'ivy staff'.[16]

However, it is from Apollodorus that we get the most detailed account of the Gigantomachy.[17] None of the early sources give any reasons for the war but the scholia to the *Iliad* mention the rape of Hera by the Giant Eurymedon and according to scholia to Pindar's *Isthmian 6*, it was the theft of the cattle of Helios by the Giant Alcyoneus that sparked the war. Apollodorus, who also mentions the cattle theft, suggests a mother's revenge as the motive for the war, saying that Gaia bore the Giants because of her anger over the Titans who had been vanquished and imprisoned by the Olympians. The late fourth-century CE Latin poet Claudian expands on this in his *Gigantomachia* with Gaia, 'jealous of the heavenly kingdoms and in pity for the ceaseless woes of the Titans', who gave birth to the Giants, urging them to war, saying 'Up, army of avengers, the hour is come at last, free the Titans from their chains; defend your mother.'[18] As soon as the Giants were born they began hurling 'rocks and burning oaks at the sky.'[19] The Giants started as they meant to go on.

Unfortunately for the Olympians, in order to eliminate the Giants, they had received an oracle ordaining that they would have to enlist the support of a mortal to deal the fatal blow.[20] Enter Heracles, fathered by Zeus through a mortal woman, Alcmene, in what must have been one of the most baffling cases of paternity in Greek mythology, not least for Amphitryon – Alcmene's husband – who believed his wife to be a virgin but miraculously presented him with twins: Heracles by Zeus and Iphicles by himself.

In a bid to foil the prophecy, Gaia scoured the earth for a particular herb (*pharmakon*) that would protect the Giants even against a mortal helper. Before Gaia or anyone else could find this plant, Zeus forbade Eos

(Dawn), Selene (Moon) and Helios (Sun) to shine, harvested all supplies of the plant himself and then had Athena enlist the help of Heracles.

According to Apollodorus, Alcyoneus and Porphyrion were the two strongest Giants and both came to sticky ends. Heracles stole up on Alcyoneus as he slept and disabled him with a volley of arrows and blows from his club. Alcyoneus fell to the ground, but then revived since he was immortal within the borders of his native land, Thracian Pallene. So Heracles, on Athena's advice, dragged him beyond the borders of Pallene where Alcyoneus promptly died. Porphyrion attacked Heracles and Hera, but Zeus caused Porphyrion to fall in love with Hera, who Porphyrion then tried to rape. Zeus struck Porphyrion with his thunderbolt and Heracles killed him with an arrow. The other giants – twenty-four according to Hyginus – were then picked off one after another by the gods in league with Heracles; some of them were buried by their assailants under volcanic islands. (Euripides, *Cyclops* 7; Diodorus Siculus 4, 21; Servius, *ad Aeneid* 8, 578.)

Apollodorus tells us about other Giants and their fates: Ephialtes was blinded by an arrow from Apollo in his left eye, and another arrow from Heracles, not to be outdone, in his right; Eurytus was killed by Dionysus with his *thyrsus* (spear), Clytius by Hecate with her torches and Mimas by Hephaestus with 'missiles of red-hot metal' from his forge; Athena crushed Enceladus under Sicily and flayed Pallas, using his skin as a shield; Poseidon broke off a piece of the island of Kos called Nisyros and threw it on top of Polybotes (Strabo also relates the story of Polybotes buried under Nisyros but adds that some say Polybotes lies under Kos instead);[21] Hermes, wearing Hades' helmet, killed Hippolytus, Artemis slew Gration, and the Moirai (Fates) murdered Agrius and Thoas with bronze clubs. The rest of the giants were 'destroyed' by thunderbolts thrown by Zeus, with each Giant being shot with arrows by Heracles for good measure.

Powerful as they were, the Giants were not without their vulnerabilities, as described by Hyginus:

Pseudo-Hyginus, *Astronomica* 2. 23 (trans. Grant): 'According to Eratosthenes another story is told about the donkeys. After Zeus had declared war on the Giants, he summoned all the gods to fight them, and Dionysos, Hephaestus, the Satyrs, and the Sileni (Silens) came riding on donkeys. Since they were not far from the enemy, the asses were terrified, and individually let out a braying such as the Gigantes had never heard. At the noise the enemy took hastily to flight, and thus were defeated.'

There is a story similar to this about the shell of Triton. He, too, when he had hollowed out the trumpet he had invented, took it with him against the Gigantes, and there blew strange sounds through the shell. The Gigantes, fearing that some wild beast had been brought by their adversaries, took flight, and thus were overcome and came into their enemies' power.

However, Plato, for one, was somewhat sceptical regarding the historicity of it all:

Plato, *Euthyphro* 6b (trans. Fowler): '(Socrates): And so you believe that there was really war between the gods, and fearful enmities and battles and other things of the sort [i.e. the war of the Gigantes], such as are told of by the poets and represented in varied designs by the great artists in our sacred places and especially on the robe which is carried up to the Acropolis at the great Panathenaia for this is covered with such representations. Shall we agree that these things are true, Euthyphro?'

Plato, *Republic* 378c (trans. Shorey): 'Neither must we admit at all,' said I, 'that gods war with gods...still less must we make battles of gods and Giants the subject for them of stories and embroideries [i.e. the War of the Giants] woven on the pelos of Athena at the Panathenaic festival.'

Centuries later the scepticism was still alive and well with Cicero. Cicero, *De Natura Deorum* 2, 28 (trans. Rackham): 'According to the myths they [the gods] even engage in wars and battles...they actually fought wars of their own, for instance with the Titans and the Giants. These stories and these beliefs are utterly foolish.'

Also with Philostratus, up to a point:

Philostratus, *Life of Apollonius of Tyana* 5, 16 (trans. Conybeare):
'Now I admit that Giants have existed, and that gigantic bodies are
revealed all over earth when tombs are broken open; nevertheless I
deny that they ever came into conflict with the gods; at the most they
violated their temples and statues, and to suppose that they scaled
the heaven and chased away the gods therefrom, – this it is madness
to relate and madness to believe.'

As noted, the beginning of the fourth century BCE sees the first portrayal
of the Giants as somewhat less than human in form, with legs that are
coiled serpents having snake heads at the ends in place of feet, rather like
Typhon. This became the standard for the rest of antiquity, culminating
in the monumental Gigantomachy frieze of the second-century BCE
Pergamon Altar. Measuring nearly 400ft long and over 7ft high, here the
Gigantomachy receives its most extensive treatment, with more than 100
figures.

Ovid adds to the variants when he gives a brief account of the
Gigantomachy in his *Metamorphoses*.[22] As we have seen, Ovid includes
the Aloadae's assault on Olympus as part of the Gigantomachy, with the
Giants attempting to seize 'the throne of Heaven' by piling 'mountain on
mountain to the lofty stars' but Jupiter (the Roman Zeus) destroys the
Giants with his thunderbolts, overturning 'from Ossa huge, enormous
Pelion'.[23] Ovid adds that from the blood of the Giants came a new race of
beings in human form. Gaia did not want the Giants to perish without a
trace, so 'reeking with the copious blood of her gigantic sons', she gave
life to the 'steaming gore' of the blood-soaked battleground. These new
offspring, like their fathers the Giants, also hated the gods and possessed
a bloodthirsty desire for 'savage slaughter'.

Later in the *Metamorphoses*, Ovid refers to the Gigantomachy as 'the
time when serpent-footed giants strove to fix their hundred arms on
captive Heaven.'[24] This is where Ovid apparently conflates the Giants
with the Hundred-Handers who, though in Hesiod fought alongside
Zeus and the Olympians, in some traditions fought against them.[25]

Various places have been associated with the Giants and the
Gigantomachy. As noted, Pindar has the battle occur at Phlegra ('the
place of burning'), as do other early sources,[26] and the Gigantomachy

were also often associated, by later writers, with a volcanic plain in Italy, west of Naples and east of Cumae, called the Phlegraean Fields. The third-century BCE poet Lycophron apparently locates a battle of gods and Giants close to the volcanic island of Ischia off the coast of Naples, where he says the Giants (along with Typhon) were 'crushed' under the island. At least one tradition placed Phlegra in Thessaly.[27]

Strabo provides an interesting fact in relation to Aphrodite Apatouros, Aphrodite the Deceitful:

> Strabo, *Geography* 11. 2. 10 (trans. Jones): 'There is also in Phanagoreia [on the Bosporus] a notable temple of Aphrodite Apatouros. Critics derive the etymology of the epithet of the goddess by adducing a certain myth, according to which the Giants attacked the goddess there; but she called upon Heracles for help and hid him in a cave, and then, admitting the Gigantes one by one, gave them over to Heracles to be murdered through treachery.'

The war of the Giants has been a very popular theme, to say the least, in the fine arts. From the sixth century BCE onwards more than 600 representations are catalogued in the *Lexicon Iconographicum Mythologiae Classicae* (LIMC).

The Gigantomachy was depicted on the new *peplos* presented to Athena on the Acropolis of Athens as part of the Panathenaic festival celebrating her victory over the Giants. The numerous vases featuring Giants depict large battles, including most of the Olympians, and contain a central group which consists of Zeus, Heracles, Athena and sometimes Gaia. Zeus, Heracles and Athena are attacking Giants to the right. Zeus mounts a chariot brandishing his thunderbolt in his right hand; Heracles, in the chariot, bends forward with drawn bow and left foot on the chariot pole; Athena, beside the chariot, strides forward towards one or two Giants and the four chariot horses trample a fallen Giant.

The Gigantomachy was still an extremely popular motif in late sixth-century and fifth-century sculpture. Highlights include the north frieze of the Siphnian Treasury at Delphi (ca.525 BCE), with more than thirty figures named by inscription; the west pediment of the Alkmeonid Temple of Apollo at Delphi; the pediment of the Megarian Treasury at

Gustave Doré's (1832–1883) 1857 illustration to Dante's *Inferno*, Plate LXV, Canto XXXI: The titans and giants. 'This proud one wished to make experiment/Of his own power against the Supreme Jove' (Longfellow). [From the title page:] Dante's *Inferno* translated by the Reverend Henry Francis Cary, MA, from the original of Dante Alighieri, and illustrated with the designs of M. Gustave Doré, New Edition, With Critical and Explanatory Notes, Life of Dante, and Chronology. Cassell, Petter, Galpin & Co., New York, London and Paris. The book was printed ca.1890 in America. Look at the relative size of Dante and Virgil to the Giants and Titans.

Poseidon attacks the giant Polybotes with Gaia on the left looking on. Red-figure cup, late fifth century BC. (*Antikensammlung Berlin F2531*)

Wenceslaus Hollar (1607–1677), the Greek gods: Typhon. Thomas Fisher, Rare Book Library. (*University of Toronto Wenceslas Hollar Digital Collection. Plate number P267, ca.1608*)

A fine depiction of Zeus with thunderbolt at the ready rushing at Typhon. Chalcidian hydria, ca.540 BCE, Munich Antikensammlungen.

Centaur mosaic (120 CE–130 CE). (*Altes Museum, Berlin; Level Etruscan and Roman Art Room Roman Villas – Luxury as a Lifestyle*)

Antonio Canova (1757–1822), 'Theseus defeats the Centaur'. Between 1805 and 1819, Rome. Kunsthistorisches Museum, Vienna. This was commissioned by Napoleon for the Corso in Milan, bought by Emperor Franz I in Rome and in 1822/23 brought to Vienna for the specially-built Theseustemple in the Volksgarten. Since 1891 it has resided in the Kunsthistorisches Museum, Vienna. (*Photographer: own work, Georges Jansoone, taken on 22 June 2006*)

Amazonomachy scene on a *lekythos*. The patterned leggings and short tunics together with crescent-shaped shields give the Amazons away as being 'Persian'. Date ca.420 BCE. Now in the Metropolitan Museum of Art, New York.

Off with her head. Heracles grabs the Phrygian hat of an Amazon while wielding his sword. She raises an axe to defend herself, and may have had a sword in her other hand. Heracles shows his skill in battle by treading on the Amazon's foot to immobilize her. (*Relief; metope from Selinus*)

Caivano Painter: scene from *The Seven Against Thebes* by Aeschylus. Capaneus scales the city walls to overthrow King Creon who looks down from the battlements. Campanian red-figure neck-amphora, ca.340 BCE. (*Getty Villa Collection; photographer Wolfgang Sauber*)

A beautiful Attic red-figure volute-krater from Spina graphically showing the Seven Against Thebes. At the bottom we can see the chariot of Amphiaraus sinking into Hades. Ca.440 BCE.

An infant Heracles strangling a snake. Marble, Roman artwork, second century CE. (*Capitoline Museums, Rome, Palazzo Nuovo*)

The Death of King Laius, artist unknown (seventeenth or eighteenth century). (*National Gallery of Scotland*)

Heracles grabs Nessus by the hair and plants his foot firmly on his back ready to stab him. Attic black–figure amphora, ca.620 BCE.

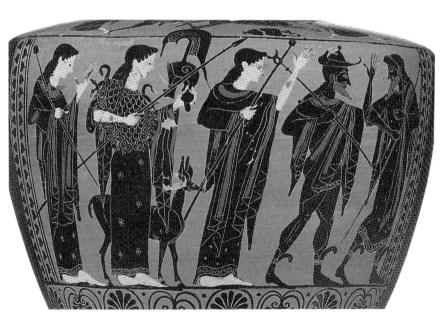

This is how the Trojan War began, with the judgement made by Paris. Here it is on an Attic black–figure hydria from about 540 BCE. Paris is on the far right facing Hermes and the goddesses: Aphrodite, Athena with deer, holding her helmet and Hera far left.

Jacob Jordaens (1593–1678), 'The Wedding of Thetis and Peleus/The Golden Apple of Discord'. The classical world's most significant apple, 1633. (*Museo del Prado, Madrid accession number P001634*)

Menelaus and Meriones lifting Patroclus' corpse on a cart while Odysseus (on the right, wearing the pilos hat and a shield) looks on. Alabaster urn, Etruscan artwork, second century BCE. From Volterra. Stored in the Museo Nazionale Archeologico Nazionale in Florence. (*From the Iliade Exhibition at the Colosseum, September 2006–February 2007; author Jastrow*)

Franz von Matsch (died 1942), 'Triumphant Achilles: Achilles dragging the dead body of Hector in front of the gates of Troy'. The original painting (1892) is a fresco on the upper level of the main hall of the Achilleion at Corfu, Greece. (*Photographer/user: Dr K.*)

Ajax with the body of Achilles. Hoping to receive Achilles' armour, in exchange for his protecting and retrieving the body of his friend, Ajax returns the remains of Achilles from the battlefield to the Achaean camp. Crafty Odysseus, however, has other thoughts and designs on the coveted armour. When he fails, Ajax commits suicide. Black-figure vase. (*Classical Art Research Centre and the Beazley Archive at Oxford University*)

Olympia; the east pediment of the Old Temple of Athena on the Acropolis of Athens; and the metopes of Temple F at Selinous.

Phidias used the theme for the metopes of the east façade of the Parthenon (ca.445 BCE) and for the interior of the shield of Athena Parthenos. Phidias' work perhaps marks the beginning of a change in the way the Giants are presented, moving from typical portrayals as hoplite warriors armed with the standard issue helmets, shields, spears and swords to a less handsome appearance, primitive and wild, clothed in animal skins or naked, often without armour and using boulders as weapons. This was, no doubt, an attempt to distance the regular Greek armies – representative of civilization – and to align the Giants more closely with the barbarians of the world.

What does the Gigantomachy actually symbolize? Along with the Titanomachy it probably reflects the 'triumph' of the new imported gods of the insurgent Greek-speaking peoples from the north from around ca.2000 BCE over the old gods of the native peoples of the Greek peninsula. For the Greeks, the Gigantomachy represented victory for order over chaos: the victory of the contemporary divine order and rationalism of the Olympian gods over the discord and excessive violence of the earth-born chthonic Giants. More specifically, for sixth- and fifth-century BCE Greeks, it symbolized a victory for civilization over barbarism, and as such was an ideal theme as a symbol of civilization and high culture for Phidias to portray on the metopes of the Parthenon, for it to be woven into Athena's *peplos* as presented to her statue at the Panathenaia, and for the shield of Athena Parthenos to symbolize the recent victory of the Athenians over the Persians. We have already noted the ubiquity of the Gigantomachy on other major temples at Delphi, Eretrea and Corcyra. To drive this anti-barbarian message home, the Giants' iconography is shown on the shield of Athene Parthenos as increasingly wild and uncivilized with skins, not armour, and rocks, not weapons. It is perhaps no coincidence that Athens, now an emerging major power in the region, had endured and survived the tyranny of Peisistratos and had another reason to use the attempted coup by the Giants to symbolize and celebrate good over evil, order over disorder, future over past. Later the Attalids – the Hellenistic dynasty that ruled Pergamon between 283 and 129 BCE – similarly used the Gigantomachy on the Pergamon Altar to symbolize their victory over the Galatians of Asia Minor.

The attempt of the Giants to overthrow the Olympians also represented the ultimate in hubris, with the gods themselves punishing the Giants for their arrogant and presumptuous challenge to their divine authority. The Gigantomachy can also be seen as a continuation of the eternal struggle between Gaia and Uranus and thus as part of the primal conflict between female and male. Plato compares the Gigantomachy to a philosophical dispute about existence, wherein the materialist philosophers, who believe that only physical things exist, like the Giants, wish to 'drag down everything from heaven and the invisible to earth.'[28]

The Romans introduced some interesting interpretations regarding the role and symbolism of the Giants whom they often conflated with the Titans, Typhon and the Aloadae. Cicero allegorizes the Gigantomachy as 'fighting against Nature'.[29] Rationalist Epicurean Lucretius, for whom such things as lightning, earthquakes, volcanic eruptions and other such phenomena had natural rather than divine causes, used the Gigantomachy to celebrate the triumph of philosophy, science and reason over mythology and superstition. In the triumph of science and reason over traditional religious belief, the Gigantomachy was for Epicurus storming heaven. Lucretius represents the Giants as heroic rebels against the tyranny of Olympus.[30] Virgil restores the conventional meaning, making the Giants once again enemies of order and civilization. Horace adds a contemporary historic symbolism when he equates the victory of Octavian (later Augustus) at the Battle of Actium as a victory for the civilized West over the barbaric East as represented by Cleopatra VII, and by other unsettling exotic influences.[31]

In his *Metamorphoses*, Ovid describes mankind's moral decline through the ages of gold, silver, bronze and iron, with the Gigantomachy a key player in the slide to rack and ruin, the descent from natural order into mayhem.[32] Lucan, in his *Pharsalia*, has the Gorgon's gaze transmogrify the Giants into mountains, while Valerius Flaccus, in the *Argonautica*, makes the *Argo* (the world's first ship) a Gigantomachy-like offence against natural law, and an example of the last word in hubris.[33]

In the fourth-century CE Clodian's *Gigantomachia*, the battle was viewed as a metaphor for vast geomorphic change: 'The puissant company of the giants confounds all differences between things; islands abandon the deep; mountains lie hidden in the sea. Many a river is left dry or has altered its ancient course....robbed of her mountains Earth sank into level plains, parted among her own sons.'[34]

As we have seen, geology and, more specifically, vulcanology are also implicated in the myth of the Giants; a number of locations associated with the Giants and the Gigantomachy were areas of volcanic and seismic activity such as the Phlegraean Fields west of Naples. The defeated Gigantes were reputed to be buried under volcanos and when they stirred they were said to be the cause of volcanic eruptions and earthquakes.[35]

The Giant Enceladus lay buried under Mount Etna, the volcano's eruptions being the breath of Enceladus and its tremors caused by the Giant rolling over from side to side beneath the mountain. The monster Typhon and the Hundred-Hander Briareus were also buried under Etna. The Giant Alcyoneus along with 'many giants' were said to lie under Mount Vesuvius, while Prochyte (modern Procida), one of the volcanic Phlegraean Islands, was supposed to cover the Giant Mimas, and Polybotes was pinned beneath the volcanic island of Nisyros, supposedly a piece of the island of Kos broken off and thrown by Poseidon.

When Mount Vesuvius famously erupted in 79 CE, burying the towns of Pompeii and Herculaneum, Cassius Dio would have us believe that many Giant-like creatures appeared on the mountain followed by violent earthquakes and the final cataclysmic eruption, saying 'some thought that the Giants were rising again in revolt (for at this time also many of their forms could be discerned in the smoke and, moreover, a sound as of trumpets was heard).'[36]

The revolt of the Aloadai

The giants Otos and Ephialtes (the tallest men who were ever nurtured by the grain-giving earth according to Homer (*Odyssey* 11, 306–20) and their separate assault on Olympus can be seen as a coda to the Gigantomachy proper. We have already met them in our account of Ares which shows them to have previous when it came to annoying the gods: namely containing Ares in a jar (*pithos*), and in the various confusions in which they are included in descriptions of the Giants in general. They were the sons of Poseidon and Iphimideia, wife to Thessalian Aloeus; according to Apollodorus (1, 53) Iphimideia stalked Poseidon for some time on the seashore, tempting him by scooping sea water over her vagina, until one day he emerged and made love to her. Giants indeed Otos and Ephialtes were: by age 9 they were growing 2ft in width and 6ft in length and were 14ft wide and 50ft+ tall (Apollodorus 1, 53). Pliny adds (*Natural History* 7, 73): 'When a mountain in Crete was split open by an earthquake a body 69 feet in height was found, which some thought must be that of Orion and others of Otus.' In beauty only Orion was better-looking. The name Aloadai is derived from the Greek verb *aloaô* meaning 'to crush'. Individually they were named 'nightmare' (*ephialtês*) and 'doom' (from *oitos*) or 'horned-owl' (*ôtos*).

The Aloadai had designs on world domination, threatening to change land into sea and sea into land; accordingly they hatched an attack on Olympus and attempted to pile Mount Ossa upon Olympus and Pelion upon Ossa. They would have succeeded, says Homer, had they been allowed to grow to manhood; but Apollo destroyed them before they began shaving (*Odyssey* 11, 305). Another version (Callimachus, *Hymn 3 to Artemis*) attributes their downfall more to sexual desire than to conflict. Ephialtes went for Hera, while Otos gave unwelcome attention to Artemis. Artemis was having none of this, so she changed herself into a deer and ran between the two brothers when they were out hunting on Naxos. An early example of friendly fire did for both of them when their spears pierced each other instead of the disguised Artemis. Some sources conflate or confuse this with the story of Ares' imprisonment in the jar: Ares was only released when Artemis offered herself up to Otos, making Ephialtes jealous and leading to a fight. Artemis transformed herself into a doe and jumped between them, thus attracting the blue on blue.

Diodorus Siculus has a different denouement:

'Aloeus dispatched his sons Otos and Ephialtes in search of his wife [Iphimedia] and daughter [Pankratis], and they, sailing to Naxos, defeated the Thracians and reduced the city. Some time afterwards Pankratis died, and Otos and Ephialtes tried to take the island as their home and to rule over the Thracians, and they changed the name of the island to Dia. But later they quarrelled, and joining battle they slew many of the other combatants and then destroyed each other, and from that time on these two men have received at the hands of the natives the honours accorded to heroes.' (Diodorus Siculus, *Library of History* 5, 51, 1.)

According to Hyginus, the punishment meted out in Hades involved being tied back-to-back by snakes to a column on which perched the nymph of Styx masquerading as a blood-sucking screech owl, presumably to drive them to eternal distraction by its interminable screeching.

Pausanias (9, 29, 1) confounds the traditional picture of these malcontents when he says that they were the first of all men who worshipped the Muses on Mount Helicon and to have consecrated this mountain to them; they worshipped only three Muses – Melete, Mneme and Aoide – and founded the town of Ascra in Boeotia. As evidence he cites sepulchral monuments of the Aloadai (9, 22, 5) near the Boeotian town of Anthedon. Their bones were also seen in Thessaly (Philostratus 1, 3).

A roll-call of Giants:

We have names for many of the Giants. Vian and Moore have a definitive list with more than seventy entries, and the following are some of them:[37]

Aegaeon: shot by Artemis with her arrows.

Agrius: According to Apollodorus, he was clubbed to death by the Moirai (Fates) with bronze clubs.[38]

Alcyoneus: The king of the Thracian Gigantes. Again, according to Apollodorus, he was, with Porphyrion, the greatest of the Giants.[39] He guarded the Isthmus of Corinth at the time when Heracles drove away the oxen of Geryon. The giant attacked him, crushed twelve wagons and twenty-four of Heracles' men with a huge boulder. Heracles himself was able to deflect the stone with his club. The boulder was visible on the isthmus for many a year.

As we have seen, Alcyoneus was immortal on his native soil within the confines of Pallene. Pindar records that he was a herdsman and, in a separate battle from the Gigantomachy, was killed by Heracles and Telamon while they were travelling through Phlegra.[40] Alcyoneus' seven mourning daughters were transformed into a flock of kingfishers (Greek *alkyones*).

Alektos/Allektos: Named on the late sixth-century Siphnian Treasury and the second-century BCE Pergamon Altar.

Aristaeus: According to the Suda, he was the only Giant to survive the war against the gods.[41] His mother Gaia hid him away in the guise of a dung beetle. His is probably the name on an Attic black-figure dinos by Lydos dating from the second quarter of the sixth century BCE, fighting Hephaestus.[42]

Asterius ('Bright One' or 'Glitterer'): A Giant (also called Aster), killed by Athena whose death, according to some accounts, was celebrated by the Panathenaea,[43] probably the same as the Giant Astarias named on the late sixth-century Siphnian Treasury. Probably also the same as Asterus, mentioned in the epic poem *Meropis*, as an invulnerable warrior killed by Athena. In the poem, Heracles, while fighting the Meropes, a race of Giants, on Kos, would have been killed but for Athena's intervention.[44] Athena killed and flayed Asterus and used his impenetrable skin for her aegis. Other accounts name others whose hide provided Athena's aegis: Apollodorus has Athena flay the Giant Pallas, while Euripides' *Ion* has Gorgon, here considered to be a Giant, as Athena's victim.[45]

Clytius: According to Apollodorus, he was killed by Hecate with her torches.[46] Because he was born to be the anti-Ares, he was everything Ares was not, resulting in a peaceful Giant.

Damasen: Because he too was born to be everything Ares was not, Damasen was a pacifist and did not, some say, participate in the war.

Damysus: The fleetest of the Giants. Chiron exhumed his body, removed the ankle and grafted it into Achilles' burned heel.[47]

Enceladus: A Giant named Enceladus, fighting Athena, is attested in art as early as an Attic black-figure pot dating from the second quarter of the sixth century BCE (Louvre E732).[48] Euripides has Athena fighting him with her 'Gorgon shield', her aegis.[49] Apollodorus says he was crushed by Athena under the Island of Sicily.[50] Virgil has him struck by Zeus' lightning bolt, and both Virgil and Claudian bury him under Mount Etna.[51] For Philostratus Enceladus was buried in Italy.[52]

> Philostratus the Elder, *Imagines* 2. 17 (trans. Fairbanks) (ca. third century CE): '[From a description of an ancient Greek painting depicting a volcanic island:] The neighbouring island, my boy, we may consider a marvel; for fire smoulders under the whole of it, having worked its way into underground passages and cavities of the island, through which as through ducts the flames break forth and produce terrific torrents from which pour mighty rivers of fire that run in billows to the sea.... The painting, following the accounts given by the poets, goes farther and ascribes a myth to the island. A Giant, namely, was once struck down there, and as he struggled in the death agony the island was placed as a bond to hold him down, and he does not yet yield but from beneath the earth renews the fight and breathes forth this fire as he utters threats. Yonder figure, they say, would represent Typhon in Sicily [i.e. beneath Mount Etna] or Enceladus here in Italy [i.e. buried beneath Mount Vesuvius], Gigantes that both continents and island are pressing down, not yet dead indeed but always dying. And you, yourself, my boy, will imagine that you have not been left out of the contest, when you look at the peak of the mountain; for what you see there are thunderbolts which Zeus is hurling at the Gigante, and the giant is already giving up the struggle but still trusts in the earth, but the Earth has grown weary because Poseidon does not permit her to remain in place. Poseidon has spread a mist over the contest, so that it resembles what has taken place in the past rather than what is taking place now.'

According to Pausanias and Euripides, he was killed by the chariot of Athena (Pausanias 8, 47, 1) or by the spear of Seilenus. (Euripides, *Cyclops*, 7.)

Nonnus, *Dionysiaca* 48, 6ff: 'Dionysos raised himself and lifted his fighting torch over the heads of his adversaries, and roasted the Gigantes' [Giants'] bodies with a great conflagration, an image on earth of the thunderbolt cast by Zeus. The torches blazed: fire was rolling all over the head of Enceladus and making the air hot, but it did not vanquish him – Encelados bent not his knee in the steam of the earthly fire, since he was reserved for the thunderbolt.'

Ephialtes: Probably not the same as the Aload Giant who was also called Ephialtes. According to Apollodorus he had both his eyes shot out by a salvo of arrows from Apollo and Heracles.[53] He is named on three Attic black-figure pots (Akropolis 2134, Getty 81.AE.211, Louvre E732) dating from the second quarter of the sixth century BCE. On Louvre E732 he is, along with Hyperbios and Agasthenes, opposed by Zeus, while on Getty 81.AE.211 his opponents are apparently Apollo and Artemis. He is also named on the late sixth-century BCE Siphnian Treasury, where he is probably one of the opponents of Apollo and Artemis, as well as on what might be the earliest representation of the Gigantomachy, a pinax fragment from Eleusis (Eleusis 349). He is also named on a late fifth-century BCE cup from Vulci (Berlin F2531), shown battling Apollo. Although the usual opponent of Poseidon among the Giants is Polybotes, one early fifth-century red-figure column krater (Vienna 688) has Poseidon attacking Ephialtes.[54]

Euryalus: Named on a late sixth-century red-figure cup (Akropolis 2.211) and an early fifth-century red-figure cup (British Museum E 47) fighting Hephaestos.

Eurymedon: According to Homer, he was a king of the Giants and father of Periboea (mother of Nausithous, king of the Phaeacians, by Poseidon), who 'brought destruction on his forward people'.[55] He was possibly the Eurymedon who raped Hera, producing Prometheus as offspring (according to an account attributed to the Hellenistic poet Euphorion). He is probably named on Akropolis 2134.[56] He may be mentioned by Propertius as an opponent of Jove.[57]

Eurytus: According to Apollodorus, he was killed by Dionysus with his pine-cone-tipped *thyrsus*.[58]

Gration: According to Apollodorus, he was killed by Artemis.[59]

Hippolytus: Apollodorus says he was killed by Hermes with his sword, wearing the helmet of invisibility.[60]

Hopladamas or **Hopladamus**: Possibly named (as Hoplodamas) on two vases dating from the second quarter of the sixth century BCE, on one (Akropolis 607) being speared by Apollo, while on the other (Getty 81.AE.211) attacking Zeus.[61] Mentioned as Hopladamus by Pausanias as being a leader of Giants enlisted by the Titaness Rhea, pregnant with Zeus, to defend herself from her husband Cronus.[62]

Lion or **Leon**: Possibly a Giant, he is mentioned by Photius (as ascribed to Ptolemy Hephaestion) as a giant who was challenged to single combat by Heracles and killed.[63] The hero made a protective cloak from his leonine skin. Lion-headed Giants are shown on the Gigantomachy frieze of the second-century BCE Pergamon Altar.

Mimas: According to Apollodorus, he was killed by Hephaestus, appropriately enough, with a volley of molten iron.[64] Euripides has Zeus burning him 'to ashes' with his thunderbolt.[65] According to Apollonius of Rhodes and Claudian he was killed by Ares.[66] He was reputedly buried under Prochyte.[67] Mimas is possibly the same as the Giant named Mimon on the late sixth-century BCE Siphnian Treasury, as well as on a late fifth-century BCE cup from Vulci (Berlin F2531) shown fighting Ares. Several depictions in Greek art, though, show Aphrodite as the opponent of Mimas.

Pallas: According to Apollodorus, he was flayed by Athena, who used his skin as a shield (the aegis).[68] Euripides' *Ion* has Gorgon, here considered to be a Giant, as Athena's victim.[69] Claudian names him as one of several Giants turned to stone by Minerva's Gorgon shield.[70]

Pelorius: Fought the gods wielding Mount Pelion. According to Claudian, he was killed by Mars, the Roman equivalent of Ares.[71]

Periboea: The youngest daughter of the king of the Gigantes. She was probably a giantess.

Phoetius: A Gigante slain by Hera.

Picolous: A Giant who had become infatuated with Circe and attempted to capture her, only to be killed by Helios after fierce fighting on the Isle of Aiaia. The magical moly plant first sprang forth from Picolous' blood as it seeped into the ground:

> Ptolemy Hephaestion, *New History Book 4* (summary from Photius, Myriobiblon 190) (trans. Pearse): 'The plant "moly" of which Homer speaks; this plant had, it is said, grown from the blood of the Giant killed in the isle of Circe; it has a white flower; the ally of Kirke who killed the Gigante was Helios; the combat was hard (*malos*) from which the name of this plant.'

Polybotes: According to Apollodorus, he was crushed under Nisyros, a piece of the island of Kos broken off and thrown by Poseidon.[72] He is named on two sixth-century BCE pots, on one (Getty 81.AE.211) he is opposed by Zeus; on the other (Louvre E732) he is opposed by Poseidon carrying Nisyros on his shoulder.[73]

> Strabo, *Geography* 10. 5. 16 (trans. Jones): 'They say that [the island of] Nisyros is a fragment of Kos and they add the myth that Poseidon, when he was pursuing one of the Giants, Polybotes, broke off a fragment of Kos with his trident and hurled it upon him, and the missile became an island, Nisyros, with the Gigante lying beneath it. But some say that he lies beneath Kos.'

Porphyrion: Apollodorus has it that he was (along with Alcyoneus), the pre-eminent Giant of Pallene. He attacked Heracles and tried to rape Hera on the battlefield but Zeus 'smote him with a thunderbolt, and Hercules shot him dead with an arrow.'[74]

According to Pindar, who calls him 'king of the Giants', he was slain by an arrow from the bow of Apollo.[75] He is named on a late fifth-century BCE cup from Vulci (Berlin F2531), where he is battling with Zeus. He was also probably named on the late sixth-century BC Siphnian Treasury.[76] Others maintain that he tried to hurl the island of Delos at the gods.

Syceus: a Gigante pursued by Zeus to Cilicia where Gaia transformed him into a fig-tree to escape the god.

Thoas *or* **Thoon**: According to Apollodorus, he was killed by the Moirai (Fates) with bronze clubs.[77]

Typhoeus: a Gigante slain by Dionysus.

The aftermath of the war

According to Ovid, the Giants failed to learn from their hubris and defeat:

> Ovid, *Metamorphoses*, 1. 151 (trans. Melville): 'There they [the Gigantes] lay, grim broken bodies crushed in huge collapse, and Gaia, drenched in her children's weltering blood, gave life to that warm gore; and to preserve memorial of her sons refashioned it in human form. But that new stock no less despised the gods and relished cruelty, bloodshed and outrage – born beyond doubt of blood.'

In the third century BCE Lycophron had added a bizarre footnote to the Giants:

> Lycophron, *Alexandra* 688ff (trans. Mair): 'The island [of Sicily] that crushed the back of the Giants and the fierce form of Typhoeus… an island boiling with flame, wherein the king of the immortals established an ugly race of apes, in mockery of all who raised war against the sons of Cronus.'

Gaea, understandably piqued at the humiliation of her children, sought a strange kind of solace. Pseudo-Apollodorus, *Bibliotheca* 1. 39 (trans. Aldrich): 'The defeat of the Giants by the gods angered Gaia all the more, so she had sex with Tartaros and bore Typhoeus in Cilicia.'

The Renaissance and after

The Giants and their Gigantomachy enjoyed a revival in the Renaissance, not least in the frescos of the Sala dei Giganti in the Palazzo del Te,

Mantua. These were painted around 1530 by Giulio Romano and his students, and aimed to give the observer the unnerving feeling that the large hall was about to collapse. The subject was also popular in Northern Mannerism around 1600, especially among the Haarlem Mannerists, and continued to be painted into the eighteenth century.

Chapter Five

The Typhonomachy: Zeus Wins the Day, and Every Day Thereafter

Τhe long struggle for the global succession was all but over: Zeus, via Cronos, had dealt conclusively with the Titans and put paid to the hubristic ambitions of the Giants; his grandfather and father had been vanquished and his third generation of gods and goddesses were in charge atop Mount Olympus and down among the dead men in Hades. Zeus, however, still had one more attempt at his superiority to deal with and eliminate in what must have seemed an endless war of succession for the king of the Olympians. This emerged in the shape of serpentine, autochthonous Typhon, one of Greek mythology's more savage and evil monsters. So powerful was he that he could contemplate taking on the entire Olympic order single-handed.

We have already met Typhon briefly in his struggles with Ares, Athena and Zeus, and have seen how he was buried under either Etna or the island of Ischia. As with the Giants, Typhon had his eye on the top job: ruling the cosmos. Typhon and Zeus came up against each other in a cataclysmic battle, which Zeus won by deploying his thunderbolts. A beaten Typhon was cast down into Tartarus but he still retains control of hurricanes, hence typhoon: Chinese *ta feng* ('big wind').

Typhon is also implicated with Python, the serpent killed by Apollo: this and the Typhon's role in the succession myths probably share a Near Eastern origin. Typhon (from ca.500 BCE) also mirrored the Egyptian god Set: a god of chaos, the desert, storms, disorder, violence and foreigners.

Hesiod's *Theogony* says that Typhon was the son of Gaia and Tartarus; Apollodorus adds that Gaia bore Typhon because she was livid at the gods for their destruction of her Giants. The *Homeric Hymn to Apollo* has it that Typhon was the child of Hera. Hera, angry that Zeus had given birth to Athena without her involvement, implored Gaia, Uranus and the Titans to give her a son stronger than Zeus, and became pregnant at the slap of the ground. Hera gave the infant Typhon in adoption to the serpent Python to bring up: Typhon grew up to become a major problem for mortals. Several sources including Pindar, Aeschylus (*Prometheus Bound*), Apollodorus and Nonnus give Typhon's birthplace and home in Cilicia.

What was this monster like? Hesiod describes Typhon as 'terrible, outrageous and anarchic', prodigiously powerful, his shoulders armed with 100 snake heads that spat out fire and all manner of commotion:

> Strength was with his hands in all that he did and the feet of the strong god were untiring. From his shoulders grew a hundred heads of a snake, a fearful dragon, with dark, flickering tongues, and from under the brows of his eyes in his marvellous heads flashed fire, and fire burned from his heads as he glared. And there were voices in all his dreadful heads which uttered every kind of sound unspeakable; for at one time they made sounds such that the gods understood, but at another, the noise of a bull bellowing aloud in proud ungovernable fury; and at another, the sound of a lion, relentless of heart; and at another, sounds like whelps, wonderful to hear; and again, at another, the high mountains re-echoed with his hissing. (Hesiod, *Theogeny*, 306–307, 823–835.)

The *Homeric Hymn to Apollo* describes Typhon as 'vicious' and 'cruel', and like neither gods nor men. Three of Pindar's poems have Typhon as 100-headed (as in Hesiod), while a fourth relegates him to only 50 heads, but 100 heads for Typhon became the norm. A Chalcidian hydria (ca.540–530 BCE) depicts Typhon as a winged human from the waist up, with two snake tails below. Aeschylus calls Typhon 'That destructive monster of a hundred heads (*hekatonkaranos*), impetuous (*thouros*) Typhon. He withstood all the gods, hissing out terror with horrid jaws, while from his eyes lightened a hideous glare.' (Aeschylus, *Prometheus Bound*, 353ff (trans. Weir Smyth).)

For Nicander, Typhon was a monster of enormous strength and strange appearance, with many heads, hands and wings, and with huge snake coils coming from his thighs.[1] Apollodorus describes Typhon as a huge winged monster, whose head 'brushed the stars', human in form above the waist, with snake coils below, and fire flashing from his eyes:

In size and strength he surpassed all the offspring of Earth. As far as the thighs he was of human shape and of such prodigious bulk that he out-topped all the mountains, and his head often brushed the stars. One of his hands reached out to the west and the other to the east, and from them projected a hundred dragons' heads. From the thighs downward he had huge coils of vipers, which when drawn out, reached to his very head and emitted a loud hissing. His body was all winged: unkempt hair streamed on the wind from his head and cheeks; and fire flashed from his eyes. (Apollodorus 1, 6, 3.)

Nonnus in his *Dionysiaca*, however, caps them all: he frequently references Typhon's serpentine nature, lending him a 'tangled army of snakes', snaky feet and hair. Typhon was a 'poison-spitting viper' whose 'every hair belched viper-poison', and Typhon 'spat out showers of poison from his throat; the mountain torrents were swollen, as the monster showered fountains from the viperish bristles of his high head', and 'the water-snakes of the monster's viperish feet crawl into caverns underground, spitting poison.'[2]

Nonnus also endows Typhon with many heads, adding various animal heads to the snake heads including leopards, lions, bulls, boars, bears, cattle, wolves and dogs, which combine to make a cacophony of 'the cries of all wild beasts together', and a 'babel of screaming sounds'. Nonnus also gives Typhon 'legions of arms innumerable', and where Nicander had only said that Typhon had 'many' hands and Ovid had given Typhon 100 hands, Nonnus awards him 200.[3]

Typhon was part of a family made up of similar unsavoury monsters: Hesiod's *Theogony* tells that Typhon 'was joined in love' to Echidna, a monstrous half-woman and half-snake, who bore Typhon 'fierce offspring':[4] Orthrus, the two-headed dog who guarded the Cattle of Geryon[5]; Cerberus, the multi-headed dog who patrolled the gates of Hades,[6] and the Lernaean Hydra, the many-headed serpent who, when one of its heads was cut off, grew two more.[7] The *Theogony* also mentions an ambiguous 'she' – Echidna? – as the mother of the Chimera: a fire-breathing beast that was part lion, part goat, and had a snake-headed tail with Typhon the father.[8]

While mentioning Cerberus and 'other monsters' as being the offspring of Echidna and Typhon, the sixth-century BCE mythographer Acusilaus adds the Caucasian Eagle that feasted on the liver of Prometheus. The mythographer Pherecydes of Leros (fifth century BCE) also names Prometheus' eagle[9] and adds Ladon (though Pherecydes does not use this name), the dragon that guarded the golden apples in the Garden of the Hesperides.[10] The lyric poet Lasus of Hermione (sixth century BCE) adds the Sphinx to this odious company of monsters.[11]

Apollodorus, as well as naming as their offspring Orthrus, the Chimera (citing Hesiod as his source), the Caucasian Eagle, Ladon and the Sphinx, also adds the Nemean lion (no mother is given), and the Crommyonian Sow, killed by Theseus.[12]

Such is the monster which squared up to Zeus to win the greatest prize of all: world domination.

The battle with Zeus

Hesiod's *Theogony* provides the first account of the battle. He says that had it not been for the quick action of Zeus, Typhon would have 'come to reign over mortals and immortals'.[13]

> [Zeus] thundered hard and mightily: and the earth around resounded terribly and the wide heaven above, and the sea and Ocean's streams and the nether parts of the earth. Great Olympus reeled beneath the divine feet of the king as he arose and earth groaned thereat. And through the two of them heat took hold on the dark-blue sea, through the thunder and lightning, and through the fire from the monster, and the scorching winds and blazing thunderbolt. The whole earth seethed, and sky and sea: and the long waves raged along the beaches round and about at the rush of the deathless gods: and there arose an endless shaking. Hades trembled where he rules over the dead below, and the Titans under Tartarus who live with Cronos, because of the unending clamour and the fearful strife. (Hesiod, *Theogeny*, 839–852.)

Zeus, making good use of his thunderbolts, has no problem overcoming Typhon, who is thrown down to earth in a ball of flame:

So when Zeus had raised up his might and seized his arms, thunder and lightning and lurid thunderbolt, he leaped from Olympus and struck him, and burned all the marvellous heads of the monster about him. But when Zeus had conquered him and lashed him with strokes, Typhoeus [*sic*] was hurled down, a maimed wreck, so that the huge earth groaned. And flame shot forth from the thunderstricken lord in the dim rugged glens of the mount, when he was smitten. A great part of huge earth was scorched by the terrible vapour and melted as tin melts when heated by men's art in channelled crucibles; or as iron, which is hardest of all things, is shortened by glowing fire in mountain glens and melts in the divine earth through the strength of Hephaestus. Even so, then, the earth melted in the glow of the blazing fire. (Hesiod, *Theogony*, 853–867.)

A vanquished Typhon is despatched to Tartarus by an angry Zeus.[14]

So much for Hesiod's account. There are many others. Epimenides (seventh or sixth century BCE) relates a different version of the story, in which Typhon enters Zeus' palace while Zeus is asleep; Zeus wakes up and kills Typhon with a thunderbolt.[15] Pindar had the gods, in order to escape from Typhon, transform themselves into animals, and flee ignominiously to Egypt; an example of Egyptian theriomorphism. This has its origins in the Egyptian myth of Seth who, with his followers, changed into animals to escape Horus. Pindar calls Typhon the 'enemy of the gods', and says that he was defeated by Zeus' thunderbolt. In another poem Pindar has Typhon held prisoner by Zeus under Etna, and in another says that Typhon 'lies in dread Tartarus', stretched out underground between Mount Etna and Cumae.[16] In Aeschylus' *Prometheus Bound*, a 'hissing' Typhon, his eyes flashing, 'withstood all the gods', but 'the unsleeping bolt of Zeus' struck him, and 'he was burnt to ashes and his strength blasted from him by the lightning bolt.'[17]

Here is how Aristophanes incorporated an unpleasant encounter with Typhon in his catalogue of infernal horrors awaiting Dionysus in Tartarus:

The black-hearted Stygian rock and the crag of Acheron dripping with gore can hold you; and the circling hounds of Cocytus and the hundred-headed Ekhidna (Typhoeus) shall tear your entrails; your lungs will be attacked by the Myraina Tartesia, your kidneys bleeding with your very entrails the Tithrasian Gorgons will rip apart. (Aristophanes, *Frogs* 475ff (trans. O'Neill).)

According to Pherecydes of Leros, during his battle with Zeus, Typhon first fled to the Caucasus, which begins to burn, then to the volcanic island of Pithecussae (modern-day Ischia), off the coast of Cumae, where he is buried under the island.[18] Apollonius of Rhodes has Typhon being struck by Zeus' thunderbolt on Mount Caucasus, before fleeing to the mountains and plain of Nysa, and ending up (as in Herodotus) buried under Lake Serbonis in Egypt.[19] Like Pindar, Nicander has all the gods but Zeus and Athena transmogrify into animals for their flight to Egypt: Apollo turns into a hawk, Hermes an ibis, Ares a fish, Artemis a cat, Dionysus a goat, Heracles a fawn, Hephaestus an ox, and Leto a mouse.[20] Here is Ovid's version:

> Typhoeus, issuing from earth's lowest depths, struck terror in those heavenly hearts, and they all turned their backs and fled, until they found refuge in Aegyptus and the seven-mouthed Nile…Typhoeus Earthborn (Terrigena) even there pursued them and the gods concealed themselves in spurious shapes; 'And Zeus became a ram,' she said, 'lord of the herd, and so today great Libyan Ammon [i.e. the Egyptian god Ammon] shown with curling horns. Delius [Apollo] hid as a raven [i.e. the Egyptian god Horus], Semeleia [Dionysus] as a goat [Egyptian Osiris or Arsaphes], Phoebe [Artemis] a cat [Egyptian Bastet], Saturnia [Hera] a snow-white cow [Egyptian Hathor], Venus [Aphrodite] a fish [the Syrian goddess Ashtarte] and Cyllenius [Hermes] an ibis [Egyptian Thoth].' (Ovid, *Metamorphoses* 5. 139ff (trans. Melville).)

Hyginus has an interesting variant:

> Pisces. Diognetus Erythraeus says that once Aphrodite and her son Eros came in Syria to the river Euphrates. There Typhon, of whom we have already spoken, suddenly appeared. Venus and her

son threw themselves into the river and there changed their forms to fishes, and by so doing this escaped danger. (Pseudo-Hyginus, *Astronomica* 2. 30.)

Apollodorus leaves us with a more complicated account of the conflict.[21] Typhon, 'hurling kindled rocks', assailed the gods, 'with hissings and shouts, spewing a great jet of fire from his mouth.' Alarmed, the gods transformed into animals and fled to Egypt but 'Zeus pelted Typhon at a distance with thunderbolts, and at close quarters struck him down with an adamantine sickle (*harpe*, the one that castrated Uranus?)' A wounded Typhon fled to Mount Kasios in Syria, where Zeus 'grappled' with him. However, Typhon, entwining his snaky coils around Zeus, was able to take the injured Zeus across the sea to the Corycian cave in Cilicia where he left the she-serpent Delphyne (half snake, half beautiful maiden) to guard over Zeus and his severed sinews, which Typhon had hidden in a bearskin, but Hermes and Aegipan (Goat-Pan) stole the sinews and transplanted them back into Zeus who, his strength restored, resumed his volleys of thunderbolts against Typhon from a war chariot. Zeus chased Typhon to Mount Nysa, where the Moirai tricked Typhon into eating 'ephemeral fruits' which weakened him. Typhon then fled to Thrace, from where he hurled mountains at Zeus, which were deflected straight back to him by Zeus' thunderbolts; the mountain where Typhon stood, being drenched with Typhon's blood, became known as Mount Haemus (Bloody Mountain). Typhon then fled to Sicily where Zeus piled Mount Etna on top of him, effectively burying him, and so Zeus finally defeated Typhon.

Oppian adds a further variation when he describes how Pan helped Zeus in the battle by tricking Typhon to come out from his lair and into the open by the 'promise of a banquet of fish', thus enabling Zeus to defeat Typhon with his thunderbolts.[22]

Yet it is with Nonnus' *Dionysiaca* that we get the most detailed account of the battle. Nonnus has it that Zeus hides his thunderbolts in a cave, so that he might seduce the maiden Plouto and so produce Tantalus. However, smoke rising from the thunderbolts gives the game away and allows Typhon, helped by Gaia, to locate Zeus' weapons, steal them and hide them in another cave. Encouraged by his success in disarming Zeus,

Typhon raised 'his clambering hands into the upper air' and begins a long and concerted attack on the heavens. Then 'leaving the air' he turned his attack upon the seas. Finally Typhon tried to wield Zeus' thunderbolts, but they 'felt the hands of a novice, and all their manly blaze was emasculated'.[23]

However, Zeus' sinews had fallen to the ground during their fight; Typhon had taken them as well as the thunderbolts. Zeus hatched a plan with Cadmus and Pan to trick Typhon. Cadmus, disguised as a shepherd, enchanted Typhon by playing the panpipes; Typhon gave the thunderbolts to Gaia to look after and set out to find the source of the music. On finding Cadmus, he challenges him to a fight, offering Cadmus any goddess as a wife, but not Hera who Typhon has earmarked for himself. Cadmus then told Typhon that, given that he liked the 'little tune' coming from his pipes, then he would surely love the music his lyre could make if it were strung with Zeus' sinews. So Typhon retrieved the sinews, giving them to Cadmus, who hid them in another cave and began to play his bewitching pipes, so that 'Typhoeus yielded his whole soul to Cadmus for the melody to charm.'

Zeus took back his thunderbolts from a distracted Typhon; when Cadmus stopped playing, Typhon, the spell broken, rushed back to his cave to discover the thunderbolts gone. A furious Typhon then unleashed devastation on the world: animals are devoured (Typhon's many animal heads each eat animals of its own kind), rivers turn to dust, seas become dry land and the land is devastated.

Typhon remained unchallenged, and while the gods 'moved about the cloudless Nile', Zeus waited through the night for the coming dawn. Victory 'reproaches' Zeus, urging him to 'stand up as champion of your own children!' Dawn rises and Typhon bellows out a challenge to Zeus: a cataclysmic battle for 'the sceptre and throne of Zeus' begins. Typhon piles up mountains as battlements and with his 'legions of arms innumerable', showers volley after volley of trees and rocks at Zeus, but all are destroyed, or blown aside, or dodged, or thrown back at Typhon. Typhon unleashes torrents of water at Zeus' thunderbolts to extinguish them, but Zeus is able to cut off some of Typhon's hands with 'frozen volleys of air as by a knife', and by hurling thunderbolts is able to burn more of Typhon's 'endless hands', and cut off some of his 'countless heads'. The four winds attack Typhon, adding 'frozen volleys of jagged hailstones'. Gaia tries to help her burned and frozen son. Finally Typhon falls, and Zeus bellows out a stream of mocking taunts, telling Typhon that he is to be buried under Sicily's hills, with a cenotaph over him which will read 'This is the barrow of Typhoeus, son of Earth, who once lashed the sky with stones, but the fire of heaven burnt him up.'[24]

Chapter Six

Centauromachy:
The Wedding Guests From Hell

Centaurs

Centaurs, bull-killers, were hirsute mythological creatures who started off as gigantic, savage or feral beings, but later were typified as having the upper body of a human and the lower body and legs of a horse; they were as wild as untamed horses and inhabited Magnesia and Mount Pelion in Thessaly, the Foloi oak forest in Elis and the Malean peninsula in southern Laconia. They were born from the union of Ixion and cloud nymph Nephele when Ixion seduced Nephele. An alternative version, however, has them as children of Centaurus, a man who had sex with the Magnesian mares. Centaurus was either the son of Ixion and Nephele or of Apollo and the nymph Stilbe. If the latter, Centaurus' twin brother was Lapithes, ancestor of the Lapiths. A variant of centaurs lived on Cyprus who, according to Nonnus, were the offspring of Zeus, who, after Aphrodite had eluded him, spilled his semen on Cypriot earth. The Cyprian centaurs were horned.[1] Another tribe of Centaurs lived in the western Peloponnese where they battled with Heracles.

Then there were also the Lamian Pheres, twelve rustic spirits of the Lamos River who were deployed by Zeus to guard the infant Dionysos, protecting him from the machinations of Hera; the enraged goddess responded by transforming them into ox-horned centaurs. The Lamian Pheres later went with Dionysos in his campaign against the Indians.

With their hybrid form they were reminiscent of the sex-crazed satyrs and they embodied the unnatural. The centaur's half-human, half-horse anatomy has led writers to see them as liminal beings, halfway between the two natures they embody: they are at once the embodiment of untamed nature, as in their battle with the Lapiths and conversely, sagacious and civilizing teachers like Chiron. Chiron was famous for his medical knowledge and skill and is credited with the discovery of botany and pharmacy, the science of herbs and medicine.[2] Homer calls him 'wisest and justest of all the centaurs'.[3] He was not related directly to the other centaurs because he was the son of the Titan Cronus and the Oceanid Philyra. Many Greek heroes were taught and trained by Chiron, including Achilles, Aeneas, Ajax, Heracles, Jason, Theseus, Nestor, Odysseus and Patroclus.

Female centaurs, centaurides or centauresses make an appearance in a Macedonian mosaic of the fourth century BCE. Ovid mentions a centauress named Hylonome who committed suicide when her husband Cyllarus was killed in the war with the Lapiths.[4]

The Lapiths

The Lapiths were natives of Thessaly. One genealogy has Lapithes and Centaurus as twin sons of the god Apollo and the nymph Stilbe, daughter of the river god Peneus. Lapithes was a valiant warrior, but Centaurus was a deformed being who later mated with mares from which the race of half-man, half-horse centaurs then came.[5] Lapithes was the eponymous ancestor of the Lapith people, and his descendants include Lapith warriors and kings such as Ixion, Pirithous, Caeneus and Coronus, and the seers Ampycus and his son Mopsus.

In the *Iliad* the Lapiths posted a contingent of forty ships to join the Greek fleet in the Trojan War, commanded by Polypoetes (son of Pirithous) and Leonteus (son of Coronus, son of Caeneus). The Lapiths were horsemen in the grasslands of Thessaly, famous for its horses; the Lapiths were credited with inventing the bridle's bit. The Lapith King Pirithous was in the happy process of marrying the horsewoman Hippodamia, whose name means 'tamer of horses', when the wedding feast erupted into bloody chaos that escalated into a full-scale battle, the Centauromachy. Some sources contend that the wedding reception debacle was only a prelude to a longer war between the centaurs and Lapiths, a war which the Lapiths won, expelling their enemy from Thessaly into Arcadia.

The Centauromachy

Most centaurs, however, were uncivilized, over-sexed, wild, dissolute, violent when intoxicated and generally offensive, degenerate and delinquent. These are the centaurs that concern us in their battles against the Lapiths, their kinsmen. We have all heard stories about the wedding from hell in which drunken guests brawl with each other, abuse the bride and trash the reception venue. It may be that it was centaurs that started this unedifying tradition when they caused unbridled mayhem at the wedding of Hippodamia and Pirithous, king of the Lapithae and a son of Ixion. It is called the Centauromachy and was ignited by the centaurs' boorish attempt to carry off Hippodamia and the rest of the Lapith women. One of the guests just happened to be Theseus who fought on the side of the Lapiths by helping Pirithous in the battle. The centaurs were driven off, taking refuge on Mount Pindus on the frontiers of Epirus, but not before another Lapith hero, Caeneus, invulnerable to weapons, was literally beaten into the ground by centaurs wielding not weapons but rocks and branches:[6]

> Caeneus was originally a woman, but after Poseidon had sex with her, she begged him to become an invulnerable man. For this reason in the battle of the Centaurs, he was contemptuous of being wounded, and destroyed many of them. The remainder finally encircled him and hammered him down into the earth with fir clubs. (Pseudo-Apollodorus, *Bibliotheca* E1, 22.)

Homer had given us more detail:

> Wine is many a man's undoing, when he gulps his draught and will never drink discreetly. Wine it was that darkened the wits of Eurytion the Centaur in the palace of bold Peirithoos [*sic*]. The Kentauros [*sic*] had come to the Lapiths' country, and now with wine he clouded his understanding and in his frenzy did monstrous things in the very hall of Pirithous. The heroes were seized with indignation; they leapt up, they dragged the Kentauros across the courtyard and out of doors, they lopped off his ears and nose with the ruthless bronze,

and the frenzied creature went his way, taking his retribution with him in his still darkened mind. From this beginning came the long feud between men and Centaurs, but it was Eurytion first of all who brought chastisement on himself by his drunkenness. (Homer, *Odyssey* 21, 293ff (trans. Shewring).)

Pindar adds:

And when the Centaurs were aware of the over-powering aroma of honey-sweet wine, anon with their hands they thrust the white milk from the tables, and, drinking, unasked, out of the silver horns, began to wander in mind. But Caeneus, struck by the green fir-trees, cleft the ground with his foot, where he stood, and passed beneath the earth. (Pindar, *Fragment* 166 (trans. Sandys).)

Theognis leaves us in no doubt as to the loutish behaviour of the centaurs when he says that 'Lawlessness will destroy this city, just as it did the Centaurs, eaters of raw flesh.' (Theognis, *Fragment* 541 (trans. Gerber).) Here is Apollodorus' graphic account:

For when Peirithous was courting Hippodameia, he gave a banquet for the Kentauroi because they were related to her; but they, unused to wine, drank too much too fast and got drunk, and when the bride was ushered in they tried to rape her. So Peirithous put on full armour and with Theseus' help started a battle, and Theseus slew many of them. (Pseudo–Apollodorus, *Bibliotheca* E1, 21 (trans. Aldrich).)

Yet for melodrama, gory detail, exciting action and vividness, Ovid's description of the unrestrained mayhem cannot be beaten. It is worth quoting his version of Nestor's description at length:

And now the wedding hymn was sung, the fires smoked in the royal hall, in came the bride with wives and matronae walking at her side, supreme in beauty. Blessed indeed we called Pirithous with such a bride – and brought, nearly, thereby their wedded bliss to naught!

For Eurytus, the fiercest of the fierce Centauri, was fired by wine and by the sight of that fair girl, and drink was in command, doubled by lust. Tables were overturned, the banquet in confusion, and the bride, held by her hair, was seized and carried off. Hippodame was seized by Eurytus; the others seized what girl each would or could. The scene was like a city sacked; the house echoed with women's screams.

At once we all sprang to our feet and Theseus shouted first 'What madness, Eurytus, possesses you to provoke Pirithous while I'm alive – two men, you fool, in one!' To back his words the great-souled prince, thrusting the throng aside, rescued the ravished girl from their wild rage. No answer came from the centaur; for no words could defend such deeds. The dastard charged her champion, pummelled his noble chest and punched his chin. An antique wine-bowl chanced to stand near by, jagged with high relief; huge as it was, Theseus, still huger, lifted it and hurled it crashing on his foe. He vomited great gouts of blood with brains and wine from wound and throat, and falling backwards beat his heels upon the soaking sand. His death incensed his twiformed brothers and with one accord, each vying with the rest, 'To arms, to arms!' they shouted. Wine gave courage. In the first fighting goblets went flying and fragile jars and bowls and dishes meant for banqueting now turned to war and carnage.

[The centaur] Amycus first robbed the sanctuary, daring to seize its gifts, and first again snatched a great candlestick with clustered lights and, lifting it at arm's length like a priest straining with sacrificial axe to cleave a white bull's neck, he crashed it on the brow of the Lapith Celadon and left his face smashed beyond recognition. Both his eyes leapt out, cheek bones were shattered, nose forced back and wedged inside his mouth. Then Amycus was felled by Pelates Pellaeus who'd wrenched away a maple table-leg; his chin was forced into his chest, and as he spat dark blood and teeth a second wound sent him away down to the shades of the Underworld.

[The centaur] Gryneus next, with murder in his eyes, stood gazing at the smoking altar. 'Why don't we use this?' he cried, and lifted up its giant bulk, aglow with fires, and hurled it at a group of

Lapithae and crushed two of them, Orios and Broteas.... 'You'll pay for this, if I've a means to find a weapon!' cried the Lapith Exadius and found antlers, a votive gift on a tall pine. He reamed the double prongs in Gryneus' eyes and gouged his eyeballs. One stuck to the horn, one rolling down his beard hung caked in blood.

Then [the centaur] Rhoetus, snatching up a blazing brand of plum-wood from the altar, on the right slashes Charaxus' forehead sheltered by his auburn hair. Caught by the ravening flame the tresses blaze like sun-baked corn; the blood, scorched in the wound, hissed with a ghastly sound, the sound of red-hot iron when a smith takes it in his curved tongs and plunges it into his water-tank and down it goes, hissing and sizzling, and the water's warm. Wounded, he shook away the hungry flame from his dishevelled hair, and pulling up a slab, a threshold-stone, he shouldered it, a wagon-load, whose very weight ensured it reached no foe: yes, one of his own side, Cometes, standing near, was crushed beneath the granite block. Rhoetus could not contain his joy. 'Well done! May all your camp today,' he shouted, 'prove your prowess in that way!' And with the half-burnt brand he aimed again at his head-wound, until with blow on blow he crushed his cranium and the shattered skull collapsed and settled in a pool of brains.

Victorious Rhoetus then turned on Corythus and Dryas and Euagrus. One of them, young Corythus (his cheeks wore their first down), dropped, and Euagrus cried 'To fee a boy – what glory do you gain?' Not a word more would Rhoetus let him speak, but fiercely thrust the ruddy flame into his open mouth, right down his throat; and savage Dryas too he chased, whirling the brand above his head. But not the same end this time. As he swaggered, proud of his trail of slaughter, Dryas thrust him through a charred pointed stake where neck and shoulder join. He groaned and strained to wrench the stake from the hard bone and fled away, soaked in his own red blood...

In that din [the centaur] Aphidas lay with every vein relaxed in endless sleep, unwoken, undisturbed, sprawled on a shaggy bearskin from Mount Ossa, his wine-filled cup in his unconscious hand, out of the fight – in vain! Observing him lying apart there, Phorbas fingered firm his lance's thong: 'You'd better mix,' he cried 'your wine with Styx's water!' There and then he hurled his lance and through Aphidas' neck, as he lay sprawled face-up, the iron-tipped ash drove deep. Death came unfelt. Over the couch – into the cup – blood gushed from his full throat.

I saw [the centaur] Petraeus trying to uproot an acorn-laden oak and as his arms embraced it and he forced it to and fro, rocking its tottering trunk, Pirithous, hurling a lance that pierced Petraeus' ribs, pinned fast his writhing chest to the tough wood. The prowess of Pirithous, men say, laid [the centaur] Lycus low, laid [the centaur] Chromis low, but each gave less distinction to the victor than [the centaurs] Dictys and Helops. Helops was transfixed by a lance that struck his forehead from the right and pierced to his left ear. Dictys, in flight before the onslaught of Ixion's son [Pirithous], slipped on a mountain precipice and fell headlong; his weight broke a huge mountain-ash whose splintered spike impaled him in his groin…

Theseus' triumphs in the fight were too much for [centaur] Demeleon. He tried with a huge heave to uproot an ancient pine, a sturdy trunk, and, when his efforts failed, he snapped it off and threw it at his foe. But as the missile came Theseus drew back beyond its range, on Athene's advice (or so he'd have us think). But still the trunk did not fall idle: from tall Crantor's neck it severed his left shoulder and his breast…

When Aeacides [Peleus], at a distance, saw the lad cleft by that hideous wound, 'Crantor,' he cried, 'My favourite, at least receive from me your death-right fight!' And with his powerful arm and all his passion's strength he hurled his spear full at [the centaur] Demeleon. It broke his ribs and hung there quivering in the box of bones. The centaur wrenched the shaft away without the point (the shaft would hardly come); the point stuck in his lung. His very agony gave him wild strength. Despite the wound he reared and pounded Peleus with his horse's hooves. On helm and ringing shield Peleus received the lashing hooves and, so defended, held his lance-point levelled and with one thrust pierced the centaur's shoulder and his two-formed chest…

I [Nestor] shouted to him (anger gave me strength) 'See how your horns yield to my steel!' and threw my spear. Unable to escape, he raised his hand to shield his threatened brow, and hand was nailed to brow. A shout went up. He stood there stuck and beaten by the bitter wound, and Peleus (for he stood nearer) struck him with his sword full in his belly. Leaping fiercely forward, he trailed his guts, trampled them as they trailed, and trampling burst them, and the tangle tripped his legs and, belly empty, he collapsed...

There stands as well before my eyes the one who'd laced together six great lion-hides, [the centaur] Phaeocomes, so shielding horse and man. He hurled a log which two ox-teams could scarce have moved and crushed the skull of Tectaphos son of Olenus (Olenides). His skull's broad dome was shattered and through mouth, nose, eyes and ears the soft brains oozed like whey when curds are strained or juice that trickles from a weighted press, squeezes through a strainer's fine-meshed apertures. But I [Nestor], as he prepared to strip the spoils, (your father knows) I plunged my sword deep in the spoiler's groin...

As Nestor told this tale of battles fought between Lapithae and the half-man Centauri, Tlepolemus took offence that Alcides [Heracles] had been passed by in silence and exclaimed: 'I am surprised, my lord, that you've forgotten the feats of Hercules. Why, many a time my father used to tell me how he quelled the cloud-born (nubigenae) [centaurs].' (Ovid, *Metamorphoses* 12, 210ff (adapted from the translation by Melville).)

As with the Gigantomachy, the contests between the centaurs and the Lapiths symbolize the tensions in the struggle between Athenian civilization and Persian barbarism.

What are the possible origins of the centaur myths? Some say that the notion of centaurs was born in a non-riding culture, as in the Minoan civilization, as a response to seeing nomads who were mounted on horses; such riders would manifest as half-man, half-animal. Significantly, bull-hunting on horseback was a popular custom in Thessaly (*Schol. ad Pind.* p.31, 9, ed. Boeckh), and the early Thessalians spent the best part of their lives on horseback. The Aztecs had a similar misapprehension about

Spanish cavalrymen. Interestingly, the Lapiths of Thessaly were held to be the pioneers of horseback riding by Greek writers. The Thessalian tribes also claimed their horse breeds were descended from the centaurs.

Robert Graves (after Georges Dumézil) traced the centaurs back to the Indian *gandharva* (part-animal heavenly singers), and speculated that the centaurs were a dimly-remembered, pre-Hellenic fraternal earth cult who had the horse as a totem.[7] A similar theory was incorporated into Mary Renault's *The Bull from the Sea*.

Lucretius, in Book 5 of his *On the Nature of Things*, studiously denied the existence of centaurs based on their comparative growths, arguing that at the age of 3 years, horses are in the prime of their life while humans at the same age are still little more than infants, making hybrid animals an impossibility. Some 300 years later, Aelian was far less sceptical:

> Anybody who has seen one [i.e. an *onokentauros* or chimpanzee which was believed to be a cross between a man and a beast] would never have doubted that the race of Centaurs once existed, and that artificers did not falsify nature, but that time produced these creatures by blending dissimilar bodies into one. But whether in fact they came into being and visited us at one and the same period, or whether rumour, more ductile than any wax and too credulous, fashioned them and by some miraculous combination fused the halves of horse and a man while endowing them with a single soul. (Aelian, *On Animals* 17. 9 (trans. Schofield).)

Cicero, however, was with Lucretius: 'Who [in this day and age] believes that the Hippocentaurus (Centaur) or the Chimaera (Chimera) ever existed…. The years obliterate the inventions of the imagination, but confirm the judgements of nature.' (Cicero, *De Natura Deorum* 2. 2.)

Meanwhile Pliny, *Natural History* 7. 35 (trans. Rackham) writes that the emperor Claudius was totally convinced, as indeed was he, as he had actually seen one! 'Claudius Caesar writes that a Hippocentaurus was born in Thessaly and died the same day; and in his reign we actually saw one that was brought here from him from Aegyptus (Egypt) preserved in honey.'

The most recognizable and memorable of all the battles fought in Greek myth is undoubtedly this epic battle of the Lapiths and the

Centaurs. By the time of the Geometric period centaurs are among the first representational figures painted on Greek pottery.

As noted, the battle between Lapiths and Centaurs reflected the conflict between civilized and barbaric behaviour; symbolically, the Lapiths exercised moderation in the consumption of wine, while the centaurs drank to reckless excess. Their disgusting behaviour, however, was not just a lesson in how not to behave in a civilized society; it also contravened a revered Greek code of practice relating to the proper behaviour expected of guests and hosts, and how to conduct oneself while dining together.

The Greek sculptors of the school of Phidias made the battle of the Lapiths and Centaurs a conflict between humankind and wild monsters, and a symbol of the great conflict between civilized Greeks and 'barbarians'. Battles between Lapiths and Centaurs were depicted in the sculptured metopes on the Parthenon, recalling Athenian Theseus' treaty of mutual admiration with Pirithous the Lapith, leader of the Magnetes, and on Zeus' temple at Olympia.[8]

In the Renaissance, the battle was a popular theme for artists who vied with each other to depict bodies in violent confrontation as closely packed as possible. Michelangelo produced a marble bas-relief of the subject in Florence in about 1492. Piero di Cosimo's panel *Battle of Centaurs and Lapiths*, now at the National Gallery, London was painted during the following decade. A frieze with a Centauromachy was also produced by Luca Signorelli in his *Virgin Enthroned with Saints* (1491), inspired by a Roman sarcophagus found at Cortona, Tuscany during the early fifteenth century.

Chapter Seven

Amazonomachy Amazons: 'Those who fight like men'

'*We are armed with the bow and javelin and we ride horses. We know nothing at all about women's work.*'

Herodotus 4, 114, 3 citing the Amazons' dismissive mission statement

'*I thought I saw it all when I went to Phrygia once and saw thousands of soldiers and gleaming horses…that fated day when the Amazons swept down to fight against men.*' Priam, *Iliad* 3,196–203

Mention fighting women in the classical world and many people immediately think of the Amazons: they are the best-known female wagers of war in classical history and mythology. However, the only sure thing that can be said about the Amazons is that nothing much about them can be said for sure. Most things to do with the Amazons remain mired in controversy or shrouded in speculation, but this chapter shows what we can deduce with some confidence, mindful at the same time that Amazons were not the classical world's only women warriors.

K.A. Bisset's article 'Who Were the Amazons?', written in 1971 when he was Head of the Department of Bacteriology at the University of Birmingham, offers some fascinating light on and fresh insights into the controversies, taking time off from researching material closer to home in published papers such as 'The Swarmers of Bacillus cereus', 'Some Characters of Rhizobium Strains from Tropical Legumes' and 'Natural Antibodies in Blood Serum of Freshwater Fish'.

His article starts as follows:

Legend informs us that the Amazons were women, that they were not only warlike but successful above average as warriors, and that they had no breasts. The masculinity of the second and third characteristics ought to make us highly suspicious of the accuracy of the first, and the explanations provided by the ancient Greeks do not bear any very close examination.

Bisset then goes on to question the survival possibility of 'such a bizarre genetic constitution' due to 'continual outbreeding with normal males'. The mastectomy debate is well and truly debunked with the assertion that 'even if a pre-aseptic culture could have achieved this feat, without a forty per cent mortality rate from gangrene, it is psychologically most improbable, and in any case, quite pointless, since there is no anatomical objection to women drawing the bow.' Bisset rejects it as 'nothing but a bright idea to explain the fact that these "women" warriors were unaccountably deficient in mammary equipment. It is also in line with the distinct sex-sadistic element that pervades the whole legend.'

Bisset answers the question in his title by asserting that the Amazons owe their existence to 'the first encounter of Europeans with a beardless small-statured race of bow-toting mongoloids.' To support this he cites some of the many examples of a similar anthropological revelation: the explorers of South America's encounter with beardless, long-haired, small-statured Amerindians on the banks of the Amazon...the Vikings in Eastern Canada [who] described their first Eskimos as 'women' and an anecdote by P.C. Wren in which a drunken Scotsman in French Indo-China comes on strongly to a long-haired Tonkinese sergeant who all but kills him in his outrage.

Bisset makes the additional point that Russian excavations of the frozen tombs of southern Siberia show that the inhabitants in the first century CE were not Orientals but Europeanoids; Scythians, not Huns or Mongols. When the Huns eventually burst into Europe an element of the horror and fear they caused was due to their 'strangeness. Nobody had seen such a man before.' To this we can add a similar terror felt by the Germans in the east of their country when faced by marauding hordes of Russian troops as they rampaged their way to Berlin in 1944–45. The Huns, Bisset informs us, did not, of course, remove their right breasts but they did 'gash their faces to prevent their beards growing'. Bisset concludes that presumably 'the Europeans learned that the Amazons were not exclusively feminine…possibly the "Amazon" women fought alongside their men.'

In Greek mythology, the Amazons (Ἀμαζόνες) were redoubtable woman warriors who commanded respect from men who knew military expertise when they saw it. Herodotus believed them to be related to the Scythians and located them vaguely between Scythia and Sarmatia, roughly modern-day Ukraine. Others would put them in Pontus, Anatolia on the River Don or in Libya. The Greeks called the River Don 'Tanais', but the Scythians called it the 'Amazon', a nod to the fact that the women fighters inhabited the area. Pliny the Elder suggests the valley of the Terme River may have been their home and mentions a mountain named after them (the modern-day Mason Dagi), as well as a settlement called Amazonium; Herodotus first mentions their capital Themiscyra, which Pliny locates near the Terme.[1] Philostratus places the Amazons in the Taurus Mountains; Ammianus locates them east of Tanais, as neighbours of the Alans. Wherever they were or wherever they came from, the important fact remains, in the words of Peter Walcott, 'Wherever the Amazons are located by the Greeks…it is always beyond the confines of the civilized world. The Amazons exist outside the range of normal human experience.'[2] They are, then, strange, liminal and not normal.

This is Hippocrates' description of the origins of the Amazons:

> And in Europe is a Scythian race, living around Lake Maeotis, which is different from the other races. Their name is Sauromatae. Their women, when they are still virgins, ride, shoot, throw the javelin on horseback, and fight with their enemies. They do not surrender their virginity until they have killed three of their enemies, and they do not marry before they have performed the traditional sacred rites. A woman who takes a husband no longer rides, unless she is compelled to do so by a general expedition.[3]

How this came about is explained by Herodotus when he tells that the Sarmatians were descendants of Amazons and Scythians, and that their wives observed their ancient maternal customs, 'frequently hunting on horseback with their husbands; in war taking the field; and wearing the very same dress as the men.' He goes on to say how a group of Amazons was blown across the Maeotian Lake (the Sea of Azov) into Scythia (today's south-eastern Crimea). They mastered the Scythian language and agreed to marry Scythian men on condition that they would not be required to follow the customs of Scythian women.[4] Domesticity springs to mind as their concern. They then moved north-east, settling beyond the Tanais (Don) River, and became the ancestors of the Sauromatians. Herodotus adds that the Sarmatians fought with the Scythians against Darius the Great in the fifth century BCE.

Despite their pugnacity, Scythian women were indubitably human, with human needs. Herodotus (4, 1–4) tells us how the Scythian men came home after a long campaign fighting the Cimmerians and the 'empire of the Medes', but when they arrived home, they were confronted by another Scythian 'army'. Due to the lengthy absence of their men, the wives had been having sex with their slaves; a battle between the offspring of the slaves and the original Scythians ensued in which the Scythians cleverly exchanged their weapons for whips, and the slaves fled. Later in the same book, Herodotus explains how the Sauromates people came about (4, 110–1): the Amazons escaped from the Athenians and ended up in Scythian territory where the Scythians mistook the Amazons for men and attacked them; it was only when they were examining the corpses that they realized that their enemy had, in fact, been women. They decided then not to fight them any more; sexual relations began and the Sauromates race was born.

Lysias, the fifth-century Attic orator, describes the Amazons as the only women to wear iron armour and the first to ride horses; he adds 'they were seen as males because of their courage rather than females because of their nature'; a good example of courage being seen as an exclusively male virtue.

In Roman times Julius Caesar reminded the Senate of the conquest of large parts of Asia by Semiramis and the Amazons. Strabo compares successful Amazon raids against Lycia and Cilicia with resistance by Lydian cavalry against the invaders.[5] Gnaeus Pompeius Trogus reports how the Amazons originated from a Cappadocian colony of two Scythian princes, Ylinos and Scolopetos.

The most famous Amazons were undoubtedly Penthesilea, who served in the Trojan War, and her sister Hippolyta, whose magic belt, given to her by her father – Ares, god of war – constituted the ninth of the labours which exercised Hercules. Hippolyta was the founding queen of the race of Amazons; aptly for women very much at home on horseback, her name means 'unbridled mare'. So prominent were the Amazons in the Greek psyche and powerful on the field of battle that the Greeks had a word for conflict with Amazons: Amazonomachy, putting them up there with the Titans, Giants and Typhon; their name has become a byword for female warriors in general. Their obvious battlefield skills apart, Amazons were great colonists and civilizers: they are said to have founded many cities including Smyrna, Paphos, Ephesus and Magnesia; as natural horse-borne fighters they are also credited with inventing the cavalry.

The etymology of the word Amazon is disputed to this day: it may derive from a Greek word meaning 'without men or husbands'; alternatively, it is from ά- and μαζός, 'without breast', reflecting an aetiological tradition that Amazons cut off their right breast to facilitate their archery. Greek art does not support this, as Amazons are always depicted with both breasts intact. Hippocrates, the influential medical scientist, though, is adamant:[6]

> They have no right breasts…for while they are still babies their mothers make red-hot a bronze instrument constructed for this very purpose and apply it to the right breast and cauterize it, so that it stops growing, and all its strength and mass are diverted up to the right shoulder and right arm.

Some 800 years later Justin still agrees:[7] 'They exercised the virgins on weapon-wielding, horse-riding and hunting, and burned the children's right breasts, so that arrow-throwing wouldn't be impeded; and for such reason, they were called Amazons.'

The 'right mastectomy theory' may have just been made up to deter women from taking up archery; nevertheless, women are perfectly capable of loosing an arrow with both breasts intact. The word may well be derived from *hamazakaran*, 'to make war' in Persian.

If the Amazons spurned men and normative Greek roles and they were 'really killers of men' (*androktones*) as Herodotus would have us believe, how then did their race survive? Apparently, once a year, the Amazons called on the neighbouring Gargareans and had sex with their men for purposes of procreation. According to Hellanicus, any resulting male children were – in a reversal of the usual Greek practice where females usually suffered – either killed, sent back to their fathers or exposed; the girls, however, were retained and raised by their mothers with training in agriculture, hunting and combat. Others explain the survival of the race by asserting that when the Amazons went to war they would spare some of the men they defeated and take them as sex slaves, having sex with them to produce the girls they needed to sustain the race.[8]

Penthesilea

When Penthesilea, daughter of the war god Ares, accidentally killed Hippolyta in a deer-hunting accident, it foreshadowed Penthesilea's own death at the hands of Achilles.[9] Penthesilea was so distraught at this unintended sororicide that she wished only for death, but she had a problem. Being an Amazon, the only fitting way to die was to do so with honour and in battle. According to Quintus Smyrnaeus' *Posthomerica*, she saw the Trojan War as an opportunity to achieve this end and enthusiastically joined in on the side of Troy, vowing, somewhat overconfidently perhaps, to slay Achilles. Her military exploits were widely famous, not least because of her appearance on the doors of the temple of Juno: Aeneas was as transfixed by her fierce combat skills, equal to any man's, as he was by her protruding naked breast. Penthesilea, like Camilla, was a *bellatrix*, a woman of war.

She arrived in Troy with twelve Amazon comrades, but the omens were not good:[10] Priam saw an eagle holding a dove, a sure sign that Penthesilea would soon die. Theano, priestess of Athena, argued that to fight would be suicidal, but Penthesilea carried on regardless. She slew Podarces, one of the former suitors of Helen, and a number of other Greeks; her fight with a mocking Telamonian Ajax was inconclusive. Achilles, however, killed Penthesilea by impaling her and her horse with a single blow to her breastplate, knocking her to the ground. She begged for mercy but

Achilles was unmoved, killed her, and scoffed over her corpse, until, that is, he removed her helmet and gazed on her beauty. It was at this point that he felt remorse for what he had done and realized that rather than kill her, he should have married her.

The conflict between Achilles and Penthesilea is covered in the fragmentary *Aethiopis* written in the seventh century BCE. The death of Penthesilea was, according to Diodorus Siculus, the beginning of the end for the Amazons:

> Now they say that Penthesilea was the last of the Amazons to win distinction for bravery and that in the future the race diminished more and more and then expired; consequently in later times, whenever any writers recount their prowess, men consider the ancient stories about the Amazons to be pure fiction.[11]

Pseudo-Apollodorus[12] says that Achilles 'fell in love with the Amazon after her death and slew Thersites for mocking him about it.' In the early Roman empire Propertius, the elegiac poet, supports this notion,[13] as does travel writer Pausanias, who describes the throne of Zeus at Olympia on which Panaenus' painted image shows the dying Penthesilea expiring and being supported by Achilles.[14] Thersites' cousin Diomedes was furious at Achilles so he harnessed Penthesilea's corpse behind his chariot, dragged it and dumped it into the River Scamander. Someone, either Achilles or the Trojans, retrieved the body and gave it a proper burial.

Robert Graves has an interesting take on the incident in his *Penthesilea*:

> Penthesileia, dead of profuse wounds, was despoiled of her arms by Prince Achilles who, for love of that fierce white naked corpse, necrophily on her committed in the public view. Some gasped, some groaned, some bawled their indignation, Achilles nothing cared, distraught by grief, but suddenly caught Thersites' obscene snigger and with one vengeful buffet to the jaw dashed out his life. This was a fury few might understand, yet Penthesileia, hailed by Prince Achilles on the Elysian plain, paused to thank him for avenging her insulted womanhood with sacrifice.

According to a lost poem by Stesichorus, Penthesilea killed Hector.

Hippolyta

Hippolyta, as we have already noted, was accidentally killed by her sister Penthesilea in a hunting accident. The magic belt she wore and which caused Hercules so much trouble was a badge of office, denoting her status as an Amazon queen.[15] Hippolyta was apparently so taken with Hercules that she surrendered the belt without a fuss while visiting him on his ship. According to Pseudo-Apollodorus, however, this did not take into account Hera who, masquerading as one of the Amazons, spread a malicious rumour among them that Heracles and his crew were intent on abducting their queen; the Amazons then attacked the ship, Heracles slew Hippolyta and relieved her of the belt, beat off the attackers and sailed away.

Another Hippolyta myth involves Theseus, some versions of which say he abducted her and others that she fell in love with Theseus and badly let the Amazons down by absconding with him. In any event, she ended up in Athens where she was to marry Theseus – the only Amazon to ever marry – causing the other angry Amazons to attack Athens (their first foray into Greece) in what became known as the Attic War, a conflict which they lost to Athenian forces under Theseus or Heracles. Plutarch assures us, though, that 'the invasion of Attica would seem to have been no slight or womanish enterprise.'[16] Other versions have it that Theseus rejected Hippolyta in favour of Phaedra, so Hippolyta rallied her Amazons to attack the wedding ceremony and was killed in the ensuing fracas.

The Attic War is commemorated as an Amazonomachy in marble bas-reliefs as on the west metopes of the Parthenon or in the sculptures of the Mausoleum of Halicarnassus, reliefs from the frieze of the Temple of Apollo at Bassae, now in the British Museum, on the shield of the statue of Athena Parthenos, and on wall paintings in the Theseum and in the Stoa Poikile. Pliny the Elder records five bronze statues of Amazons in the Artemision of Ephesus.[17] Amazons are typically depicted with caps, bows, Persian trousers and axes, all redolent of Persians; weak and barbaric losers to Athens. They thus share by association, as with the Giants, the Athenian humiliation of the Persians as an uncivilized race in much of their civilizing architecture.

Hippolyta married Theseus and despite having thereby renounced her Amazonian status and nullified her credentials as an Amazon, was keen to accompany him as a warrior on his expedition against Thebes. Her 'swelling womb', however, prevented this and she was encouraged by Theseus, in a fine euphemism combining the erotic with the martial, to discard the 'cares of Mars and dedicate her retired quivers to the bedroom'.[18]

Myrina

Another queen of the Amazons, Myrina not only epitomizes the military capabilities of the Amazons but demonstrates for us what great builders, town planners and civilizers the Amazons apparently were. Her tomb in the Troad is mentioned in the *Iliad* and according to Diodorus Siculus[19] she led a military expedition in Libya and was victorious over the Atlantians, laying waste their city, Cerne. Myrina was not so successful in fighting the nearby Gorgons, failing to burn down their forests. She struck a peace treaty with Horus of Egypt, conquered the Syrians, the Arabians and the Cilicians. She subdued Greater Phrygia, from the Taurus Mountains to the Caicus River, and several Aegean islands including Lesbos; she discovered a previously uninhabited island which she named Samothrace, building a temple there and went on to found the cities of Myrina in Lemnos,[20] another Myrina in Mysia, Mytilene, Cyme, Pitane and Priene.[21] Myrina died when her army was eventually defeated by Mopsus the Thracian and Sipylus the Scythian.

Jordanes' *Getica* (written ca.560), is the earliest surviving history of the Goths. In it Jordanes tells how the ancestors of the Goths, descendants of Magog, originally inhabited Scythia, on the Sea of Azov between the Rivers Dnieper and Don and how, having repulsed a raid by a neighbouring tribe, while the menfolk were away fighting Pharaoh Vesosis, the women formed their own army under Marpesia and crossed the Don to invade Asia; Marpesia's sister Lampedo remained in Europe to guard the homeland. The invading women were in fact descended from the Amazons: they procreated with men once a year, conquered Armenia, Syria and all of Asia Minor as far as Ionia and Aeolia. Jordanes also relates how they fought with Hercules and in the Trojan War, how a contingent of them lived in the Caucasus Mountains until the time of Alexander. He mentions by name the Queens Menalippe, Hippolyta and Penthesilea.

There are at least eighty-two Amazons known to us; here are some of the more important ones:

Aello was the first to attack Heracles when he came calling for Hippolyta's belt. Unfortunately, Heracles was now clad in the lion skin acquired from his first labour, making him invulnerable. Aello, therefore, was killed. Her name means 'Whirlwind'.

Andromache was an Amazon queen. Her name translates as 'Man Fighter'.

Antiope was an Amazon queen defeated in battle by Theseus; she survived and, undeterred, she married Theseus and bore his son, Hippolytus. One version has it that Antiope was betrayed by Theseus when he married another woman; she led an attack with her Amazons on the day of the wedding, planning to massacre the guests. Theseus and Heracles killed her. Her name means 'Confronting Moon'. A similar story is ascribed to Hippolyta, as we have seen.

Lysippe: another Amazon queen, she settled her Amazons near the Black Sea. Lysippe established the policies and rules by which the Amazons lived. She was a highly intelligent woman, an excellent general and founder of the city named Themiscrya. She was killed in battle. Her name means 'She Who Lets Loose the Horses'.

Melanippe was the sister of Antiope. When Heracles came to get Hippolyta's girdle, Melanippe was taken prisoner. While in captivity, she launched a successful mutiny among the crew on one of Hercules' ships, enabling her to escape with some other captive Amazons. They commandeered the ship, killing the Greeks and dumped their bodies overboard. Unfortunately, the seafaring skills of the Amazons were somewhat inadequate and they were blown to the shores of Scythia. Here they stole horses and became career horse-rustlers. Melanippe's name means 'Black Mare'.

Pantariste pursued Heracles' soldiers when they fled; two Greek soldiers attacked her, but she killed them, one by grasping his throat until he choked. She threw her spear at Tiamides, who blocked it with his shield, but the force knocked him to the ground. She unleashed her *labrys*, a double-headed axe, and beheaded him.

Thalestris was an Amazon queen and mistress of Alexander the Great. They went lion-hunting together but, more interestingly, spent thirteen nights in lovemaking. Thirteen is significant: it is a sacred fertility number for moon worshippers, and relates to the number of moons in a year. Despite this torrid sex, Thalestris died without issue, dashing her hopes of a child by Alexander.

Valasca (or Dlasta) was a tyrannical and cruel Amazon warrior queen, who poked out and cut off the right eye and thumbs of all males to render them ineffective in battle. Her aim was to start a new era for the Amazons; only when she died did 'the nation resume its normal order'.

The Amazons were not averse to intermarrying: Herodotus tells us how they settled down with the Scythians.[22] In the *Iliad*, the Amazons are referred to as *Antianeirai*: 'those who fight like men'. They invaded Lycia only to be defeated by Bellerophon, who was sent against them by King Iobates, hoping in vain that the Amazons might kill him.[23] They attacked the Phrygians, who were assisted by Priam, then a young man.[24]

The Amazons featured prominently in religion. According to Plutarch in his *Theseus* and Pausanias, Amazon tombs are to be found scattered throughout Greek lands, including Megara, Athens, Chaeronea, Chalcis, Thessaly at Skotousa and in Cynoscephalae; statues of Amazons crop up all over Greece. Plutarch reports that there was an Amazoneum or shrine of Amazons at both Chalcis and Athens; on the day before the Thesea at Athens there were annual sacrifices to the Amazons. In historical times, Greek maidens of Ephesus performed an annual circular dance with weapons and shields that had originally been established by Hippolyta.

By and large, the Amazons received a good press when it came to assessments of their martial capabilities. When no less an authority than Priam relates his earlier war experiences to Helen of Troy, he concedes that the Amazons are the equal of men: 'Once before I visited Phrygia of the vineyards…and I myself, a helper in war, was marshalled among them on that day when the Amazon women came, men's equals.'

The military exploits of the hero Bellerophon elicit a similar assessment: '…he slaughtered the Amazons, who fight men in battle.'[25]

The first-century Greek historian Diodorus describes their revolutionary *modus vivendi* as follows:[26]

> The sovereignty was in the hands of a people among whom the women held the supreme power, and its women performed the services of war just as did the men. Of these women one [Penthesilea], who possessed the royal authority, was remarkable for her prowess in war and her bodily strength, and gathering together an army of women she drilled it in the use of arms and subdued in war some of the neighbouring peoples. And since her valour and fame increased, she made war upon people after people of neighbouring lands.

What few men and boys there were in the Amazon world had a distinctly hard time with some cruel role reversal and infant mutilation:

> But to the men she assigned the spinning of wool and such other domestic duties as belong to women. Laws were also established by her, by virtue of which she led forth the women to the contests of war, but upon the men she fastened humiliation and slavery. And as for their children, they mutilated both the legs and the arms of the males, incapacitating them in this way for the demands of war.

Diodorus subscribes to the 'right mastectomy' etymology: '…and in the case of the females they seared the right breast that it might not project when their bodies matured and be in the way; and it is for this reason that the nation of the Amazons received the appellation it bears.'

Penthesilea comes in for special praise:

> In general, this queen was remarkable for her intelligence and ability as a general, and she founded a great city named Themiscyra at the mouth of the Thermodon river and built there a famous palace; furthermore, in her campaigns she devoted much attention to military discipline and at the outset subdued all her neighbours as far as the Tanaïs river…and fighting brilliantly in a certain battle she ended her life heroically.

Her daughter, Artemis, carried on the fine Amazon tradition: training – 'she exercised in the chase the maidens from their earliest girlhood and drilled them daily in the arts of war' – and subduing as far as Thrace 'and subdued a large part of Asia and extended her power as far as Syria.'

Some 200 years later Justin more or less endorses this:[27] marrying their neighbours would for the Amazons be tantamount to slavery; they governed without men, and they put to death all the men who had remained at home. In order to continue their race they nevertheless consorted with the men of the adjacent nations, but if any male children were born, they put them to death. The girls they kept busy not by consigning them to working in wool, but training them in combat skills, the management of horses and hunting.

Chapter Eight

The Theban Wars: Complex Oedipus, the Seven Against Thebes and the Epigoni War

Thebes is a city in central Boeotia which has been inhabited for 5,000 years. Mythical Thebes vies with Troy as the origin of numerous myths, a number of which are essentially martial in nature. In particular there are first, the foundation of the Theban citadel Cadmea by Cadmus, a Phoenician king and the growth of the Spartoi or 'Sown Men' – an aetiological myth to explain the origin of the Theban nobility.

Second, there is the story of Laius, whose malfaisance culminated in the tragedy of Oedipus and the wars of the Seven Against Thebes, the Epigoni and the downfall of his dynasty. Although Laius was the rightful heir to the throne, he was usurped by Amphion and Zethus. Laius took refuge in the court of Pisa in the Peloponnese, where King Pelops welcomed him. Betraying the trust given to him as a guest by Pelops, he then raped and abducted Pelops' son, Chrysippus, and returned to Thebes, where he was restored to the throne. Laius' pederastic rape of Chrysippus was thought by some to have been the first recorded instance of homosexuality among mortals, and may have provided an etiology for the practice of pedagogic pederasty for which Thebes was famous. Later, Laius married Jocasta, but he received an oracle that he should on no account father a child or the child would kill him and marry his wife. However, one night he was so drunk that he slept with Jocasta and made her pregnant, with Oedipus.

Cadmus and the Spartoi

The Greeks attributed the foundation of Thebes to Cadmus, a Phoenician king from Tyre (modern Lebanon) and the brother of Queen Europa. Cadmus ended up in Boeotia at the end of a fruitless search for Europa who had been famously raped and abducted by Zeus in the guise of a bull. Cadmus is remembered for teaching a variant of the Phoenician alphabet which developed into ancient Greek, and for building the acropolis at Thebes, which was named the Cadmeia after him; it was an intellectual, spiritual and cultural centre; a shining example of Greek civilization.

After consulting the oracle at Delphi, Cadmus was advised to forget Europa and follow a special cow from the herd of Pelagon of Phocis, identifiable by a white full moon on her flanks, which would meet him, and to build a town on the spot where she lay down exhausted, having collapsed on her right side, the side of good omen. This done, Cadmus sacrificed the beast to Athena (thus founding the cult of Pallas Onka) and asked two of his men, Deioleon and Seriphus, to fetch lustral water from a nearby spring, which was sacred to Ares but guarded by a dragon, the Ismenian dragon, in effect a giant serpent which was also sacred to Ares.[1] The dragon killed most of his men before Cadmus slew the dragon with a rock or with his sword or both. Athena then instructed Cadmus to sew half of the dragon's teeth in the ground; fierce, armed soldiers then sprang from the earth; these were the Spartoi, the 'sown men'. A fearful Cadmus threw a stone among them; they were confused by this and started fighting each other because they thought that one of their number had lobbed the stone. Only five survived: Echion, Udaeus, Chthonius, Hyperenor and Pelorus; as the military caste of Thebes they helped Cadmus build Thebes. Cadmus had to serve Ares for a year to atone for what he did to the dragon. Ares later avenged his draconic son by transforming Cadmus and his wife into serpents.

Ovid leaves us with a wonderfully vivid and graphic account:

Gliding down out of the sky Athena appears and bids Kadmos plough the soil and plant the Dragon's teeth, from which a future people should arise. Cadmus obeys, and with his plough's deep share opens wide furrows, then across the soil scatters the teeth, the seed of humankind. The tilth – beyond belief! – began to stir: first from the furrows points of spears were seen, next helmets, bright with nodding painted plumes, then shoulders, chests and weapon-laden arms arose, a growing crop of men in mail. So, when the curtain at a theatre is raised, figures rise up, their faces first, then gradually the rest, until at last, drawn slowly, smoothly up, they stand revealed complete, their feet placed on the fringe below.

In fear of these new foemen Cadmus sprang to arms. 'Lay down your arms!' a warrior cried, one of the Earth-born (Terrigenae) regiment, 'Take no part in civil strife.' So saying, with his sword he felled a Soil-sprung (Terrigenis) brother by his side, then fell himself, struck by a far-flung lance. He too who dealt him death was dead as soon and of that new-given lifebreath breathed his last. In the same mould of madness all that host, that sudden brotherhood, in battle joined, with wound for wound fell dead. That prime of youth, whose lot was life so short, lay writhing on their mother's bloodstained bosom – all save five who survived. (Ovid, *Metamorphoses* 3, 101ff (trans. Melville).)

The other half of the dragon's teeth were planted by Jason at Colchis. Aeetes, the king of Colchis, had been given the teeth by Athena, and he forced Jason to sow them in order to win the Golden Fleece. Like Cadmus, Jason threw a stone among the Spartoi to confuse them. The Spartoi then began to fight each other over the stone. None survived the battle.

Things reached a high for Cadmus when he was duly reconciled with Ares, and Zeus married him off to Harmonia, daughter of Ares and Aphrodite. The wedding was a high-profile celebrity event with all the Olympians coming down to the Cadmeia: the Muses sang the hymns along with Apollo or the Charites, the Graces. The bride was showered with lavish gifts; not least the divine necklace (fashioned by Hephaistos) and the robe, the *peplos* gifted by Athena via Europa and Zeus; both would come back to haunt the house of Cadmus in a terrible way as the much-coveted Harmonia Necklace and the Harmonia Gown. While this wedding myth illustrates the best a mortal can do in the world, its extension later exemplifies the inescapable fact that even the most forunate mortals cannot avoid the serious trials and tribulations of life. Cadmus and Pentheus were no exception.

Pausanias records that the house of Cadmus, the bridal chamber and the place where the muses sang at the wedding could still be seen in historical times (9, 12, 13).

Pentheus and Dionysus

In Greek mythology a bewildering number of kings assumed the Theban throne between the city's foundation by Cadmus and the Trojan War, suggesting a number of competing traditions, which mythographers have had to reconcile. Thebes only became Thebes much later during the reign of Amphion and Zethus, named after the latter's wife Thebe. When Cadmus died, his son Polydorus was under age so Pentheus, a son of Cadmus' daughter Agave and one of the Spartoi, was crowned king. He met a terrible tragic end at the hands of Dionysus.

Euripides' *Bacchae* gives us the story in a tragedy demonstrating what he considered to be the inadequacy of the Greek gods and religion. When an aging Cadmus abdicated in favour of his grandson Pentheus, Pentheus wasted no time in injudiciously banning the worship of Dionysus, who was the son of his aunt Semele, and did not allow the women of Cadmeia to celebrate his rites. This annoyed Dionysus no end: he made Pentheus' mother Agave and his aunts Ino and Autonoë, along with all the other women of Thebes, rush to Mount Cithaeron (the mountain between Boeotia and Attica) in a Bacchic frenzy. Pentheus locked Dionysus up and chained him to an angry bull in the palace stable, thinking him to be just another Bacchant, but the god's chains fell off and the jail doors opened for him; Dionysus razed the palace with an earthquake and fire.

A herdsman arrived from Mount Cithaeron, where he had been herding his grazing cattle. He reported that he saw some women on the mountain behaving strangely: wandering about in the forest, giving breast to animals, twining snakes in their hair and performing magic. Pentheus' plan was to slaughter the women with his soldiers but Dionysus, disguised as a woman, lured Pentheus out to spy on the Bacchic rites, with Pentheus fully expecting to see sexual abandon in action.[2] Hallucinating under the divine power of the god, Pentheus climbed a tree for a good view. The daughters of Cadmus spotted him in the tree and, urged on by Dionysus, believed him to be a wild animal. They pulled Pentheus down and tore him limb from limb as part of a ritual, the *sparagmos*. When Pentheus was identified, the women were exiled from Thebes. Some say that his own mother had been the first to attack him, tearing his arm off and then ripping off his head. She placed the head on a pike and took it back to Thebes, but only realized whose head it was when told by her father Cadmus that it was not the head of a mountain lion she mistakenly believed it to be but was in fact the bloody head of her mutilated son. Agave and her sisters were exiled, and Dionysus decreed that Cadmus and his wife Harmonia be turned into snakes before he led a barbarian horde to plunder the cities of Greece. This is what you get – vulgar barbarians triumphing over civilized Greeks – when you vie with the gods; hubris never pays.

Never was a man so tragically well-named. 'Pentheus' means 'man of sorrows' and derives from πένθος, *pénthos*, sorrow or grief, especially the grief caused by the death of a loved one. His name certainly marked him out for tragedy. More tragedy came from the fact that before or possibly after Pentheus was killed, his wife gave birth to a son named Menoeceus, who became the father of Creon and Jocasta and the grandfather of Oedipus.

Ovid has a version which diverges from Euripides' work in several ways.[3] In Ovid's *Metamorphoses*, King Pentheus is warned by the blind seer Tiresias to welcome Bacchus or else 'Your blood [will be] poured out and defile the woods and your mother and her sisters…' Pentheus snubs Tiresias and ignores his warnings. As Thebes succumbs to the 'dementia and the delirium of the new god', Pentheus laments the fall of his kingdom and demands the arrest of Bacchus. Instead the guards arrest Acoetes of Maeonia, a sailor who confirms the divinity of Bacchus and tells how the crew of his ship were turned into dolphins after trying to kidnap the young god.

Pentheus, convinced that Acoetes was lying, tried to throw him into jail. However, when the guards tried to shackle Acoetes, the chains fell off. Raging, Pentheus hurtled through the woods straight into a bacchanal. Driven to a frenzy, the participants took Pentheus for a boar and attacked him. His mother was the first to spear him; the other bacchants then tore him to bits with their bare hands.

Things had certainly deteriorated for Cadmus and Harmonia. They were obliged now to leave Thebes and went into exile to the wind-blasted land of Illyria on an ox-drawn hand cart with the family belongings. En route, a war between Illyria and the neighbouring Encheleans ('Eel people') allowed him to win a new kingdom and home when an oracle advised the Eel people that if they took Cadmus as leader they would win their war. They duly won the war. In the end they were transported to the Elysian Fields in a chariot drawn by winged dragons after being transformed into snakes. Why this highly inconvenient metamorphosis? Ovid suggests that Ares was behind it, even visiting them in their unhappy exile in Illyria, the god still smarting from Cadmus' slaying of his dragon all those years before (*Metamorphoses* 4, 569–603).

Nycteus, Antiope, Amphion and Zethus

Polydorus eventually succeeded his nephew, but not for long. At his death, the kingdom was entrusted to his father-in-law Nycteus, who acted as guardian for the young Labdacus, the son of Polydorus and Nycteis. Nycteus and his brother Lycus were the sons of either Chthonius, one of the Spartoi (or of the nymph Clonia and Hyrieus, the son of Poseidon and the Atlantid Alkyone, or of Poseidon and the Pleiad Celaeno). Nycteus had two daughters by Polyxo: Nycteis and Antiope.

Nycteus and Lycus had fled from Euboea after they murdered King Phlegyas, settling in Hyria and then moving to Thebes because they were on friendly terms with King Pentheus. Nycteus' daughter Nycteis married Polydorus, who succeeded Pentheus; their son was Labdacus. However, Pentheus and Polydorus both died soon after and Nycteus became regent for Labdacus.[4]

After Antiope was made pregnant by Zeus, possibly masquerading as a rapacious satyr, and fled to marry King Epopeus in Sicyon, Apollodorus reports that Nycteus killed himself in shame when he discovered Antiope's pregnancy and Lycus initiated the attack because he himself desired to punish her, successfully carrying her off after the battle.[5] Pausanias writes that Nycteus waged war on Epopeus, but was wounded in battle and died after being carried back to Thebes, appointing Lycus as regent for Labdacus.[6] In any event, Antiope gave birth to the twins Amphion and Zethus courtesy of Zeus on the way back to Thebes, at Mount Cithaeron. Lycus abandoned the babies on the mountain. They were rescued by shepherds who brought them up.

Once he returned to Thebes, Lycus gained custody of his niece Antiope. She was then given by Lycus to Dirce who locked her up and tortured her. Many years later, Antiope escaped and eventually found her sons but Zethis turned her away, thinking her to be a runaway slave. While Antiope was wandering the mountain she encountered Dirce who was roaming the hills as a Bacchant; Dirce grabbed her with the intention of killing her but her twins, now in hot pursuit, managed to save their mother and tied Dirce to a bull by her long hair. The bull trampled her to death. They vowed to take revenge for what Lycus and Dirce had done to their mother, travelled to Thebes and killed him. They then sent Laius into exile.[7]

Dirce was an avid acolyte of Dionysus who was angered by her death. In retaliation he rendered Antiope mad, destined to wander through Greece in a state of advanced frenzy. Eventually she was cured of this by Phokos, son of Ornytion, who married her.

Labdacus later became king. Another war broke out, this time a boundary dispute between Thebes and Athens; once again, Thebes was defeated after the army of King Pandion I of Athens (he ruled for forty years from 1437 BCE to 1397 BCE) was reinforced by the Thracian King Tereus. Labdacus himself survived the war but tragically failed to learn from recent history when he too messed with the cult of Dionysus and was killed by Dionysus' enraged Maenads.[8] Labdacus left behind a young son, Laius. Lycus again took control of Thebes, this time as a usurper denying Laius his birthright; he reigned for twenty years.

Amphion and Zethus marched on Thebes. Lycus' death, however, did not restore Laius to the throne. Amphion and Zethus seized power, ruling as joint kings of Thebes, and expelled Laius. Amphion and Zethus extended the city, rebadged it as Thebes and built the seven great gates of Thebes which were to loom large in the myth of the Seven Against Thebes, naming them after Amphion's daughters: Thera, Cleodoxa, Astynome, Astycratia, Chias, Ogygia and Chloris. Amphion deployed his strength and practical skills in the construction, while the musically-gifted Zethus was able to magic, Orpheus-like, the stones into place by his virtuoso lyre-playing and vocal accompaniment.

Niobe

Niobe, Amphion's wife, was an arrogant woman, well-known for her hubris since at least Homer.[9] Homer tells us of the hubris she exhibited when she boasted of her fourteen children, seven male and seven female (the Niobids), to Leto who only had two children, the twins Apollo and Artemis. This slight earned her a particularly harsh punishment from Leto. She sent Apollo and Artemis to slay all of her fourteen children with their poison arrows; Artemis killed all of Niobe's daughters while Apollo slaughtered all of her sons. The dead children lay unburied for nine days (it was a terrible, unholy thing in Greece to be denied burial rites), while she half-starved herself to death. Her grief drove her back home to Lydia where she turned to stone. Amphion committed suicide after the death of his beloved children, or he may have been arrowed by Apollo for attacking the god in a rage at the fate of his children. Zethus' son and only child had died earlier through a mistake of his mother Thebe, causing Zethus to kill himself too.

Laius, Jocasta and…Oedipus

The Theban throne was now vacant so the Thebans invited Laius back from the Peloponnese where he was exiled under the protection of King Pelops; in effect this move restored the original dynasty of Cadmus. We have noted how Laius abused the hospitality shown to him by Pelops when he raped Chrysippus while teaching him how to drive a chariot, or as Hyginus records it, during the Nemean games in which Chrysippus was due to compete. Laius then was guilty not only of abusing his host's hospitality as an honoured guest but also of abusing the trust invested in him as a teacher of Chryssippus, as defined in the Greek tradition of pedagogy and pederasty. Laius carried him off to Thebes, an abduction which is thought to be the subject of one of the lost tragedies of Euripides called *Chrysippus* and given in the same trilogy that included *The Phoenician Women*. Chrysippus was so ashamed, he fell on his sword.

When Laius became king, he married Jocasta, daughter of Menoeceus, son of Pentheus. Jocasta was childless at first and Laius had been told by the Delphic oracle that he might as well forget about children as he would be murdered by any son he had. For a while Laius managed to remain celibate, but, as noted, one night drink got the better of him and a drunken Laius had sex with Jocasta…and made her pregnant with Oedipus. Laius realized the consequences of this indiscretion, especially when the baby was born; he then exposed this newborn son – Oedipus – on Mount Cithaeron, staked the infant's ankles together so binding his feet together (or maybe staking them to the ground) to deter any attempts at rescue. Oedipus was named after the swelling from the injuries to his feet and ankles. The word 'oedema' is from the Greek word for swelling: οἴδημα or oedēma. However, Oedipus survived when he was rescued by a shepherd, Euphorbos, who, unable to afford to bring him up, passed him on to the childless King Polybus and Queen Merope of Corinth, who adopted him and raised him to adulthood.[10]

Oedipus grew up in Corinth oblivious to his real parentage, assuming that he was the biological son of his putative parents Polybus and Merope. However, rumours persisted about his father and mother in the form of a drunk at a banquet who questioned his parentage, so he consulted the Delphic Oracle only to learn the dreaded news that he was fated to kill his father and to marry his mother. Fearing for the safety of the only parents known to him, Polybus and Merope, Oedipus fled Corinth to avoid committing these sins. On the 'Cleft Way', (*schiste hodos*) 'where three roads narrow', he encountered Laius, who was on his way to Delphi to consult the oracle because he had prophetically received omens indicating that his son might return to kill him. Polyphontes, Laius' herald, demanded that Oedipus give way. After an altercation, Oedipus refused to defer to the king; Laius either ran a chariot wheel over his foot or struck him with his whip; when Polyphontes killed one of Oedipus' horses, Oedipus exploded in anger, killed Polyphontes, dragged Laius from his chariot and slew him too. Laius was buried where he died by Damasistratus, the king of Plataea. Thebes was then cursed with a plague because Laius' murderer had not received due punishment.

Oedipus continued on to Thebes quite unaware of the identity of the old man he had just murdered, oblivious to the fact that he had unwittingly fulfilled the first part of the prophecy. He then learned that the king of the city (Laius) had been recently killed, and that the city was being terrorized by the Sphinx who would routinely stop all travellers to Thebes and challenge them with a riddle. If the travellers could not answer her correctly, they were killed and eaten; if they were successful, they would be free to continue on their journey. The situation got so bad for the citizens of Thebes that a desperate Creon offered the hand of former queen Jocasta and the kingdom to anyone who solved the riddle (and presumably cause the Sphinx to move on).

The riddle was: 'What walks on four feet in the morning, two in the afternoon and three at night?' Oedipus answered: 'Man: as an infant, he crawls on all fours; as an adult, he walks on two legs and, in old age, he uses a "walking" stick.' Oedipus was the first to answer the riddle correctly and, having heard Oedipus' answer, the Sphinx allowed him to proceed. However, so upset was the Sphinx by Oedipus' success that she flung herself off the acropolis in Thebes, or surrendered to Oedipus to allow him to slay her.

A grateful and relieved Thebes elected Oedipus as its new king. Oedipus took his rewards: he accepted the throne and married Laius' widowed queen Jocasta, so fulfilling the second half of the terrible prophecy. Jocasta bore him four children: two girls, Antigone and Ismene, and two boys, Eteocles and Polynices.

Years later the predicted plague struck Thebes, devastating crops, livestock and the Theban people. Oedipus was determined to end the depredation and sent his uncle, Creon, to the Oracle at Delphi for advice. Creon returned and reported that Apollo insisted that Thebes was harbouring a terrible abomination and that the plague would only be lifted when the true murderer of King Laius was killed or exiled. Oedipus swore to do this, unaware that he was himself the culprit. Oedipus then summoned Tiresias for advice, but he was initially reluctant to reveal anything. Finally Tiresias explained that Oedipus was in fact looking for Oedipus; during a heated argument, Tiresias exposed Oedipus' terrible and tragic trio of crimes: patricide, regicide and incest. Yet Oedipus was in denial and convinced that Tiresias was in league with Creon to usurp the throne. The argument brought out a worried Jocasta who mentioned that Laius was slain at a place where three roads meet, a fact that awoke Oedipus' memory of the events that day in the road and he realized, horror upon horror, that he might well be the very man he was pursuing. One of Laius' servants had survived the attack and was living out his old age in a frontier district of Thebes. Oedipus sent immediately for the man to either confirm or refute his guilt. It was then that Oedipus nervously realized that he may have murdered Laius and so caused the plague.

A messenger arrived from Corinth announcing that King Polybus had died. Oedipus was relieved as this meant that the prophecy could no longer be fulfilled if Polybus, whom he considered his birth father, was now dead.

Jocasta realized that Oedipus was her natural son; devastated and distraught, she rushed into the palace where she hanged herself. Oedipus then learned that the infant raised as the adopted son of Polybus and Merope was really the son of Laius and Jocasta. Oedipus now knew that the man he had killed at the place where the three roads met was his own father, King Laius, and that he had married his mother, Jocasta.

Differing versions exist. Sophocles says that when his city was struck by plague, Oedipus learned that it was divine punishment for his patricide and incest. Jocasta then hanged herself.[11] Euripides has Jocasta endure the disgrace and live on in Thebes, only committing suicide after her sons killed one another in a fight for the crown. In both versions Oedipus gouged out his eyes with the pins from Jocasta's dress; Sophocles has Oedipus go into exile with his daughter Antigone, finally dying at Colonus where they had been welcomed by King Theseus of Athens. Euripides and Statius have him living in Thebes, during the war between Eteocles and Polynices.[12]

In a bid to expiate his terrible sins, Oedipus cursed his ungrateful sons:

> When I was thrust from hearth and home; when I was banned and banished, they never raised a hand to help me. Then may the gods never quench their fatal feud. That neither he who holds the sceptre now may keep his throne, nor he who fled the realm return again. (Sophocles, *Oedipus at Colonus* 425.)

So, in order to deflect their father's curse, Polynices and Eteocles struck a pact that each should rule alternately one year at a time. Eteocles reneged on the pact, and Polynices was banished from Thebes, helping himself to some of the contents of the Theban treasury on the way out since they might be used to seize power again. That is how the famous and fateful Robe and Necklace of Harmonia left Thebes.[13] Polynices fled to the court of King Adrastus of Argos to raise an army which we know as the Epigoni.

In the *Thebais*, Polynices and Eteocles were cursed by their father for their disrespect towards him on two occasions. The first of these occurred when they served him using the silver table of Cadmus and a golden cup of the same origin, which he had forbidden them to use. The brothers then sent him the haunch of a sacrificed animal rather than the shoulder, which was his due. An apoplectic Oedipus prayed to Zeus that the brothers would die at each other's hands and that they never would agree as to who would become his successor on the throne of Thebes.

In Sophocles' *Oedipus at Colonus*, Oedipus wished to stay in Thebes but was expelled by Creon.[14] When Polynices met the exiled Oedipus at Colonus, asking for his father's support since an oracle had said that he who counted Oedipus as an ally would win, all he received was a renewed curse from his father, who again doomed them to kill each other and never rule: 'This curse I leave you as my last bequest: Never to win by arms your native land, nor return to Argos, but by a kinsman's hand to die and slay.' (Oedipus to Polynices. Sophocles, *Oedipus at Colonus* 1385.)

The Seven Against Thebes

Eriphyle, daughter of Talaus, was the mother of Alcmaeon and the wife of Amphiaraus. Eriphyle persuaded Amphiaraus to take part in the raid that we know as the Seven Against Thebes, though she knew full well he would not be coming home. She had been persuaded by Polynices, who offered her the necklace and robe of Harmonia for her complicity and help. As we have seen, the exiled Polynices saw fit to help himself to some of the contents of the Theban treasury for future use as a bargaining chip in his quest to take his rightful place on the throne at Thebes.

When Polynices reached Argos, he married a daughter of Adrastus. At that time, the kingdom of Argos was divided into three kingdoms with three kings: Adrastus, Amphiaraus and Iphis. Adrastus promised his new son-in-law Polynices that he would restore him to his native land, and for that purpose made ready to attack Thebes as part of a coalition force. King Iphis also agreed and sent his son Eteoclus to join the alliance. However, King Amphiaraus, who was a seer and could see that the expedition would fail, refused to participate and warned Adrastus. Now Amphiaraus was married to Adrastus' sister Eriphyle; traditionally, when there was a difference between the two men, Amphiaraus was sworn to let Eriphyle decide which way to go. King Iphis told Polynices that Amphiaraus could be forced to yield if Eriphyle happened to be bribed by the prospect of the Necklace of Harmonia. Amphiaraus had forbidden Eriphyle to accept gifts from Polynices, but Polynices prevailed and she agreed to persuade her husband to join the coalition. So, when war was advocated by Adrastus and opposed by Amphiaraus, Eriphyle, having accepted the necklace, decided in favour of Adrastus and war.

Amphiaraus reluctantly agreed to join the doomed raid, but aware of his wife's deception, asked his sons, Alcmaeon and Amphilochus, to avenge his inevitable death by killing her should he not return. This they did later as members of the Epigoni. On the way to the battle, Amphiaraus repeatedly warned the other warriors that the expedition would fail, and blamed Tydeus for starting it. After Amphiaraus died, Alcmaeon killed his mother. He was then pursued by the Erinyes in his flight across Greece, eventually reaching sanctuary at the court of King Phegeus of Psophis in Arcadia, who purified him and gave him his daughter in marriage. This was Arsinoe, or Alphesiboea, to whom Alcmaeon gave as a wedding present the Robe and Necklace of Harmonia. An exhausted Alcmaeon, driven half-mad, consulted an oracle on how to placate and shake off the Erinyes; due to his crime, Psophis became barren and an oracle told Alcmaeon to go to the springs of Achelous where the god purified him and was given the river-god's daughter, Callirrhoe, as a wife. Callirrhoe told Alcmaeon that she would not live with him if she did not possess the Robe and Necklace of Harmonia, still owned by his first wife Arsinoe. Alcmaeon then went back to Psophis and told Phegeus that it had been predicted that he should be rid of his madness when he had brought the robe and necklace to Delphi and dedicated them. Phegeus believed him and gave up the jewellery and clothing, but a servant disclosed to Phegeus that Alcmaeon was in fact taking the ill-gotten goods to Callirrhoe. So the sons of Phegeus, Pronous and Agenor (or Temenus and Axion), were despatched by their father to wait for Alcmaeon in an ambush and kill him. Their sister Arsinoe thought this was too extreme a solution and reproached her brothers; their response was to bundle her into a chest, carry her to Tegea and give her as a slave to Agapenor, falsely accusing her of Alcmaeon's murder.

Callirrhoe was now a widow in grief. She asked Zeus that the sons she had by Alcmaeon become all of a sudden full-grown in order to avenge their father's murder; Zeus, who was involved with her at the time, granted her wish. So when Pronous and Agenor, carrying their sister in a chest, along with the robe and necklace which they intended to dedicate at Delphi, arrived at the house of Agapenor, they met the surprisingly suddenly grown-up children of Alcmaeon and Callirrhoe, Amphoterus and Acarnan, who happened to arrive there at the same time. The sons of Alcmaeon immediately murdered their father's murderers, went to Psophis, entered the palace and slew both Phegeus and his wife. Amphoterus and Acarnan told their mother what had happened and then went to Delphi to dedicate the robe and necklace. After Delphi they went to Epirus and having collected settlers, colonized Acarnania.

There is an eerie coda to all this. About 750 years after these events – during the Third Sacred War (356–346 BCE) – the tyrant Phayllus of Phocis (d.351 BCE) fell in love with the wife of an Oetan leader and in order to win her, he promised her much gold and silver, inviting her to ask whatever she wished. The woman asked for the Necklace of Harmonia which was now hanging at Delphi in the sanctuary of Athena Forethought. So when Phayllus seized Delphi, he took much booty including the necklace, which he gave to the woman he was pursuing. After some time, her youngest son went mad and set fire to the house: his mother died in the blaze, and most of the family's possessions were lost. Since then there has been no trace of either the necklace or the robe.

According to Hyginus (*Fabulae* 244, 245), Phegeus himself killed his son-in-law and also his granddaughter, the daughter of Alphesiboea.

The provenance of the necklace and robe reaches all the way back to Cadmus when

Zeus gave him Harmonia as wife, daughter of Aphrodite and Ares. And all the gods left the sky, feasted in the Cadmea and celebrated the marriage with hymns. Cadmus gave her a robe and the necklace wrought by Hephaestus, which some say was given to Cadmus by Hephaestus, but Pherecydes says that it was given by Europa, who had received it from Zeus. (Apollodorus 3, 4, 2.)

In Statius' *Thebaid* (2, 265–305; 4, 188–213), Eriphyle's desire to procure the Necklace of Harmonia is one of the catalysts for the war between Argos and Thebes. In this version of the myth, however, Argia, Polynices's wife, persuades her husband to give the necklace to Eriphyle so that Amphiaraus will join the war effort.

As both sides prepared for war it became apparent that there were to be no winners: Eteocles was now widely seen as being a man who breaks his promises for power and deceives and denies a brother; Polynices was now suspected of being somewhat less than patriotic, wishing to cause his own native land's destruction. As we have seen, before he left for war, Amphiaraus ordered his sons to kill their mother to avenge him and march against Thebes as soon as they were grown up. This would be the war of the Epigoni which took place ten years later.

The armies of Polynices set off for war; they paused to water at Nemea, to celebrate the Nemean games and honour with a magnificent funeral the dead prince Opheltes who had been devoured by a dragon there when left by Hypsipyle, his nursemaid, to show the Argives the way to the spring. The army reached Cithaeron whence Tydeus was sent as envoy to Thebes to request Eteocles to cede the kingdom to Polynices as they originally agreed. Diplomacy failed: the embassy was fruitless, so the army approached the walls of Thebes with each commander stationed facing each of the seven gates, with their armies arrayed behind them. Divination was duly performed by Eteocles and his government, who decided to listen to Tiresias; he pronounced that the Thebans would be victorious if Menoeceus, son of Creon, sacrificed himself. Menoeceus slew himself before the gates.

The siege proceeded with much loss of life. An early casualty was the arrogant and proud Capaneus who bragged that he would take Thebes and put it to the torch whether Zeus wanted it or not. Eventually it was agreed that the brothers should fight in single combat; Polynices and Eteocles slew each other, thus fulfilling Oedipus' curse.

To illustrate the carnage and barbarity of the conflict we learn how Tydeus killed the Theban Melanippus, only to be mortally wounded by him in the stomach. Tydeus lay dying when Athena approached with a medicine she had received from Zeus, and by which she intended to render Tydeus, a favourite of hers, immortal. However, Amphiaraus despised Tydeus for his part in fomenting the war and set about foiling Athena's intentions. Amphiaraus decapitated Melanippus and presented his head to Tydeus, knowing that this would provoke an atrocious response. Sure enough, Tydeus cleaved open the skull and gulped down the brains. Athena was naturally utterly disgusted by this behaviour and thought better of administering the potion and the offer of immortality. Another example of atrocious and barbaric behaviour in a supposedly civilized world.

When Polynices and Eteocles were each slain by the other in the ensuing conflict, Creon took the throne and branded Polynices a traitor; Creon forbade proper burial of Polynices and his Argive allies and even prohibited mourning on pain of death by stoning. The Argive fallen were to be left to rot; a decision which offended men and gods alike.

Creon's decision here caused tragedy to be piled on top of tragedy. In Sophocles' *Antigone*, Polynices's story continues after his death. As we know, King Creon, who ascended to the throne of Thebes, decreed that Polynices was not to be buried or even mourned, on pain of death by stoning. Antigone, his sister, defied the order, but was caught. Creon imposed the death penalty, even though she was betrothed to Creon's son Haemon. Antigone's sister Ismene then declared she had helped Antigone and wanted the same fate. Creon imprisoned Antigone in a tomb; meanwhile the gods, through Tiresias, expressed their disapproval of Creon's decision, which convinced him to rescind his order. He then went to bury Polynices himself and release Antigone. However, he was too late: she had already hanged herself rather than be entombed alive. When Creon arrived at the tomb where she was to be interred, his son Haemon, implacably opposed to his father's decision regarding the burials, attacked him and then killed himself. When Creon's wife Eurydice learned of their deaths, she too took her own life.

Adrastus enlisted the help of Theseus to get the Argives buried and they eventually were, in Eleusis. Polynices, however, was laid to rest in Thebes, some say alongside his brother. The decision to deny the Argives their burial rites comes to us through a largely lost play by Aeschylus, the *Eleusinians*.

Aeschylus, Euripides and Sophocles all used the myths of the Theban dynasty as the basis for a number of their plays.

Aeschylus: *The Seven Against Thebes*

As we have seen, the two cursed sons of the now blind Oedipus, Eteocles and Polynices, agreed to rule Thebes in alternate years in order to avoid bloodshed. After the first year though, Eteocles refused to cede, inciting Polynices to raise an army of Argives captained by the eponymous Seven to take Thebes by force. Aeschylus' tragedy *The Seven Against Thebes* opens at this point. This is the third play in a trilogy produced by Aeschylus in 467 BCE; the first two plays, *Laius* and *Oedipus*, as well as the satyr play *Sphinx*, are lost.

The play gives a lengthy description of each of the seven captains that led the Argive army against the seven gates of the city of Thebes, as well as their respective shields. Eteocles, in turn, announces which Theban commanders he will send against each Argive attacker. Finally, the commander of the troops at the seventh gate is revealed to be Polynices. Eteocles now recalls the curse of their father Oedipus. Eteocles resolves to meet and fight his brother at the seventh gate. A messenger announces that the attackers have been repelled, but that Eteocles and Polynices have killed each other in battle. Their bodies are brought on stage to be mourned by the chorus.

Women play a major role in this play, in the shape of a chorus made up of Theban women, a city under siege. Much of the play comprises a troubled dialogue between the chorus and the city's king, Eteocles, brother of Polynices. Polynices is about to attack the city to claim his rightful turn as king of Thebes, denied to him by Eteocles who is overstaying his turn and time as king. The chorus is influential in the play: it offers up prayers to the gods of Thebes in defiance of Eteocles who wants to silence the chorus;[15] it pictures itself as a victim of war, fearful and frightened by the din of the siege as Eteocles formulates his plan for the defence of the city; it desperately tries to persuade Eteocles not to fight Polynices; the chorus clings to the statues of the local gods in a bid to win their protection for the city.[16] So frustrated does it all make Eteocles that he exclaims somewhat misogynistically: 'Zeus, what a race you've given us for company, these women!' to which the leader of the chorus quips in reply: 'A wretched one, just like men when their city is taken!'[17] The only benefit Eteocles can see in the womanly chorus is their support for the sacrifices which will mark his victory, the sacred lamentation and the cry of victory, the Paean.[18] The chorus vividly describes the fate that awaits them 'when a city is taken': their city is destroyed; they, young and old alike, are dragged off by their hair like horses, their clothes ripped off; virgin girls are systematically raped, a fate worse than death itself. They wish death on the bragging, conquering soldier: may he be struck down if ever he bursts into their homes to rape a virgin (452–6).

The women in the chorus are also influential in the shields scene in which Eteocles systematically allocates a Theban hero to face the seven Argive warriors who are detailed to assault the seven gates of Thebes. For the first six of the seven, the chorus, with increasing belligerence, asks the gods for their support, which they get. However, when it comes to the seventh, everything changes. Eteocles, as noted, decides that he will face Polynices; the chorus tries to persuade him not to: for the women, the stain, the miasma, of brother killing brother will live forever.[19] The last act of these powerful women immersed in a fratricidal war is to lament the two brothers united in death, fulfilling the curse inflicted on them by Oedipus and exterminating the house of Laius.

The myth of the Seven is traditionally thought to be based on Bronze Age history in the generation before the Trojan War; indeed, 'there is no reason to suppose that the tale was not based on historical fact.'[20] The myth has passed into Etruscan culture, as attested by a fifth-century bronze mirrorback inscribed with Fulnice (Polynices) and Evtucle (Eteocles) running at one another with drawn swords.[21] A sculpted terracotta relief from a temple at Pyrgi, ca.470–460 BCE, shows a highly gruesome detail from the battle in which Tydeus gnaws on the living brain of Melanippos during the siege.[22]

Euripides: *The Phoenissae*

The play gets its name from the chorus which comprises women from Phoenicia, war booty sympathetic to their Theban ancestors, and on a one-way ticket to Delphi where their fate is to be sacrificial fodder to Apollo. Unlike some of Euripides' other plays, the chorus does not play a significant role in the plot but represents the innocent and neutral people who very often are found in the middle of war situations; the women are trapped in Thebes by the war. Patriotism is a significant theme in the story as, paradoxically, Polynices talks a great deal about his love for the city of Thebes but has brought an army to destroy it; Creon is also forced to make a choice between saving the city and saving the life of his son.

Phoenicia is significant because it is the home of Cadmus and of that 'horned ancestor' Io, raped by Zeus and right there at the beginning of the tortuous sequence of events which led to the Trojan War and culminated in the curse of Oedipus bestowed on his two fratricidal sons. The play opens with a summary of the Oedipus story and its aftermath told by Jocasta, who in this version has obviously not committed suicide. She explains that after her husband blinded himself upon discovering that he was her son as well as her husband, his sons Eteocles and Polynices locked him away in the hope that the people might forget the dreadful events. He curses them, proclaiming that neither would rule without killing his brother. To avert this, as we know, they have agreed to split the country; Polynices allows Eteocles to rule for one year. When the year expired, Eteocles was to abdicate, permitting his brother to rule for a year. Eteocles refused to do so, forcing his brother into exile instead. While exiled, Polynices went to Argos, where he married the daughter of Adrastus, king of the Argives. He then persuaded Adrastus to send a force to help him reclaim the city. Jocasta has arranged for a cease-fire so that she can mediate between her two sons.

The Phoenician women, though, are not the only powerful women in the play: Jocasta, until her suicide after the deaths of her two sons, and her daughter Antigone also loom large in the action. Indeed, importantly, they open the play: Jocasta provides the back story by relating the history of the house of Cadmus and the origins of the curse of Oedipus and his descendants; Antigone has her teichoscopy in which she describes the army besieging her city from the terrace of her palace.

Jocasta soon takes control by taking command. Assuming the role of a military commander, she, desperate for reconciliation, orders a truce between the opposing armies, but Eteocles is intractable and refuses to compromise, adamant as he is that he will retain power in the land, rightfully Polynices' power at that specific time and rightfully Polynices' land. Jocasta's sagacious appeal to fairness and equality falls on deaf ears.[23] Instead, she is forced to witness an unpleasant exchange in which the brothers verbally mutilate each other, both parting with the promise of killing the other in an impious and sacrilegious prayer which leaves Jocasta with nothing but the prospect of two dead sons and a ruined city.

Tiresias reveals that Creon must sacrifice his son Menoeceus. He explains that the city was founded by men who had sprung from the ground where Cadmus sowed the teeth of a serpent he had killed, but the serpent was sacred to Ares, who would punish Thebes unless a sacrifice was made. As only Creon and his son were pure-blooded descendants of the men who sprouted from the ground, Menoeceus was the only choice. Creon is told he can only save the city by sacrificing his son, and instructs Menoeceus to flee to the oracle at Dodona; Menoeceus agrees but secretly goes to the serpent's lair to sacrifice himself and appease Ares.

When Jocasta learned of the impending duel between her sons she is determined, with the help of Antigone, to battle her way between her sons but arrives too late; both are dead. Seizing a 'bronze-hammered' sword lying between the bodies of Eteocles and Polynices, she stabs herself and dies a soldier's death as she falls on the bodies of her boys. This battlefield death in no man's land between two armies, effected with a soldier's sword, is the death of a militaristic woman falling in battle.

Antigone gets her first taste, and view, of battle and war from the vantage point of the palace terrace from which she describes the military activity going on below in a teichoscopy. Like Medea in Valerius Flaccus' *Argonautica*, Antigone is initially untouched by the ways of war and is frightened by the horror of it all, although, at the same time, she is awed by the scale and magnificence of the weaponry worn by the warriors.[24] She curses them, predicting the servitude their martial behaviour will impose on the Theban women. This all changes, however, when she reluctantly descends to the battlefield with Jocasta amid the carnage engendered by the duel between her two brothers.[25] Antigone is now face to face with the horrors of war. Things go from bad to worse when her mother takes her own life and Antigone is left to perform the crucial funeral rites for all three relatives and to break the terrible news to a pathetic Oedipus.

Both Jocasta and Antigone show immense courage and tenacity in their ultimately unsuccessful attempts to deflect or mitigate the sins and mistakes of their kin. However, they are not just up against the fickleness and vainglory of mortal men: the gods are in control here and nothing the women can do can thwart the will of the gods. Jocasta and Antigone boldly intrude into the male world of war, but to no avail; so all that was left to Antigone was to report the bad news and perform the traditionally female role of lamenting and organizing the funerals.

Euripides: *The Suppliant Women*

The action of this play, first performed in 423 BCE, revolves around the dire predicament the bereaved mothers of slain warriors, the Seven Against Thebes, find themselves in when they are prohibited by Creon from performing funeral rites and burying their sons, all in contravention of divine law and ancient custom. The execution of funeral rites and the organization of proper burial was one of the few significant responsibilities allowed to women in a society which precluded them from public activity in most other areas of civic life. Creon's prohibition here would, therefore, have resonated badly with the grieving women. Eventually they prevail on Theseus, king of Athens, through Aethra his mother to intercede. He attacks Thebes, although the women are fearful of yet more loss of life; Theseus himself washes the corpses of the dead sons and prepares them for burial. The women are naturally grateful that the bodies have been recovered, but distressed at the prospect of seeing them as corpses, agreeing that it would have been better had they never married. Theseus cremates and obtains the ashes of the fallen heroes, shielding the women from the horrific sight of the mutilated and rotting corpses.

Like Perseus, Cadmus and Heracles, Theseus was a modernist, a reformer and an agent for change who came into conflict with the old, conservative socio-religious order. Theseus was a unifying king and can lay claim to establishing the *synoikismos* (dwelling together) – the political unification of Attica under Athens – represented, like Heracles, by his labours, slaying ogres and monsters.

As the women continue their lamentations they see Capaneus' wife Evadne in her wedding dress climbing the rocks above her husband's tomb, declaring her plan to join her husband in the flames of the pyre. Her father Iphis tries to talk her down, but she leaps to her death. As Iphis dies, the orphaned youths hand over the ashes of their fathers to their grandmothers. The boys' lamentations are mingled with promises of revenge and more war.

War is undoubtedly a high price to pay, but such is the strength of duty and feeling experienced by the bereaved suppliant women that it is considered a price worth paying to see their sons accorded the appropriate funeral rites and a proper burial.

Sophocles: *Antigone*

Antigone was written in 441 BCE, the third of the Theban trilogy plays following on where Aeschylus' *Seven Against Thebes* ends. As we have seen, it is another dramatic expression of the tragic predicament in which women found themselves when prohibited from carrying out the funeral rites and burial of their kin: Antigone is forbidden by Creon to bury her brother, Polynices. The corpse is to remain on the field of battle to be picked over by carrion: a fate worse than death for all directly concerned, including the shade (spirit) of Polynices if he remains unburied. The defiant and brave Antigone goes to bury her brother herself, despite her sister Ismene's refusal to help.

When Creon learned that Polynices had received funeral rites and a symbolic burial effected with a thin covering of earth, he was incandescent with rage and ordered that the culprit be found and brought to book; Antigone is duly discovered and admits her guilt, comparing the morality of Creon's edict with the morality of her own actions. A still angry Creon assumes Ismene to be implicated; she is summoned and confesses falsely to the crime, wishing to die with her sister; Creon orders that the two women be imprisoned.

Haemon, Creon's son and Antigone's fiancé, pledges allegiance to his father and tries tactfully to persuade him to spare Antigone, claiming that 'under cover of darkness the city mourns for the girl'. Things go badly and Haemon leaves, vowing never to see Creon again. Creon's cruel reaction is to spare Ismene and to entomb Antigone alive in a cave. She is taken away to her living death, midst lamentations from the Chorus over her impending doom.

Tiresias, the blind prophet, warns Creon that Polynices should be buried: the gods are displeased to such an extent that they are refusing all sacrifices or prayers from Thebes. Creon accuses Tiresias of corruption, to which the seer responds that Creon will lose 'a son of [his] own loins'. All of Greece will despise him; a terrified Chorus asks Creon to take their advice: he agrees and frees Antigone and buries Polynices. However, in the meantime, Antigone has hanged herself; Haemon tries and fails to stab Creon, then turns the knife on himself. Creon's wife, Eurydice, commits suicide and, with her dying breath, curses her husband.[26]

Jean Anouilh's tragedy *Antigone* was inspired by both Sophocles' play and the myth itself. Anouilh's play premièred in Paris at the Théâtre de l'Atelier in February 1944 during the Nazi occupation of France and produced under the constraints of Nazi censorship. The play is ambiguous with regard to the rejection of authority (represented by Antigone) and the acceptance of it (Creon). The parallels to the French Resistance and the Nazi occupation are evident.

The fate and actions of women as a consequence of war are also explored in Aristophanic Greek comedy. The famous example is, of course, the *Lysistrata*, one of a number of plays based on fantasy situations in which the norms of Athenian society are absurdly contravened and contraverted.

Aristophanes: *Lysistrata*

Lysistrata – the name translates as 'Army Disbander' – was performed in 411 BCE, and is the story of one woman's extraordinary but mad mission to end the Peloponnesian War. Lysistrata persuades the women of Greece to withhold sex from their husbands and lovers until they negotiate a peace; however, all it does in the end is excite a battle between the sexes. However, Aristophanes manages to show how inept some men can be and the theoretical ability of women to intrude into the traditional territory of men.

In the beginning, a solemn oath is struck over a wine bowl in which the women renounce all sexual pleasure, including the 'Lioness on the Cheese Grater', an obviously satisfying sexual position. Early success comes in the capture of the Acropolis, home to the treasury; the women are now able to freeze the funds which are needed to finance the ongoing war. The magistrate turns up looking for a means to pay for oars and then proceeds to trot out the usual pejorative, misogynistic stereotypes, deploring the hysterical nature of women, their bibulous behaviour, their predilection for promiscuous sex and attraction to strange and exotic cults; he also censures his fellow men for not controlling their women. Lysistrata responds by delineating the frustration felt by women during war when the men make stupid decisions that affect the whole population while their wives' opinions are ignored. She feminizes him, covering his head with her headdress, and gives him a basket of wool – traditional accoutrements of women – and tells him that from now on war – men's work – is now women's business. She explains the plight of young, childless women who sit at home, growing old while the men are away fighting endless campaigns, alluding to the double standard whereby women are obliged to marry very young and men can marry when they choose, having played the field to their heart's content. To Lysistrata, the magistrate, and everything he stands for, might as well be dead. Nevertheless, reconciliation eventually ensues and everyone is happy. The war continues apace, but Euripides has at least allowed the women a voice to adumbrate the inequalities they face in Greek society, to voice an opinion about the war and the suffering it causes the women left at home, and to criticize the handling of the war by the men of Athens.

The *Lysistrata* was not the only comedy in which women were on top. We know of two plays called *Gynaikokratia* – one by Alexis (PCG 2, frr 42–43) and one by Amphis (PCG 2, fr.8) – plus *Tyrannis* by Pherecrates (PCG 7, frr 150–154) and Theopompus' *Stratiotides* (PCG 7, frr 55–59).

In Aristophanes's *Birds* (829–831) Euelpides objects to a similar gender reversal when he complains that Athena, a female deity no less, protects the city in a suit of armour while so-called warrior Cleisthenes is portrayed as an effete man armed with his shuttle; bellicosity apart, Athena is also patron of wool-working and other women's crafts. The line here is a parody of Euripides' *Meleager* fr. 522: 'if work with shuttles were to be the concern of men, while women were seized with the delights of weaponry.'

The war of the Epigoni

The Theban wars, however, did not end with the assault of the seven on Thebes. The Epigoni (offspring) were the sons of the Argive heroes who had fought and died in the first Theban war. This, the second Theban war, occurred ten years later, when the Epigoni, intent on avenging the deaths of their fathers, successfully attacked Thebes and razed the city walls. Apollodorus and Pausanias are our chief sources, and tell the story of the war with some differences. According to Apollodorus,[27] the Delphic oracle had promised victory if Alcmaeon, son of Amphiaraus, was chosen as leader, and so he was. Aegialeus, son of Adrastus, was killed by Laodamas, son of Eteocles, but Alcmaeon killed Laodamas. The Thebans were defeated and, on the advice of Tiresias, fled their city. Pausanias, however, maintains that Thersander, son of Polynices, was their leader, that Laodamas fled Thebes with the rest of the Thebans, and that Thersander became king of Thebes.[28]

As we have seen, the catalyst for the wars was Eriphyle allowing herself to be bribed, first by Polynices who gave her the Necklace of Harmonia, and later by Thersander, son of Polynices, who gave her the Robe of Harmonia. The first bribe resulted in Amphiaraus, her husband, reluctantly going to war with both wife and husband knowing full well that he would not return; on leaving for Thebes in the first war he ordered his sons to slay their mother and march for a second time on Thebes.

Alcmaeon was appointed as their commander-in-chief on the strength of an oracle that predicted victory under his leadership. He quickly appointed, as before, seven champions to lead the attack against Thebes, one for each of the seven city gates. This time they were not going to make the same mistakes as ten years before, ensuring that the army marching against Thebes would be strong enough by reinforcing their task force from Argos with contingents from Messenia, Arcadia, Corinth and Megara.

The Epigoni first devastated the surrounding villages; a battle took place at Glisas in which Laodamas was killed by Alcmaeon, and Aegialeus, son of King Adrastus of Argos, was also slain. With Laodamas dead, the Thebans fled within the city walls.

All was practically lost for the Thebans; Tiresias told the Thebans to send a herald to discuss surrender terms with the Epigoni. This they did while at the same time loading their children and women on wagons under cover of the night, and fleeing from the city. Tiresias fled with his fellow citizens, but he died soon after they arrived at the spring called

Tilphussa. The Theban refugees built a new city, Hestiaea, where they settled.

Meanwhile, the Epigoni took a deserted Thebes, plundered it and flattened the walls. Most of the Argive commanders returned rich with booty to their respective countries after handing the throne to Thersander. In a variant, after the capture of Thebes, Alcmaeon found out that his mother Eriphyle had been bribed by Polynices' son Thersander with the Robe of Harmonia; he was livid and killed his mother on his return.

Jocasta's brother Creon, who before had governed Thebes after the death of Laius and after the exile of Oedipus, then became regent for Eteocles' son Laodamas. Heracles was born with Creon as his guardian; Creon gave his daughter Megara in marriage to Heracles. In return, Heracles later defended Thebes in two more wars: the first against King Erginus of Minyan Orchomenus, then against King Pyraechmus of Euboea.

Eteocles' son Laodamas came of age, and Thersander was installed as king of Thebes. King Laodamas was killed during the war by Alcmaeon after he had killed Aegialeus.[29]

In an alternative myth narrated in Sophocles' *Antigone*, Laodamas murdered his aunts Antigone and Ismene, whom he had arrested for burying Polynices. They sought refuge in the temple of Hera, but Laodamas set fire to it and they burned to death.[30]

Thersander later joined up with the Greek forces in the Trojan War a generation or so later, but he was killed by Telephus, a son of Heracles on the shores of Mysia before ever reaching Troy. Thersander's son Tisamenus was too young at the time to assume command of the Theban contingent, but he later came of age during the war and entered the conflict near its end.

There was an *Epigoni*, an early Greek epic on this subject which was a sequel to the *Thebaid*, part of the Theban Cycle. As well as the fragments ascribed to the *Epigoni*, we have seven extant fragments assigned to a play by Sophocles called *Eriphyle*. This may be an alternate title for *Epigoni*, to which these seven fragments would apply. However, it is possible that *Eriphyle* is an entirely separate play from *Epigoni*, in which case it is possible that both were part of a connected trilogy, with the other tragic play in the trilogy being *Alcmaeon* and the satyr play being *Amphiaraus*. Sophocles also composed a tragedy, also the *Epigoni*, now lost.

Chapter Nine

Heracles: Not labouring but battling

Heracles was both hero and god at the same time, or as Pindar has it *heros theos*, a veritable demi-god. He was the son of Zeus and Alcmene, foster son of Amphitryon; he was a great-grandson and half-brother of Perseus. A paragon of masculinity, the epitome of an alpha male and a champion of the Olympian order against chthonic monsters. He can lay claim to being Gatekeeper of Olympus; god of strength, heroes, sports, athletes, health, agriculture, fertility, trade, oracles and divine protector of mankind. As an alpha male and 'A'-class celebrity, if he were alive today he would be the man that every man loved to hate. He was also often invoked as a patron for men, especially young men. He was considered the ideal man/hero/god to have on your side in warfare; he presided over gymnasiums (γυμνάσιον) – those athlete training, fitness-cum-literary clubs – like institutions for adult males, and *palestrae* (wrestling schools); and he looked after men in military training. He was right up there with Achilles, Hector and Theseus. Like many a male Olympian, he was notorious for his sexual prowess and indeed was himself the result of heteropaternal superfecundation, where a woman carries twins sired by different fathers: Zeus had made love to the mortal Alcmene disguised as her husband Amphitryon on the same night that Amphitryon returned home from a long war.

It has been suggested that the myths surrounding Heracles were based on the life of a real person or an amalgam of several people whose accomplishments became embroidered and exaggerated over time. He is, of course, most famous for his efficient and clinical execution of the Twelve Labours (*athloi*), but he can also add a number of successful wars and battles (among his activities, *praxeis*) to his voluminous and glowing *curriculum vitae*.

Heracles sacks Troy

Even before the Greek heroes set sail to besiege Troy, Heracles had
been there and sacked it.[1] This is shown on the Eastern pediment of
the Temple of Aphaea which is within a sanctuary complex dedicated
to the mother goddess Aphaia on Aegina in the Saronic Gulf; it depicts
Heracles fighting against the king of Troy, Laomedon, with Telamon
figuring prominently as he fights alongside Heracles.

When Laomedon refused to give the gods Apollo and Poseidon a
promised reward for building the walls of Troy, they responded with
a plague and a sea monster to ravage the land. An oracle decreed to
Laomedon that the only way to save Troy would be to sacrifice his daughter
Hesione, so Hesione was bound to a rock to await her death. Heracles was
just returning from his expedition against the Amazons when he spotted
a forlorn and forsaken Hesione bound to that rock on the shore; taking
pity on her, he duly turned up in Troy along with Telamon and Oicles
and agreed to kill the monster Poseidon had sent if Laomedon would
give him the divine horses he got from Zeus as compensation for Zeus'
kidnapping of Ganymede. Laomedon agreed. Heracles slew the monster
with a fish-hook or salvo of arrows. However, Laomedon reneged on the
deal. Heracles had other matters to attend to at the time, but vowed that
he would be back to complete this unfinished business:

> Poseidon sent a Ketos (Cetus, Sea-Monster) which would come
> inland on a flood-tide and grab people on the plain. Oracles
> proclaimed that there would be release from these adversities if
> Laomedon were to set his daughter Hesione out as a meal for the
> Ketos, so he fastened her to the rocks by the seaside. When he saw
> her lying there, Heracles promised to save her in return for the
> mares which Zeus had donated as satisfaction for the abduction of
> Ganymedes. Laomedon agreed to this, and so Heracles slew the
> monster and rescued the girl. (Apollodorus 2, 103 (trans. Aldrich).)

So, in a later expedition to fulfil his promise to avenge Hesione, Heracles
sailed with eighteen ships and sacked Troy, killing Laomedon outside
the walls, and all of Laomedon's sons except Podarces, who took the new
name Priam, saving his skin by giving Heracles a golden veil Hesione had

made. Telamon nearly got himself killed by Heracles when he sprinted into the city ahead of him. This, of course, was Heracles' prerogative; he threatened Telamon with his sword but Telamon eased the tension when he explained the indiscretion away by asserting that he was rushing to erect an altar to Heracles the Noble Victor (Kallinikos). Heracles made amends when he offered Hesione to Telamon as a war prize and concubine; they had a son, Teukros.

On the way home, Heracles had to contend with a storm conjured up by the malevolent Hera. The fleet ended up on Cos where the Coans took Heracles' force to be pirates. They bombarded the 'pirates' with stones, but to no avail. Heracles landed by night and killed the king of the Coans, Eurypylos.

The war with Augeas

Augeas was very rich, and he had many herds of cows, bulls, goats, sheep and horses; every night the cowherds, goatherds and shepherds drove the thousands of animals to the stables which were becoming clogged up with piles of fetid excrement. Hercules approached King Augeas and offered to clean out the disgusting stables in one day if Augeas would give him a tenth of his fine cattle. This was the fifth of the Twelve Labours Heracles completed: a huge amount of dung (ἡ ὄνθος) had to be shifted as the Augean stables had not been cleaned out for more than thirty years and 3,000 cattle lived there. Heracles diverted the rivers Alpheus and Peneus to wash out the filthy mess.

However, Hercules was none too pleased when Augeas failed to deliver the promised reward. In the end, at Cleonai, Heracles ambushed and killed the Molionides, Euryatos and Kteatos, Augeas' generals. He then launched a second invasion. This time he marched into Elis, sacked it, slaying King Augeas in the battle. To celebrate his victory, Heracles founded the Olympic Games near the Eleian town of Pisa.

If Ibycus, a sixth-century BCE lyric poet, is to be believed, Euryatos and Kteatos were born from a single silver egg after their mother Molione, wife of Aktor, was seduced by Poseidon in the guise of a bird. Euryatos and Kteatos were Siamese twins joined at the hip with four arms, four legs and two heads between them. They proved a formidable challenge to

Heracles, inflicting on him a rare defeat, hammering his army and killing Iphikles, Heracles' half-brother, and forcing the hero to withdraw to the Argolid. Heracles showed just how duplicitous and sacrilegious he could be when he ambushed the Molionides' army at Cleonai while they were en route to the Isthmian Games as envoys of the Elians and under the protection of a religious truce. The Elians demanded compensation and, when it was refused, never attended the Isthmian Games again. Heracles took Elis and killed Augeas and all his sons bar Phyleus who was in exile for testifying on Heracles' behalf. Heracles recalled him and made him King of Elis.

Neleus

Neleus was the son of Poseidon and Tyro. Tyro was originally married to Cretheus, but was secretly in love with the river god Enipeus. However, Enipeus showed no interest. Poseidon lusted after Tyro so he disguised himself as Enipeus and seduced her; Pelias and Neleus, twins, were the result; Tyro exposed her sons on a mountain to conceal her sin, but the boys were found by a horsekeeper and raised by a maid.

When they were grown up, Pelias and Neleus located Tyro and then killed her stepmother, Sidero, for having mistreated their mother. Sidero hid in a temple to Hera for sanctuary but Pelias killed her regardless, thus winning for himself Hera's undying hatred and his own inevitable doom. Neleus and Pelias then fought for the throne of Pylos; Neleus was banished to Messenia but eventually became King of Pylos.

Heracles came to Neleus in Pylos to receive purification for his murder of Iphitus, the man who gave Odysseus his famous bow. However, Neleus refused on account of his friendship with Iphitus' father Eurytus; others maintain that Heracles wanted purification for having murdered his own wife Megara. Iphitus was the son of King Eurytus of Oechalia.

When Heracles had completed his twelve labours, he came to Oechalia to compete in archery for the hand of Iole; he won and yet he was refused the bride by Eurytus and his sons, except Iphitus who said that Heracles should get Iole on the grounds that he could once more kill his offspring as he had done to his children by Megara. Soon after, some cattle were stolen by the thief Autolycus, for which Heracles got the blame. However,

Iphitus did not believe this and invited him to go and look for the cattle with him. Heracles promised to do so, but suddenly went berserk and threw Iphitus from the walls of Tiryns to his death.

During his later military campaigns in the Peloponnese, Heracles invaded Messenia (after the conquest of Elis, but before he attacked Lacedaemon) to repay Neleus' refusal to purify him. Others say that Neleus died because he tried to rob him of the cattle of Geryon. Heracles took Pylos, and in the battle killed Neleus and eleven of his twelve sons; only Nestor, the youngest, was spared.[2] One of Neleus' other sons, Periklymenos, was granted by his grandfather Poseidon the ability to change himself into any kind of animal or tree; another source limits his choices to an eagle, ant, bee or snake. Heracles either swatted him with his club when he was a bee or a fly settling on the yoke of his chariot, or shot him with an arrow when he took the shape of an eagle.[3]

During the same war Hera, Poseidon and Hades were allies of Neleus, while Athena and Zeus assisted Heracles. Ares fought on the side of Neleus until Heracles wounded him in the thigh with a spear thrust and forced him to withdraw. Heracles also wounded Hades in the shoulder with an arrow, and he shot Hera in the right breast with a three-pronged arrow that caused her 'incurable pain'. The intensity of her suffering was due to the fact that Heracles tipped his arrows with the poison of the Hydra, the monster which Hera herself had raised against Heracles. By wounding Hera in the breast, Heracles gained symbolic revenge for her rejection of him from her breast when he was an infant; his 'retroactive' poisoning of her breast appropriately punished her refusal to give him the nurture he desired.

Hippocoon

Heracles' next enemies were King Hippocoon of Sparta and his sons; they had been allies of Neleus and had killed Heracles' cousin Oionos, son of Alkmena's brother Likymnios. This occurred as Oionos was gazing at the palace of Hippocoon when a guard dog ran out and bit him; when he threw a stone at the dog, the sons of Hippocoon rushed out and clubbed him to death.

Heracles was with Oionos in Sparta; the Spartans wounded him in the hand or the thigh, but Asclepios patched him up and he returned with an army. First, however, he went to Tegea in Arcadia and asked King Kepheus and his twenty sons to help him; Kepheus refused, afraid that in his absence the Argives would invade his country. Heracles gave Kepheus' daughter Sterope a lock of Medusa's hair which he had received from Athena and told her that it was certain to put any enemies to flight if she held it up three times from the walls, her eyes averted. Kepheus then agreed to help Heracles, but in the battle at Sparta he and all his sons were killed along with Hippocoon and his sons and Heracles' brother Iphikles. Heracles now brought back Tyndareos, who had been expelled by his brother Hippocoon, and gave him the kingdom.

Nessus

Nessus is known for his role in the story of the Tunic of Nessus, the poisoned shirt (*chiton*) that killed Heracles. It was Nessus' allegedly divinely appointed job to carry people over the River Eunos in Anatolia for a fee; he was a kind of upper-world Charon. Heracles had been married to Deianeira for nearly three years when, at a feast in the house of Oeneus, he accidentally killed Eunomus, the son of Architeles. Heracles, in accordance with the law, went into exile with his wife Deianeira, arriving at the river during their wanderings.

Nessus told Heracles of his upstanding character and was given permission to carry Deianeira over the river. After carrying Deianeira over, Nessus, charlatan that he was, tried to rape her. Heracles heard his wife's screams and saw what was going on from the other bank. He shot a Hydra-poisoned arrow into Nessus' heart. As the centaur lay dying, as a final act of malice, knowing that his blood was now infected with the Hydra's venom, Nessus told Deianeira (her name means husband killer) that his blood would make a failsafe love potion if mixed with some of the semen he had spilt during the attempted rape. It would always ensure that Heracles was true to her.

Ovid can always be relied upon to provide a vivid account:

And now on the far bank and stooping for the bow he'd thrown,
he heard a voice, his wife's, calling and sure that Nessus had in

mind a breach of trust, 'You raping ravisher!' he cried, 'Where are you going? So confident in your four feet! Nessus Two-Formed (biformis), listen! Hold off from me and mine. Maybe you feel no dread of me – at least your father's [Ixion's] wheel should hold you back from lust and lechery. Trust horse-strength if you will, you'll not escape. With wounds not feet I'll follow!' His last words were proved at once: an arrow flew and pierced the fleeing centaur's back: out from his breast the barbed point stuck. He wrenched the shaft away, and blood from both wounds spurted, blood that bore the Lernaean's [Hydra's] poison. Nessus scooped it up. 'I'll not die unavenged,' he thought and gave his shirt soaked in warm gore to Deianira, a talisman, he said, to kindle love... (Ovid, *Metamorphoses* 9, 101ff (trans. Melville).)

Deianeira believed him. Later, when she began to have doubts about Heracles' fidelity because of Iole, she spread the centaur's blood on a robe and gave it to her husband. Iole was the beautiful young daughter of King Eurytus of Oechalia and was ripe for marriage. According to Apollodorus, Iole was claimed by Heracles for a bride, but Eurytus refused her hand. Iole was, in effect, indirectly the cause of Heracles' death because of Deianeira's jealousy of her. Heracles went to a gathering of heroes, where his passion got the better of him. Meanwhile, Deianeira accidentally spilled a portion of the centaur's blood onto the floor. To her horror, it began to smoke by the light of the rising sun. She realized it was poison and sent her messenger to warn Heracles, but it was too late. Heracles lay dying a slow and painful death as the robe corroded his skin. Heracles was then taken to Mount Olympus by Zeus and welcomed among the gods for his heroic exploits. Sophocles' play *Trachiniae* is largely based on this myth.

The Tunic of Nessus or imitations thereof have enjoyed an interesting, if tragic, history since the days of ancient Greece. During the Anabaptist Münster Rebellion of 1534, a 15-year-old girl named Hille Feyken tried to deceive Münster's Prince Bishop Franz von Waldeck who had been leading a protracted siege of the city. Her plan was to pretend to defect and tempt von Waldeck with details of the city's defences while giving him a fine shirt soaked in poison. Before her plan could be carried out she was betrayed by another defector, who warned the bishop; Feyken was tortured and killed.

In Act 4.12 of Shakespeare's *Antony and Cleopatra*, Mark Antony is incensed after losing the Battle of Actium and exclaims, 'The shirt of Nessus is upon me.'

Major General Henning von Tresckow was one of the conspirators in the 20 July plot to assassinate Adolf Hitler; he famously referred to the 'Robe of Nessus' when he realized that the assassination plot had failed and that he and others involved in the conspiracy were now doomed: 'None of us can complain about our own deaths. Everyone who joined our circle put on the "Robe of Nessus".'[4]

Cycnus

Cycnus, son of Ares, was a bloodthirsty beast of a man; he was never the greatest of hosts since he was in the habit of murdering his guests, that is until Heracles killed him when Cycnus had challenged him to a fight.[5] Cycnus had seized control of the sacred grove of Apollon at Itonos in southern Thessaly from where he indulged his penchant for challenging any man he met to a fight, tearing off their heads and using their skulls as building material in the ongoing construction of a temple to Ares. As Heracles donned his armour, Athena warned Heracles that, should he kill Cycnus, he must not take his armour as spoils, but instead keep an eye out for Ares, as he would surely try to avenge Cycnus' death.

Cycnus hurled his spear at Heracles' shield, but it bounced off, after which Heracles drove his spear through Cycnus' neck, killing him. Cycnus was afterwards transformed into a swan (*kyknos*, English cygnet). Ares was, as predicted, angered by his son's death and moved to kill Heracles when Athena intervened, urging him to control his anger and stop fighting. Ares ignored her, however, and again charged at Heracles, hurling his spear at his shield; Athena, however, diverted the spear.

Ares then drew his sword and leaped at Heracles, who, seeing his chance, thrust his spear into Ares' thigh; the god fell to the ground; Ares' twin sons, Phobos and Deimos, appeared on the scene, rescued him and carted him ignominiously back to Mount Olympus. Heracles then helped himself to Cycnus' armour.

Chapter Ten

The Trojan War:
The Battle for Helen and the Great Sulk

By the time of the Trojan War, mighty Zeus and Gaia were beginning to grow tired of and irritated by all those mortals swarming over their beloved Earth, and, not being immortal, they were beginning to clog up Hades too. What is more, many humans were getting insolent, fractious and decidedly hubristic; it was enough having to deal with his disputatious and cantankerous fellow gods on Mount Olympus without these annoying mortals challenging him all over the place. It wasn't for this that he had swatted off the challenges from the Titans, Giants and Typhon to establish his unquestioned superiority. Zeus had had enough and wanted a fresh, cathartic start, so he conceived a spot of genocide which would rid the mortal world of mortals. He would do this through some impromptu climate change, deploying his fiery thunderbolts and causing an almighty flood. Thankfully for us, though, less extreme counsel was on hand in the guise of the more moderate Momos, the last word in fault-finding, who criticized Zeus' extermination plan, advising something less cataclysmic than Zeus' universal ethnic cleansing: the population had already been thinned out somewhat through the casualties from the Theban Wars. Another war should do the trick, a war between Europe and Asia; a world war indeed in which death and destruction would rid Zeus of a good number of those annoying mortals.

So, to effect this, it was decided that the sea nymph Thetis would marry a mortal and that Zeus would father the most beautiful woman who ever walked the earth. Enter Helen, and the sumptuous wedding of Thetis and Peleus attended by all the gods. Eros, Strife incarnate, was there to spoil the party when she mischievously rolled an apple inscribed 'to the most beautiful' among the guests. This had the desired effect of enraging Aphrodite, Hera and Athena and causing an almighty row as each considered herself to be the fairest of them all. Hermes was delegated to lead the three to Mount Ida in Troy where they would be judged in a divine beauty contest by Paris. Paris was persuaded by Aphrodite who promised him the hand of the world's most beautiful woman and daughter of Zeus, rejecting the regal power and military success offered by Hera and Athena.

Paris, of course, was blithely unaware of the curse under which he had lived since birth; Hecabe (Hecuba), his mother was doomed to deliver a son who would be responsible for the fiery destruction of Troy. In a bid to avert this inevitability, the infant was exposed on Mount Ida where he was raised by a she-bear and subsequently found by a shepherd. Paris grew up and when he returned to Priam's Troy to take part in games in his memory, his identity was confirmed by his sister Cassandra, and he was welcomed back into the family fold.

Paris's somewhat whimsical decision at the beauty contest had serious consequences: Helen, of course, was already married and her appropriation would involve relieving her husband, Menelaus no less – King of Sparta and brother of Agamemnon, only the most powerful man in Greece – of his wife and her complicity in a plan to abscond to Troy with Paris. Furthermore, the suitors of Helen were all bound by the Treaty of Tyndareus by which they were obliged to assist each other militarily should Menelaus ever find himself bereft of Helen. Paris would run away with a willing Helen; a cuckolded Menelaus would raise a huge Greek army to retrieve her. The stage was now nicely set for the Trojan War.

Aphrodite told Paris to build ships to enable him to sail to Greece to abduct Helen. This he did, despite warnings of the dire consequences not just from sister Cassandra but also from his own wife, for he too was already married to the prophetic nymph Oinone. Aeneas was delegated by Aphrodite to accompany Paris. The two arrived in Sparta and were warmly welcomed by Helen and Menelaus. Menelaus, however, had to leave after nine days to attend the funeral in Crete of the former Spartan king Katreus. Paris saw his chance, successfully wooed an increasingly besotted Helen and eloped with her, but not before he had loaded much of the Spartan royal treasure onto his ships. The affair was consummated, and despite some infelicitous inclement storms brewed up by Hera in her role as protector of the institution of marriage, the happy couple finally

'The Wrath of Achilles' (1847) by François-Léon Benouville. Achilles is seen sulking after Agamemnon had appointed his war prize, Briseis. (*Fabre Museum, Montpellier*)

Athena detail from a silver kantharos with Theseus in Crete, 440–435 BCE, part of the Vassil Bojkov collection, Sofia, Bulgaria. (*Author Gorgonchica*)

Jacques-Louis David (1748–1825), 'The Figwht Between Ares and Athena', date 1771. (*Louvre Museum Room 932; accession number INV 3695*)

Cornelis van Haarlem (1562–1638): 'The Fall of the Titans', 1588. (*Statens Museum, Copenhagen*)

Follower of Francisco Goya (1746–1828), formerly attributed to Goya. 'The Colossus' (Giant) circa 1818–25. Museo del Prado, Madrid, accession number P002785 (Museo del Prado). References https://www.museodelprado.es/coleccion/galeria-on-line/galeria-on-line/obra/el-coloso (*Source/photographer http://www.museodelprado.es/uploads/tx_gbobras/1a_01.jpg*)

Gilt-bronze Enceladus by Gaspar Mercy in the Bosquet de l'Encelade in the Gardens of Versailles. *Encelade écrasé sous les rochers et se transformant en l'Etna*, author Coyau. This photograph was taken during the partnership between the Château de Versailles and Wikimédia France.

An angry Polyphemus towers over wily Odysseus in the Cyclops' cave. From *Stories from Homer* (1885).

Guido Reni 'Polyphemus', the blinded Polyphemus seeks vengeance on Odysseus (1639). (*Capitoline Museums, Rome; accession number PC 241*)

Woodcut illustration (leaf [c]9v, f. [xix]) of Niobe, Amphion and their dead sons, hand–coloured in red, green, yellow and black, from an incunable German translation by Heinrich Steinhöwel of Giovanni Boccaccio's *De mulieribus claris*, printed by Johannes Zainer at Ulm ca.1474. One of seventy-six woodcut illustrations. (*Author, kladcat*)

Dante Gabriel Rossetti, 'Helen of Troy', 1863. Helen of Troy ελεναυσ, ελανδροσ, λεεπτολισ destroyer of ships, destroyer of men, destroyer of cities. What an epitaph. Rossetti painted 'Helen of Troy' in 1863, a year after the death of his wife from an overdose of laudanum. The model he used was Annie Miller. Original cost: £60. (*Current location: Kunsthalle, Hamburg Catalogue Number: 2469*)

Four years after Rossetti painted his Helen, Frederick Sandys (1829–1904) painted his 'Helen of Troy' and caused tensions between the two artists; astonishingly Rossetti believed that Sandys' version was too much like his own. Did Sandys have his tongue stuck in his cheek by any chance? Good art it undoubtedly is, but this triumph of petulance and teenage angst would certainly have sunk as many ships as it launched. (*Walker Art Gallery, Liverpool, accession number WAG 2633*)

Mykonos vase 670 BCE. Archaeological Museum of Mykonos, Inv. 2240. Decorated pithos found at Mykonos, Greece, showing one of the earliest known renditions of the Trojan Horse. (*Source https://www.flickr.com/photos/travellingrunes/2949254926/ Author Travelling Runes*)

Asmus Jacob Carstens, 'Sorrowful Ajax with Termessa and Eurysakes', 1791, contemplating suicide. (*Source http://www. projekte.kunstgeschichte.uni-muenchen.de/dt_frz_malerei/41-dt-franz-malerei/studieneinheiten/1780_1789_d/1a/gruppe_1/b. htm. Author file: James Steakley; artwork: Asmus Jacob Carstens*)

'Achilles fighting against Memnon', Leiden Rijksmuseum voor Oudheden, Nederlands. (*Author Jona Lendering*)

'Aeneas and his Father [Anchises] Fleeing Troy', ca.1635 by Simon Vouet. (*San Diego Museum of Art*)

Peter Paul Rubens (1577–1640): 'The Death of Hector' (between 1630 and 1635). (*Museum Boijmans Van Beuningen, Rotterdam*)

Johann Georg Trautmann (1713–69), 'The Burning of Troy' (1759/62). (*From the collections of the grand dukes of Baden, Karlsruhe. Photographer http://www.zeller.de*)

John Flaxman (1755–1826), 'Apollo Preceding Hector with His Aegis, and Dispersing the Greeks'. (*Fuseli's Lectures, Yale Center for British Art*)

Polymestor kills Polydorus. Engraving by de Bauer for Ovid's *Metamorphoses*, Book 13, pp.430-438.

East Frieze detail representing a scene from the battle of Troy: Achilles against Memnon. (*Reproduction of the Treasury of Siphnos, Delphi, Archaeological Museum of Delphi. Author: Marsyas*) The Bassae Frieze is made from a set of twenty-three marble panels that were in the Temple of Apollo at Bassae. They were carved just before 400 BCE. The stones are on permanent display in a specially-constructed room in Gallery 16 in the British Museum in London. Copies of this frieze decorated the walls of the Ashmolean Museum and London's Travellers Club. (*Collection British Museum, blue pencil.svg wikidata: Q6373 Achilles (left) and Penthesilea (on the ground)*)

arrived in Troy via Sidon in Phoenicia. The lost epic *Cypria*, the first poem in the Epic Cycle and a prequel to the *Iliad*, covered this and the flight to Troy by Paris and Helen.

When told by Iris of his wife's infidelity, Menelaus sprang into action and immediately began mustering the Greek forces to help him in his recovery operation. Aulis, on the east coast of Boeotia, was command headquarters and it was here that the seer Calchas interpreted a rather disturbing portent which must have given some of the Greeks pause for thought. A serpent slithered under the altar during a sacrifice to Apollo, slid up a tree and devoured eight sparrow chicks nesting there along with their distraught mother. Calchas gloomily revealed that this meant a nine-year war before Troy would finally fall in the tenth year.

Even then, all was not plain sailing. Maritime geography and navigation were obviously not strong points aboard the Greek ships. The Greeks mistook neighbouring Mysia for Troy and devastated the land, much to the annoyance of the king there, Telephus – son of Heracles and Auge – who charged the Greeks back to their ships with much loss of Greek life. The Greeks went on their way but were scattered by a destructive storm, forcing them to disperse back to their respective homelands. The task force, according to the *Cypria*, delayed for a further ten years before resuming operations.

Even then there was more trouble and delay. Agamemnon fell foul of Artemis when he hubristically claimed to be a more accomplished hunter than her; she punished him most cruelly by demanding that he sacrifice one of his unmarried daughters. Iphigenia drew the short straw and was summoned from Mycenae on the equally cruel and sly pretext that she was chosen to marry Achilles. At the last minute, Artemis must have felt pangs of conscience because she replaced the girl on the slab with a stag, sent her to the lands of the Taurians and elevated her to a goddess. The Greeks went on their way, stopping at Tenedos where they were met with a salvo of stones and, according to Plutarch (*Quaestiones Graecae* 28), Achilles raped Hemithea, sister of the ruler Tenes, who tried to stop him and was slaughtered for his pains.

On arriving off Troy the Greeks began their landing. Protesilaus was first ashore, only to be killed instantly by Hector. When Achilles followed him he confronted Cycnus, son of Poseidon. Cycnus was something of a challenge for Achilles because Poseidon had rendered his son invulnerable to piercing wounds. He was possibly an albino if the references to his 'white head' in the Hesiodic *Catalogue* (fragment 237) and the description of him as white-skinned from birth by Hellanicus (4F148) are anything to go by. Achilles then had to be creative if he was to kill him: Apollodorus (393B) says that he threw a rock at his head; Ovid writes that Achilles lost his temper when his sword and spear were ineffectual, so he battered his face in with the hilt of his sword. In the end Achilles knelt on his chest, crushing his ribcage with his shield and then garotting him with his helmet straps. Ovid ends the story by telling us that Poseidon turned Cycnus into a swan, hence our 'cygnet' (*Metamorphoses* 12, 70–140).

The Greeks soon established a beachhead and advanced onto the plain, killing Trojans as they advanced, and approached the city of Troy. Their ten-year siege had begun.

It is Homer's *Iliad* which provides us with our most detailed account of a very short but very decisive episode in the tenth year of the Trojan War; this is extended by fragments of the Epic Cycle of poems and the so-called Homerica, the Greek tragedians and Aristophanes, Apollodorus and the Roman poets Ovid and Virgil, Horace and Propertius, all of whom tell us about the aftermath and the experiences of some of the protagonists in the war and their relatives. One question is how much of this is mythology and how much is based on real historical events?

Despite accepting some poetic licence and hyperbole on the part of Homer, many classical authors, including Thucydides and Dio Chrysostom,[1] believed the Trojan War to be historical, that it took place around the Dardanelles in the thirteenth or twelfth century BCE. Scepticism had set in by the mid-nineteenth century when the war and the city of Troy itself were relegated to mythology. However, in 1868 German archaeologist Heinrich Schliemann was persuaded by Frank Calvert that Troy was a real city located near modern-day Hisarlik in Turkey. This is now widely accepted on the basis of excavations conducted by Schliemann, among others.

Scholars who advocate the historicity of the Trojan War prefer a date in the twelfth century BCE, as given by Eratosthenes; this corresponds with archaeological evidence for a destructive conflagration at Troy VIIa, Hisarlik and with the end of the Bronze Age. Excavations have revealed

Troy VIIa to be a walled city with fortified towers up to 30ft high with foundations 59ft deep. Troy VII covered 50 acres or so with a population between 5,000 and 10,000 inhabitants; it was, by the standards of the day, a major city. Michael Wood notes that scholarly scepticism about Schliemann's identification has been dispelled by the more recent archaeological discoveries, linguistic research and translations of clay-tablet records of contemporaneous diplomacy: 'Now, more than ever, in the 125 years since Schliemann put his spade into Hisarlik, there appears to be a historical basis to the tale of Troy.'[2] Further excavations have revealed that Troy was full of bins and pits dug for the emergency storage of grain and other staples, dragged in by country folk seeking refuge and making preparations for a long siege. The numerous shanties discovered were just as indicative of a city preparing to sit out a protracted blockade.

So, while it is very likely that a war and a siege of some kind did take place, it is equally likely that the descriptions given by Homer and other literary sources bear little relation to actual events in that war.[3] Joachim Latacz has identified the 'Achaioi' of the *Iliad* with the inhabitants of Ahhiyawa, believing that 'the *Iliad* preserved through oral hexameters the memory of one or more acts of aggression perpetrated by the Ahhiyawans (Hittite for Achaeans) against Wilusa (Hittite for Troy) in the thirteenth century B.C.'[4]

This is Manfred Korfmann's illuminating article; at the time he wrote this he was Director of Excavations at Hissarlik:[5]

Troy appears to have been destroyed around 1180 B.C. (this date corresponds to the end of our excavation of levels Troy VI or VIIa), probably by a war the city lost. There is evidence of a conflagration, some skeletons, and heaps of sling bullets. People who have successfully defended their city would have gathered their sling bullets and put them away for another event, but a victorious conqueror would have done nothing with them. But this does not mean that the conflict was the war – even though ancient tradition usually places it around this time. After a transitional period of a few decades, a new population from the eastern Balkans or the north-western Black Sea region evidently settled in the ruins of what was probably a much weakened city...

The main argument against associating these ruins with the great city described in the *Iliad* has been that Troy in the Late Bronze Age was a wholly insignificant town and not a place worth fighting over. Our new excavations and the progress of research in south-eastern Europe have changed such views regarding Troy considerably. It appears that this city was, by the standards of this region at that time, very large indeed.

According to the archaeological and historical findings of the past decade especially, it is now more likely than not that there were several armed conflicts in and around Troy at the end of the Late Bronze Age. At present we do not know whether all or some of these conflicts were distilled in later memory into the 'Trojan War' or whether among them there was an especially memorable single 'Trojan War'. However, everything currently suggests that Homer should be taken seriously, that his story of a military conflict between Greeks and the inhabitants of Troy is based on a memory of historical events, whatever these may have been. If someone came up to me at the excavation one day and expressed his or her belief that the Trojan War did indeed happen here, my response as an archaeologist working at Troy would be: 'Why not?'

In a letter to *The Times*,[6] M.L. West said:

Hisarlik is the major prehistoric site in north-west Anatolia.... There is no doubt that it is 'Homer's Troy' at least in the sense that the poet of the *Iliad* knew the place and assumed its topography in his narrative. There is archaeological evidence that it had been destroyed by an enemy force in the 12th century BC. Nearly all scholars accept that the Greek tradition about the Trojan War is based on some memory of this.

On the other hand, we know that an epic tradition is liable to grossly distort the facts and to be all but worthless as an historical source. We must therefore remain sceptical on such questions as who exactly destroyed Troy, in what circumstances and from what motive. Troy probably fell to a much smaller group of attackers in a much shorter time.

So, we can probably quite safely take it that elements of the Trojan War and the siege of Troy were historical, but that the facts as known and events were embroidered considerably with the interweaving of various myths and stories to heighten their entertainment value.

C.B. Armstrong has helpfully collected the casualty lists in the Trojan War: he finds that the number of casualties among officers is 238 plus 26 unnamed of whom 24 were just wounded rather than killed. Homer does not give other ranks. Hector comes top with 28 killings to his credit plus those slain in his *plethos*. Diomedes comes next with 22 named and 12 unnamed; Patroclus bagged 27 and Achilles 23. Telamonian Ajax could lay claim to 20 kills and 12 woundings. Odysseus and Agamemnon took 17 and 14 Trojans respectively.

Much of the Trojan War can be told through the actions of the combatants. Here are some of the main (male) participants in the Trojan War; first the Trojans:

Priam

King Priam of Troy had seen the last of his fighting days when the war began. He was, nevertheless, a crucial source of battlefield knowledge and imparter of sound military advice. Moreover, as the father of some twenty-two sons mentioned in the *Iliad* alone, he was an important source of high-calibre recruits to the Trojan cause; pre-eminent among these were Hector and Paris. His military record is impressive: he tells Helen that he once helped King Mygdon of Phrygia in a battle against the Amazons, specifically Otrera, mother of Penthesilea; after the death of Hector he persuaded a ruthless Achilles to return Hector's mutilated and desecrated body so that he is permitted to give his son a proper burial and funeral games during a twelve-day truce. Despite winning respect from both sides in the war for his piety, he is finally slaughtered, sacrilegiously, by Neoptolemus, Achilles' son, when seeking refuge on the altar of Zeus in his own palace, as described in the lost *Iliu Persis* and by Virgil in Book 2 of the *Aeneid*.

Hector

Hector was Troy's greatest fighter as leader of the Trojans and their allies in the defence of Troy, 'killing 31,000 Greek fighters' according to Hyginus (*Fabulae* 115). We have seen how Hector fought Protesilaus in single combat right at the start of the war and killed him. This was in fulfilment of a prophecy which said that the first Greek to land on Trojan soil would surely die. In Book 7 of the *Iliad* (43–305), Hector challenged any one of the Greeks to single combat. There was at first much reluctance, but eventually nine Greek heroes stepped up to the plate and drew lots to see who was to face Hector. Ajax won and fought Hector all day long, ending in a stalemate. There was mutual admiration for each other's courage, skill and strength: Hector gave Ajax his sword, which, ironically, Ajax later used to kill himself. Ajax gave Hector the belt that Achilles would later attach to his chariot to drag Hector's corpse around the walls of Troy.

In year ten of the war, Hector chided Paris for the trouble he had visited on his country and for now refusing to fight. Paris responded to this goad when he proposed single combat between himself and Menelaus, with the victor winning Helen and thus bringing an end to the war. The duel, however, was inconclusive because Aphrodite evacuated Paris from the field of battle. The Greeks attacked and drove the Trojans back, inciting Hector to lead a counter-attack. Before he does, however (*Iliad* 6, 390–480), his wife Andromache, with their son Astyanax in her arms, meets Hector at the gate in one of the most moving and sensitive scenes in the entire epic, pleading with him not to go out for her sake as well as his son's. Hector knows all along that Troy and the house of Priam are doomed to fall and that the wretched fate of his wife and infant son will be to die or go into slavery in a foreign land. Hector's gleaming bronze helmet startles little Astyanax and makes him cry. Hector removes it, embraces his wife and son, and for his sake prays aloud to Zeus that his son might be commander after him, become more glorious in battle than he, that he will bring home the blood of his enemies and make his mother proud. Once gone, those in the house begin to mourn as they know he will not return. Hector and Paris go through the gate and rally the Trojans, causing consternation among the Greeks.

The Trojans forced the Greeks back into their camp and were within an ace of capturing their ships, but Agamemnon personally rallied the Greeks. The Trojans are driven off, night falls, and Hector resolves to take the camp and burn the ships the next day. The Trojans camp in the field (*Iliad* 8, 542ff). The next day Agamemnon rallied the Greeks again and drove the Trojans 'like a herd of cows maddened with fright when a lion has attacked them'. Then it was Hector's turn to rally the Trojans: the Trojans swept down on the wall and hammered on it; they tried to pull down the ramparts while the Greeks rained arrows down on them. Hector smashed open a gate with a boulder, cleared the gate and urged the Trojans to scale the wall.

The battle raged on inside the camp. Hector fell, struck by a stone thrown by Ajax, but aided by Apollo he recovered and ordered a chariot attack. Hector then captured Protesilaus' ship and called for fire, but the Trojans could not deliver as Ajax was killing everyone who tried. Eventually, Hector broke Ajax's spear with his sword, forcing him to give ground, and he set the ship on fire.

Patroclus, Achilles' closest comrade, disguised in the armour of Achilles, entered the fray leading the Myrmidons and the rest of the Achaeans to force a Trojan withdrawal. After Patroclus has routed the Trojan army, Hector killed Patroclus, gloating: 'You wretch! Achilles, great as he is, could do nothing to help you.' A dying Patroclus foretells Hector's own death: 'You yourself are not one who will live for long, but now already death and powerful destiny are standing beside you, to go down under the hands of Aiakos' great son, Achilles.'

Hector strips the armour of Achilles off the corpse of Patroclus and gives it to his men to take back to the city. Glaucus accuses Hector of cowardice for not challenging Ajax. Stung by this, Hector calls for the armour to be brought back, puts it on, and uses it to rally the Trojans. Zeus is not pleased: he sees the donning of a hero's armour as an act of insolence by a fool about to die, but it gives Hector strength for now.

The next day, the enraged Achilles rejoins the battle and routs the Trojans, forcing them back into the city. Hector, though, elects to remain outside the gates of Troy to face Achilles. When he sees him, however, Hector is fearful and turns to flee. Achilles chases him around the city three times before Hector overcomes his fear and turns to confront Achilles. However, Athena, in the guise of Hector's brother Deiphobus, has fooled Hector. He requests of Achilles that the victor should return the other's body after the duel, though Hector himself was planning to throw the body of Patroclus to the dogs, but Achilles refuses. Achilles looses his spear at Hector, who dodges it, but Athena brings it back to Achilles' hands without Hector noticing. Hector then throws his own spear at Achilles; it hits his shield but does no harm. When Hector turns to face his supposed brother to retrieve another spear, there is no one there. This is when Hector realizes that he is going to die. Hector decides that he will go down fighting so that men might talk about his bravery in years to come.

Hector draws his sword, now the only weapon left to him, and charges, but Achilles takes aim with his spear and pierces Hector's collarbone, the only part of his body not protected by the stolen armour of Achilles. The wound was fatal, but Hector was still able to implore Achilles for an honourable funeral. Achilles replies that he will let dogs and vultures scavenge on Hector's corpse. Hector dies, but not before he prophesied that Achilles' own death would follow soon.

Achilles slit Hector's heels and passed the belt that Ajax had given Hector through the gashes fastening it to his chariot and dragged Hector to the Greek camp. For the next twelve days, Achilles desecrates the body, but it remains preserved by Apollo and Aphrodite. After the end of the twelve days, the gods can stand it no longer and despatch two messengers: Iris and Thetis, the mother of Achilles. Thetis told Achilles to allow King Priam to come and take the body for ransom, a ransom that included twelve robes, twelve white mantles, several richly embroidered tunics, ten bars of yellow gold, a special gold cup and several cauldrons. Priam himself goes to claim his son's body, protected by a charm that will make anyone who looks at him fall asleep.

Achilles, as we have seen, is sufficiently moved by Priam and returns Hector's body to Priam and promises him a truce of twelve days to allow the Trojans to perform funeral rites for Hector. Priam returns to Troy with the body of his son.

Aeneas

Comparatively speaking, Aeneas, son of Anchises and Aphrodite and cousin of Hector, though an important leader, takes a rather low profile role in the Trojan War, but there again he has much bigger fish to fry since he is to be called on to found the Roman state as described in detail in Virgil's *Aeneid*, a direct ancestor, no less, of Romulus and Remus. Nevertheless, he fights important duels with Achilles and Diomedes and is only saved through divine intervention.

We learn the details of his birth from the *Homeric Hymn to Aphrodite*; Aphrodite has made Zeus fall in love with mortal women so, to get his own back, Zeus fills the goddess with passion for Anchises, who is minding his own business tending his cattle on the hills near Mount Ida. When Aphrodite sees Anchises she is truly smitten, dresses up as for a wedding and shows herself off to him. He too is smitten, supposing her a goddess, but Aphrodite is pretending to be a Phrygian princess. They make love and Aphrodite reveals her true identity to Anchises who becomes anxious that there may be consequences to his having sex with a goddess. Aphrodite assures him that he will be protected, and tells him that she will bear him a son who will be called Aeneas. However, she cautions that he must never tell anyone that he has slept with a goddess. When Aeneas was born, Aphrodite took him to the nymphs of Mount Ida who she instructed to raise him to the age of 5, then take him to Anchises. Some would have it that Anchises boasted about his liaison with Aphrodite, and as a result was struck in the foot by a thunderbolt courtesy of Zeus. This makes him lame and that is why Aeneas has to carry him from the flames of Troy.

In the *Iliad* Aeneas is forever needing to be rescued and, as such, fills the role of a hero awaiting a greater destiny; indeed, we know that becoming king of the Trojans and founder of Rome are his destiny. A sometimes reluctant warrior at Troy, he was angry with Priam because he believed that, despite his bravery, he was being denied his due share of honour. Nevertheless, he led an attack against Idomeneus to recover the body of his brother-in-law Alcathous at the urging of Deiphobus. Aphrodite and Apollo rescued Aeneas from combat with Diomedes of Argos, who almost killed him, and carried him away to Pergamos to recuperate. He was wounded by Diomedes and, having passed out, would have died had not his mother come to his rescue. Aphrodite herself was wounded by Diomedes, but then Apollo took over the protection of Aeneas, removing him from the battle to the citadel, where his temple was located. In the sanctuary, Leto and Artemis healed Aeneas and made him even stronger. However, for those fighting, Apollo fashioned a phantom of Aeneas, so that Achaeans and Trojans killed each other round it until the real Aeneas, having recovered, returned to the field.

Even Poseidon, who is usually pro-Greek, came to Aeneas' rescue. Apollo urged Aeneas to challenge Achilles to fight with him in single

combat. Aeneas was almost killed, but Poseidon rescued him, explaining
to the other gods:

> Even Zeus might be angry if Achilles killed Aeneas, who after all
> is destined to survive and to save the House of Dardanus from
> extinction…. Priam's line has fallen out of favour with Zeus, and
> now Aeneas shall be King of Troy and shall be followed by his
> children's children in the time to come. (Poseidon to the gods.
> Homer, *Iliad* 20,300.)

Some say that Aeneas was allowed by the Achaeans, on account of his
piety, safe passage to leave the city whence he took refuge on Mount Ida,
according to the *Iliu Persis*. Aeneas also took his son Ascanius (later Iulus),
and his household gods, the *penates*, but his wife Creusa became separated
from him in the chaos. Some claim that Aeneas took the Palladium with
him to Italy as well, eventually getting it to Rome. The Palladium had
fallen to Earth from the sky; it was an ancient cult image on which the
safety of Troy, and later Rome, depended: the wooden statue (*xoanon*) of
Pallas Athena that Odysseus and Diomedes stole from the citadel of Troy
and was later taken to the future site of Rome by Aeneas where it was in
the care of the Vestal Virgins. It was made by Athena to commemorate
the death of Pallas, as part of the city's founding myth. Diomedes and
Odysseus went to the citadel in Troy by a secret passage and carried off
the Palladium; the Greeks were then able to enter Troy and lay it waste
with the help of the duplicitous Trojan Horse. Odysseus, according to the
epitome of the *Little Iliad*, went to Troy at night disguised as a beggar, but
Helen recognized him and revealed the whereabouts of the Palladium.
He and Diomedes then re-entered the city and stole the Palladium.

Aeneas fled the burning city of Troy, father on his back, and reached
Mount Ida, where he was joined by other refugees from the war. The hope
was to return home when the enemy had sailed away, but the Achaeans
were set on eliminating all refugees. The Trojans sent heralds to the
Achaeans and an agreement was reached, which allowed Aeneas, as well
as his people and property, to leave the Troad, once he had surrendered
all arms to the Achaeans. Aeneas and his followers built a fleet of twenty
ships, sailing away in the early summer.

Apollodorus tells that '…the Greeks let him alone on account of his piety', and it is piety that is his defining characteristic: *pius* Aeneas shows *pietas* in his attitude to gods, country and family and that is what makes him an eminently suitable founder of Rome.

Hyginus (ca.64 BCE–CE 17) in his *Fabulae* (115) tells us that Aeneas killed twenty-eight enemies in the Trojan War. Aeneas also features in the Trojan narratives attributed to Dares Phrygius (*De excidio Troiae*) who describes him as 'auburn-haired, stocky, eloquent, courteous, prudent, pious, and charming' and to Dictys of Crete. In the sixth century John Malalas' eighteen-book *Chronographia* declares Aeneas to be somewhat less than heroic: 'short, fat, with a good chest, powerful, with a ruddy complexion, a broad face, a good nose, fair skin, bald on the forehead, a good beard, grey eyes.'

Aeneas built his fleet in Antandrus. He sailed first to Thrace where he met Polydorus' ghost. Then, after having been received in Delos by King Anius, he attempted unsuccessfully to settle in Crete. Later, having stopped in the Strophades Islands and Zacynthos and sailed past Ithaca, Aeneas came to Buthrotum in Epirus. From there, he crossed to Italy, skirting the waters of Tarentum, Lacinium and the Sicilian coast. On first reaching Drepanum, Aeneas lost his father. From Drepanum he sailed to Carthage where he met Dido. After his love affair with the queen, Aeneas returned to Drepanum, later crossing to Italy. In Cumae he descended to the Underworld in his famous *katabasis*, ending his journey soon after in the harbour of Caieta.

Deiphobus

Deiphobus was a son of Priam and Hecuba. He was a prince of Troy and the greatest of Priam's sons after Hector and Paris. In the *Iliad* Deiphobus and his brother Helenus led a sortie at the siege of the newly-built Argive wall and killed many Greeks, even wounding the Achaean hero Meriones. We have seen how, when Hector was fleeing Achilles, Athena assumed the shape of Deiphobus and goaded Hector to make a stand and fight.

After the death of Paris, Deiphobus was given Helen of Troy as a bride for his deeds in the war, outbidding his other brother, Helenus. During the sack of Troy, Deiphobus was slain and his body mutilated. Virgil claims that he was betrayed by Helen.

Helenus

Helenus was the twin brother of the prophetess Cassandra and brother of Deiphobus. He also went by the name Scamandrios. Cassandra, having been given the power of prophecy by Apollo, taught it to her brother. Like Cassandra, he was always right, but unlike her, others actually believed him.

At the end of the Trojan War, as we have seen, Helenus lost the chance of Helen's hand to his brother Deiphobus. Somewhat annoyed by this, Helenus retreated to Mount Ida, where Odysseus later captured him. As a seer he was able to reveal to Odysseus – probably still smarting at the loss of Helen – how they could take Troy: he confided that they would win if they stole the Trojan Palladium, brought the bones of Pelops to Troy and persuaded Neoptolemus and Philoctetes, with his bow, to join the Greek side.

Neoptolemus gave Andromache, Helenus' sister-in-law and Hector's widow, to Helenus after the fall of Troy, and fathered Molossus, Pielus and Pergamus with her. Helenus prophesied Aeneas' founding of Rome when he and his followers stopped at Buthrotum, as described by Virgil in *Aeneid* Book III.

Now the Greeks:

Achilles

The anger of Achilles (μῆνις Ἀχιλλέως) is the central theme and purpose of the *Iliad*. This is how Homer introduces it:

> Μῆνιν ἄειδε θεὰ Πηληϊάδεω Ἀχιλῆος
> :οὐλομένην, ἣ μυρί' Ἀχαιοῖς ἄλγε' ἔθηκεν, [...]

> Sing, Goddess, of the rage of Peleus' son Achilles,
> the accursed rage that brought great suffering to the Achaeans.

Homer, *Iliad*, 1, 1–2

Achilles came to Troy with fifty ships, each with a complement of fifty Myrmidons. He appointed five commanders so each leader was in charge of 500 Myrmidons: Menesthius, Eudorus, Peisander, Phoenix and Alcimedon (*Iliad* 16, 168–197). The Myrmidons had won themselves a reputation for their loyalty to their leaders; so much so that the word 'myrmidon' carried some of the same connotations that 'robot' does today. 'Myrmidon' later came to mean 'hired ruffian'.

When Agamemnon reluctantly agreed to return Chryseis to her seer father in order to end the plague visited on the Greeks, and when he arrogantly took Briseis, Achilles' war booty woman, as a replacement in his bed, he could have had no idea of the ructions this would cause and the effect that it would have on his military objectives at Troy.

So began Achilles' great sulk: incandescent at the shame of having his booty and glory snatched away and, as he admits later, because he loved Briseis (*Iliad* 9, 334–343), he, urged on by his mother Thetis, petulantly withdrew his support for the Greek cause, so compromising any successful outcome for his fellow Greeks. At the same time, Achilles selfishly prayed to Thetis to convince Zeus to help the Trojans gain ground in the war, so that he may salvage his honour.

Later, Nestor revealed the truth that everyone in the Greek camp already knew but did not want to admit: the Trojans were winning because Agamemnon had upset Achilles; the king should, therefore, make amends. Achilles, despite inducements from Agamemnon with wily Odysseus as intermediary, remained obdurate and recommended that all the Greeks sail for their respective homes as he himself intended to do. Agamemnon, to appease Achilles, offered seven tripods, seven women, seven cities and lots more gifts besides Briseis; without the participation of Achilles in the war, the only prospect was defeat.

Hector, meanwhile, led the Trojans in a push that saw the Greek army forced back to the beaches and their ships attacked. Annihilation loomed but Patroclus responded and led the Myrmidons into battle wearing Achilles' armour. He managed to repulse the Trojans, but was killed by Hector before he could lead a concerted assault on the city of Troy.

Achilles was devastated by his comrade's death. A comforting Thetis persuaded Hephaestus to make new armour for him, to replace the armour that Patroclus had been wearing and which had been plundered by Hector. The new armour included the Shield of Achilles, which Homer describes in detail.

Achilles' fury at Agamemnon was then replaced with rage over the death of Patroclus. Achilles returned to the fray, killing many men in his frenzy but ever on the lookout for Hector. He even took on the river god Scamander, who was annoyed that Achilles was clogging his waters with all the corpses of the men he had killed. The god tries to drown Achilles but is restrained by Hera and Hephaestus. Zeus observes Achilles' anger and sends the gods to calm him down so that he does not sack Troy before the time ordained for its destruction. Achilles eventually finds Hector and, as we have seen, chases Hector around the wall of Troy three times before Athena, in the form of Hector's brother, Deiphobus, persuades him to stop running away and face up to Achilles. After Hector realizes the trick, he knows that combat is inevitable. Wanting to go down fighting, he charges at Achilles with his only weapon, his sword, but misses. Accepting his fate, Hector begs Achilles not to spare his life but to treat his body with due respect after he has killed him. An implacable Achilles tells Hector that 'my rage, my fury would drive me now to hack your flesh away and eat you raw – such are the agonies you have caused me.' Achilles kills Hector.

There are many different accounts of the death of Achilles. His death does not feature in the *Iliad*, although other sources tell us that he was killed towards the end of the war by Paris, who shot him in that vulnerable heel with an Apollo-guided arrow. Statius in the first century CE in his *Thebaid* says that Achilles was invulnerable in all of his body except for his heel because, when his mother Thetis dipped him in the river Styx as an infant to give him invulnerability, she held him by one of his heels. After death, his bones were mixed with those of Patroclus, and funeral games were held.

Another version tells that he fell in love with one of the Trojan princesses, Polyxena. Achilles asked Priam for Polyxena's hand in marriage; Priam had no objections because it would mean the end of the war and an alliance with the world's greatest warrior. However, Paris, who would have to give up Helen if Achilles married his sister, is lurking in the bushes and shoots Achilles with a deadly arrow.

Many paintings on pottery show Achilles and Ajax playing a board game (petteia); so absorbed in the game are they that they are oblivious to the surrounding battle raging around them.

Aeschylus wrote a trilogy of plays about Achilles, christened *Achilleis* today. The tragedies describe the actions of Achilles during the Trojan War, including his defeat of Hector and his death. The first part of the trilogy, *The Myrmidons*, focuses on the relationship between Achilles and the chorus, who represent the Achaean army and try to convince Achilles to renounce his quarrel with Agamemnon; only a few lines survive today. Sophocles wrote *The Lovers of Achilles*. Achilles gets a bad press from Euripides in his *Hecuba*, *Electra* and *Iphigenia in Aulis*.

Agamemnon

By dint of the fact that he was King of Mycenae, Agamemnon was a powerful player in the Trojan War. He was the son of King Atreus and Queen Aerope of Mycenae, the brother of the cuckolded Menelaus, the husband of Clytemnestra and the father of Iphigenia, Electra, Orestes and Chrysothemis. After Helen was abducted by Paris, Agamemnon became commander-in-chief of the Greek armed coalition in the ensuing Trojan War.

Murder, treachery, pederastic rape and incest blemished Agamemnon's life. Atreus murdered the sons of his twin brother Thyestes and fed them to Thyestes after discovering Thyestes' adultery with his wife Aerope. Thyestes fathered Aegisthus by his own daughter Pelopia; Aegisthus vowed revenge on Atreus' children: Aegisthus murdered Atreus, took possession of the throne of Mycenae and jointly ruled with Thyestes. During this time, Agamemnon and his brother Menelaus took refuge with Tyndareus, King of Sparta. There they married Tyndareus' daughters Clytemnestra and Helen. Menelaus succeeded Tyndareus in Sparta, while Agamemnon, with his brother's assistance, drove out Aegisthus and Thyestes to recover his father's kingdom, becoming the most powerful prince in Greece.

As we have seen, Agamemnon mustered the Greek task force to sail for Troy, himself contributing 100 ships, but all did not go to plan when Agamemnon's forces incurred the wrath of Artemis. How depends on where we look: in Aeschylus' *Agamemnon*, Artemis is angry for the sake of the young men who will die at Troy, whereas in Sophocles' *Electra*, Agamemnon has ill-advisedly slain a stag sacred to Artemis, and exacerbated the situation when he boasted that he was Artemis' equal in hunting. A plague and an absence of wind prevented the army from sailing. The prophet Calchas announced that the wrath of the goddess could only be propitiated by the sacrifice of Agamemnon's daughter Iphigenia. Her death appeased Artemis, and the Greeks set sail for Troy.

During the fighting at Troy, Agamemnon killed Antiphus and fifteen other Trojan troops (Hyginus, *Fabulae* 114), but the *Iliad* has it that he slew hundreds more in Book 11 during his *aristeia* (day of glory). This shows that he was no mean warrior:

> As when annihilating fire falls on a thick forest scrub, and the wind carries it billowing all over, and the bushes are brought down headlong in the flames' overwhelming onslaught, so the fleeing Trojans went down under Agamemnon, son of Atreus, and many strong-necked horses rattled empty chariots along the avenues of battle, missing the noble charioteers they knew: but they lay dead on the ground, a sight now to gladden vultures, not their wives. (*Iliad*, 11, 155–162.)

Agamemnon is one of the three volunteers fancied to face Achilles in a duel; Agamemnon was the only major warrior on either side never to need the gods' direct intervention to augment his strength or give him any unfair advantages in battle and yet he still caused incredible carnage, almost as much as Achilles.

Agamemnon, of course, is central to the *Iliad*: as we know, he claimed Chryseis, daughter of Chryses, one of Apollo's priests, as a war prize and in so doing set in motion the events which led to the end of the war and victory for the Greeks.

After Troy fell, Agamemnon was allocated Cassandra, the daughter of Priam, when the booty was shared out. Apart from in the *Iliad*, Agamemnon features in Euripides, *Electra*; Sophocles, *Electra*; Seneca, *Agamemnon*; Aeschylus, *The Libation Bearers*; Homer, *Odyssey* 1, 28–31; 11, 385–464; Aeschylus, *Agamemnon*; Apollodorus, *Epitome*, 2, 15–3, 22; 6, 23.

Diomedes

Diomedes was the son of Tydeus and Deipyle and later became King of Argos, succeeding his maternal grandfather Adrastus. In the *Iliad* Diomedes rates alongside Ajax the Great as one of the foremost warriors in the Achaean alliance, after only Achilles. He was one of the Seven Against Thebes. Later, he went on to found ten or so Italian cities and was deified after his death.

In the Trojan War, Diomedes contributed a fleet of 80 ships, third only to Agamemnon's 100 ships and Nestor's 90. When fighting Telamonian Ajax in an armed sparring contest where the winner was he who drew blood first, Ajax unsuccessfully attacked Diomedes where his armour covered his body. Ajax owned the biggest set of armour and the tallest shield which covered most of his body, leaving only two places vulnerable: his neck and armpits. So Diomedes manoeuvred his spear above Ajax's shield and went for his neck, drawing blood. The Achaean leaders were scared that another such blow would kill Ajax, so they stopped the fight. Diomedes received the prize for the victor. He later overcame and could have killed Aeneas. Diomedes was the favourite warrior of Athena, who even drove his chariot once. He was also the only hero except Heracles to attack and wound Olympian gods, including Ares, who he struck with his spear, and Aphrodite, both on the same day. He was even granted divine vision in order to identify immortals. The god Hephaestus made Diomedes' cuirass for him.

Apart from his obvious prowess as a warrior, Diomedes exhibited considerable maturity and intelligence and was an active and wise participant in war counsels.

Menelaus

Menelaus is probably best known as the man whose wife ran away with Paris, thus triggering the Trojan War when her beautiful face launched a thousand ships in the operation to restore her to Menelaus. Relatively speaking, he was a 'gentle warrior' (*Iliad* 17, 588), generally less savage than other warriors but honourable and brave and inclined to clemency, as in his desire to spare Adrastus until countermanded by Agamemnon.

The *Iliad* tells us what happened next. In Book 3, Menelaus challenged Paris to a duel, the winner of which would regain or retain the Spartan queen. Menelaus easily beat Paris, but before he could kill him and claim Helen back, Aphrodite evacuated Paris back inside the walls of Troy. In Book 4, while the Greeks and Trojans squabbled over who was the winner, Athena inspired the Trojan Pandarus to shoot Menelaus with his bow and arrow. However, Athena never intended for Menelaus to die, so she deflected the arrow. Menelaus is nevertheless wounded in the stomach and the fighting resumes. Later, in Book 17, Menelaus enjoyed an extended *aristeia* in the course of retrieving the corpse of Patroclus from the battlefield.

According to Hyginus, Menelaus killed eight men in the war and was one of the Greeks concealed inside the Trojan Horse. During the sack of Troy, Menelaus killed Deiphobus, who had married Helen after the death of Paris.

Tragedy did Menelaus no favours. In Euripides' *Trojan Women* he is depicted as weak, lacking the stomach to kill his errant wife; Sophocles' *Aias*, Euripides' *Andromache* and *Orestes* all portray him as a rather odious individual. The *Helen* has him as more sympathetic. Herodotus (2, 119) describes how he sacrificed two Egyptian children.

Nestor

Nestor has a busy history with an admirable war record: he was an Argonaut; he fought the centaurs as a Lapith fighting alongside other non-Lapiths like Theseus and Peleus (*Iliad* 1, 260ff); he took part in the hunt for the Calydonian Boar and after Heracles butchered Neleus and all of Nestor's siblings he was the sole survivor of the family and became King of Sandy Pylos (*Iliad* 2, 77). In the war between Pylos and Elis Nestor earned his spurs as a renowned warrior. The Eleans took advantage of the previous war between Pylos and Heracles, a war in which the best Pylian warriors had perished, in order to oppress the city, stealing their cattle and their horses. So when the Pylians reacted accordingly, Elis sent an army against them, including the Molionides, twins who had their bodies joined to one another. When the army camped, Athena came from Olympus and instructed the Pylians to array themselves for battle. Neleus could not prevent Nestor from going into battle.

According to Nestor himself, he killed the Elean Itymoneus, son of Hypeirochus, with a spear. He also slew Mulius, who was the son-in-law of King Augeas. Nestor could not kill the Siamese twins because Poseidon had enveloped them in a fog. Later, the Pylians waged war against the Arcadians, who included in their ranks Ereuthalion, the squire of King Lycurgus (*Iliad* 4, 319f); when Lycurgus grew old, he gave his armour to Ereuthalion; while he wore this armour no man dared to challenge him, except Nestor, who, although the youngest in the army, defeated and slew Ereuthalion, or so he says.

He and his sons, Antilochus and Thrasymedes, fought on the side of the Achaeans in the Trojan War, contributing an impressive ninety ships (*Iliad* 2, 590ff). Nestor was already very old (about 70) when the war began (*Iliad* 1, 250ff), but he was noted for his past bravery, sagacity, loquaciousness and eloquence, offering advice to the younger warriors and advising Agamemnon and Achilles to make up their differences (*Iliad* 1, 254ff). However, his wise counsel fell on two pairs of deaf ears:

Agamemnon:

All these things, old man, to be sure, you have spoken as is right. But this man wishes to be above all others; over all he wishes to rule and over all to be king, and to all to give orders; in this, I think, there is someone who will not obey.

Achilles:

Surely I would be called cowardly and of no account, if I am to yield to you in every matter that you say. On others lay these commands, but do not give orders to me, for I do not think I shall obey you any longer. (Homer, *Iliad* 1, 285.)

Odysseus

Quick-witted Odysseus, King of Ithaca, was the only son of Laertes of Ithaca, a former Argonaut, and Anticlea, the only daughter of Autolycus. Autolycus, Odysseus' grandfather, was a son of Hermes and was infamous as an uncatchable, skilful thief being 'able to transmogrify whatever he stole into some other form – from white to black, or from black to white, from a hornless animal to a horned one, or from horned one to a hornless – indeed, Shakespeare's 'snapper-up of unconsidered trifles' in *The Winter's Tale*. Odysseus inherits much of this and is, therefore, famous for his intellectual brilliance, guile and mental agility (*polytropos*); he is often known by the epithet 'Odysseus the Cunning' (μῆτις).

He is just as famous for his *nostos* or 'homecoming', his long and winding journey home which took him ten eventful years after the decade-long Trojan War. Odysseus is not just synonymous with Mediterranean travel; he is also inextricably linked with serial adultery. While Penelope waited patiently and virtuously at home for twenty years, swatting off so many salacious suitors and working her wifely wool, wily Odysseus took the long way home, enjoying ten years of adventure, tourism and extended horizontal collaboration with two of the region's more voluptuous but excitingly dangerous women, notably witchy Circe and sexy Calypso.

The male sexual freedom exercised here no doubt reflected the norm in Homer's day, and probably was common practice in the heroic age he was writing about centuries before. As such, the message from the epic poems and their myths would have resonated down the ages as generation handed them down through the generations; it would become routine for men to philander and mandatory for women not to. Indeed, Calypso is very reluctant to give up Odysseus and indignantly complains about the Olympian sexual double standards in which a god can pursue a mortal woman or man *ad libitum* while her own case demonstrates that a goddess has little hope of capturing a mortal man. She cites the precedent set by Iaision in his dalliance with Demeter in that 'thrice-ploughed field' when he paid the ultimate price courtesy of a thunderbolt from Zeus.

So, by our modern standards he was a bit of a cad, but Odysseus could also be a cruel man. His most brutish act was just after Troy had fallen when he demanded that Astyanax, Hector's little boy, be murdered, concerned no doubt that one day he might come back seeking retribution for the death of his father and the hideous enslavement of his mother. The *Iliu Persis* says that Odysseus hurled the infant to his death from Troy's walls.

One of the cunning stunts Odysseus pulled off was to feign lunacy in a bid to avoid the draft: the call to arms in response to the abduction of Helen and the fulfilment of the oaths made at the Treaty of Tyndareus.

The *Cypria* records how Odysseus tried to avoid his obligation by feigning lunacy, as an oracle had prophesied a long-delayed return home for him if he went to war. So Odysseus hooked a donkey and an ox to his plough because, as every sane person knows, they have different stride lengths and thus compromise the efficiency of the plough when yoked together. Should anyone still doubt his sanity, he craftily sowed his fields with salt. Palamedes, at the behest of Agamemnon, was having none of it and in a bid to expose Odysseus' feigned madness and trickery placed Telemachus, Odysseus' infant son, in the path of the plough (Hyginus, *Fabulae* 95, 2). Odysseus intuitively swerved the plough away from the boy, thus revealing his deceit. Odysseus never forgave Palamedes for dragging him away from his home. Apollodorus (*Epitome*, 3, 7) says that Palamedes threatened the infant with a sword.

In the Trojan War Odysseus is a powerful and influential force on the side of the Greeks: he holds off the rout of the Greeks at *Iliad* 11, 310–488; he is brave and resourceful in the *Doloneia* in Book 10. Along with Nestor and Idomeneus he is one of the most trusted and wise counsellors and advisors as exemplified by his holding together the fragmenting (*Iliad* 2, 169–355) Greek army. Odysseus is forever championing the Achaean cause, raising morale and urging victory.

After Patroclus was killed, it is Odysseus who counsels Achilles (*Iliad* 9, 223–306) to let the Achaean men eat and rest rather than follow his rage-driven desire to keep on fighting – and kill Trojans – immediately. Odysseus is often seen as the opposite to Achilles in the *Iliad*: while Achilles' wrath is all-consuming and self-destructive, Odysseus is frequently viewed as a measured man, a voice of reason, renowned for his self-restraint and diplomacy. He is also the antithesis to Telamonian Ajax (Shakespeare's 'beef-witted' Ajax, *Troilus and Cressida*): Ajax is all brawn, but Odysseus is an eloquent speaker and has a nuanced, intellectual and entrepreneurial quality about him as evidenced by his inspired idea of the Trojan Horse.

The Trojan Horse was a capacious wooden sculpture whose hollow belly accommodated the cream of Greece's celebrated heroes. After leaving the horse near the Gates of Troy, the Greeks pretended to sail away; initially confused by this stratagem, the Trojans soon started believing that the war was over and that the horse had been a divine gift, so they wheeled the contraption inside their city gates. They spent the whole day partying, celebrating their phantom victory and dancing around the deceptive horse. However, once night fell, the Greek warriors emerged from the beast and opened the gates to admit the rest of the Greeks, who had sailed back to the shore. The Greeks attacked the drunk and defenceless Trojans, butchering many of them and winning a conclusive victory.

Odysseus can also claim to have procured the recruitment of Achilles to the Achaean cause. It had been prophesied by Calchas that victory for the Greeks was impossible without Achilles, so Odysseus and other envoys acting for Agamemnon travelled to Scyros to enlist his support. Thetis, Achilles' mother, disguised her son as a woman to conceal him from this press gang because another oracle had predicted that Achilles would either live a long, uneventful life or achieve everlasting glory but die young. Cross-dressing was probably not the ideal start for a boy on the verge of becoming an alpha male warrior of the highest calibre. When he arrived in Scyros Odysseus immediately saw through the disguise, exposing Achilles as the only 'female' present when his eye was caught by the weapons hidden among a selection of jewellery and musical instruments brought for the daughters of their host. Odysseus made sure of his man by sounding the battle bugle, at which Achilles' natural reaction was to grab a weapon for defence and show his military training and natural belligerence. Disguise blown, Achilles joined Agamemnon's call to arms.

Along with Diomedes, Odysseus captured and killed the Trojan spy Dolon and slew the Thracian King Rhesus during a dangerous night raid on the Trojan camp. He also captured the Trojan seer Helenus in order to glean intelligence from him on what the fall of Troy depended.

Physically, Odysseus was no Hercules; we learn from a discussion between Priam and Helen in the *Iliad* that Odysseus was shorter by a head than Agamemnon but broader in his chest and shoulders. Physically unimpressive, 'thou wouldest have deemed him a churlish man and naught but a fool' on sight, claims Priam. 'But whenso he uttered his great voice from his chest, and words fell like snowflakes on a winter's day, then could no mortal man beside vie with Odysseus; then did we not so marvel to behold Odysseus' aspect.' 'He knoweth all manner of craft and cunning devices,' agrees Helen, this illustrious 'Odysseus of many wiles.'

Odysseus features in the poems of the Epic Cycle. As we have seen, the *Cypria* reveals his feigned madness in a failed bid to avoid his obligation to the Treaty of Tyndareus and join the task force against the Trojans; the *Iliu Persis* shows Odysseus hurling little Astyanax from the walls of Troy to his death to snuff out any later recriminations by the son of Hector and Andromache. The *Little Iliad* describes how Odysseus and Diomedes steal the Palladium and thus expose Troy to its fate, with some sources claiming that Odysseus tried to kill Diomedes on the way home. The spat with Aias over the arms of Achilles first heard of in the *Iliad* (11, 543–541) comes in the *Aethiopis* and the *Little Iliad*, with Pindar (*Nemean* 8, 23–34) asserting that Odysseus procured the arms through guile.

The tragedies were no kinder to Odysseus. He features in a number of the extant plays by Aeschylus, Sophocles (*Ajax*, *Philoctetes*) and Euripides (*Hecuba*, *Rhesus*, *Trojan Women*, *Cyclops*). In his *Ajax*, Sophocles portrays Odysseus as a fine, upstanding man; a modern voice of reason compared to the title character's rigid, entrenched attitudes. In his *Philoctetes* he is, conversely, a cynic devoid of morals.

Plato in his *Hippias Minor* examines a question about whom Homer intended to portray as the better man, Achilles or Odysseus.

Palamedes

Trojan War apart, Palamedes is remembered for his invention of the dice. According to Pausanias (*Description of Greece* 2, 20, 3) there is in Corinth a Temple of Fortune in which Palamedes dedicated the dice that he had invented.

As we have seen, Odysseus never forgave Palamedes for exposing his sham madness and ensuring his participation in the ten-year-long war. One source has it that Odysseus forged a letter from Priam purporting to be from Palamedes. A sum of gold greased the captive's palm. However, he never got to spend it as he was murdered by Odysseus who then concealed the gold in Palamedes' tent, making sure that the letter was found by Agamemnon, whose discovery of it led the Greeks to the gold. Palamedes was stoned to death as a traitor (Apollodorus, *Epitome* 3, 8;

Hyginus, *Fabulae* 105). Another source says that Odysseus and Diomedes persuaded Palamedes to go down a well with the promise of finding treasure at the bottom. When Palamedes reached the bottom, the two buried him with stones, eventually killing him. Pausanias holds that two warriors drowned him during a fishing expedition (Pausanias 10, 31, 2, citing the *Cypria*). Palamedes' father Naupius got his revenge when he caused some of the returning Greek heroes' wives to be unfaithful or by lighting false beacons off Cape Caphareus in Euboea and shipwrecking some of the Greek fleet (Apollodorus, *Epitome* 6, 7–8).

Telamonian Ajax (Αἴας ὁ Τελαμώνιος), or Ajax the Great

A significant figure in the Trojan War, as distinguished from Ajax, son of Oileus, Ajax the Lesser, rapist of Cassandra. Ajax the Great was a giant of a man, the strongest of all the Achaeans according to Homer (*Iliad* 3, 226–9; 2, 786–9) and known as the 'bulwark (*erkos*) of the Achaeans' (*Iliad* 6, 5); he was trained by the centaur Chiron, at the same time as Achilles. Ajax was fearless, strong and powerful with not a little combat intelligence. Ajax typically commanded his army wielding a huge shield made of seven cow-hides with a layer of bronze. When Achilles was slain in battle by Paris, it is Odysseus and Telamonian Ajax who retrieve the warrior's body and armour amid heavy fighting. According to Hyginus, Ajax killed twenty-eight Greeks at Troy (*Fabulae* 114).

Ajax's prodigious strength and courage is no better evident than in his duels with Hector. In Book 7, as we have seen, Ajax was chosen by lot to meet Hector in a duel which lasted the best part of a day (7, 181–305). The second fight occurred when Hector burst into the Greek camp and fought with the Greeks. In Book 14 (408–417), Ajax threw a giant rock at Hector which almost killed him. In Book 15, Hector was restored to strength by Apollo and returned to attack the ships. Ajax, wielding an enormous spear and leaping from ship to ship, held off the Trojan armies virtually single-handed. In Book 16, Hector and Ajax come to blows again. Hector disarms Ajax and Ajax is forced to retreat, seeing that Zeus is clearly favouring Hector. Hector and the Trojans succeed in burning one Greek ship, the culmination of an assault that almost brings the war to an end.

As we have seen, Ajax and Odysseus are the heroes who fight the Trojans to get to Achilles' body and bury it with the body of Patroclus. Ajax recovered the body and carried it to the ships, while Odysseus fought off the Trojans (*Odyssey* 5, 309f). After the burial, the *Little Iliad* tells us how each claimed Achilles' armour, forged on Mount Olympus by Hephaestus; Ajax laid claim to it in recognition of his heroic efforts. Odysseus, however, is the more eloquent, and with the aid of Athena, wins the armour. Ajax is furious, goes berserk and slaughters the Achaeans' herds of captured livestock, believing them to be his enemies. Unable to cope with this apparent hallucination, he falls on his own sword, 'conquered by his [own] sorrow', and commits suicide (Lesches of Mitylene, the *Little Iliad*). In this version, Ajax is denied his funeral rites and is still fuming when Odysseus meets him in his nekyia: Ajax ignores him completely in another of literature's great sulks (*Odyssey* 11, 543–564).

In Sophocles' *Ajax*, after the armour is awarded to Odysseus, Ajax feels so insulted that he has an urge to kill Agamemnon and Menelaus. Athena intervenes and fogs his mind and vision so that he slaughters a flock of sheep, imagining they are the Achaean leaders, including Odysseus and Agamemnon. When he comes to his senses, blood-splattered, he realizes the enormity of what he has done: he has diminished his honour, and decides to kill himself rather than live in shame. He does so with the very sword that Hector gave him.

Pausanias records that a gigantic skeleton, its kneecap 13cm in diameter, appeared on the beach near Sigeion, on the Trojan coast; the bones were identified as those of Ajax.

The women of the Trojan War

It is with Homer that we first meet the widely-held axiom in the classical Greek and Roman worlds that war is men's work while wool-working is the preserve of women: the two lie at different poles of Greek and Roman society and gender convention and, according to most Greeks and Romans, never should the two meet or be confused. The one informs men, the other women; war is a badge of maleness, wool and looking after the *oikos* or *domus* are emblems of the good wife, the *matrona*, and home-maker. Hector and Telemachus vocalize this quite emphatically in Homer, and ever since it has echoed down through classical life and literature as a mantra to normal life and the much-desired establishment status quo. At the same time, though, it has come under attack from a small but momentous and significant gender role reversal in which women go off warring and, occasionally, men are left holding the bobbins and shuttles. It first manifests in Homer, specifically with Penthesilea the Amazon fighting Achilles.

The world, as we know, is not always normal. For example, Herodotus is staggered to report that Egyptians are all crazy: the women go to market and men stay at home and weave (the exact opposite to Greek practice). Women even urinate standing up and men sitting down. Aristophanes' *Lysistrata* attests that war is as much the responsibility of women as of men: she turns the state upside down and upsets the status quo when she dresses up the *proboulos* in women's clothes and teaches him the ways of wool while she and her comrades take over the running of the city, the complicated and challenging affairs of which include the Peloponnesian War, a conflict which can be disentangled as easily as a ball of wool (*Lysistrata* 567ff). Elsewhere, an armoured Athena, female goddess that she is, protects Athens while effeminate Cleisthenes has his shuttle.

Diodorus (3, 53) reports that the Amazon men of Libya stay home, weave and look after the children while the women go out fighting wars; Pindar's Cyrene eschews the loom and prefers to slay wild beasts with her sword (*Pythian* 9, 19–22); Euripides' Auge goes one better, getting self-fulfilment by slaughtering animals with her bare hands (*Bacchae* 1236); the Bacchants too have deserted the loom for a life much more exciting; when he observes Artemisia's military excellence and belligerence, a bemused Xerxes reflects that his men are acting just like women and she like a man. The warlike Amazons consign their men to a life of woolworking. Throughout Greek and Roman history exceptional women are described as exhibiting *andreia* or *virtus*, with all the connotations of manliness and bravery.

Men, of course, were the protagonists in the Trojan War: Homer's *Iliad* tells the story of the ten-year conflict with Achilles, Patroclus, Hector, Agamemnon, Ajax, Aeneas and Deiphobus among the many alpha male warriors. However, there would not have been a Trojan War without the involvement of women, both as the very *casus belli* itself and as characters who influenced the action and direction of the war. Helen, Queen of Sparta, must take responsibility for causing the war when she allowed herself to be abducted by Paris, while Briseis and Chryseis both played a role far more influential than their relegation to spoils of war would suggest. Hector's wife, later war widow, Andromache tried to influence her husband's actions and strategy with some cogent advice in how to prosecute the war, while the ever-patient, faithful army wife Penelope, in the *Odyssey*, endured virtual widowhood for twenty years as she waited and waited in the hope that Odysseus would come back to her and dispel the repellent suitors circling around her shark-like, with more than just an eye on her virtue. Achilles' mother Thetis was a significant influence in her son's agonizing decision: to fight or not to fight in the war against Troy.

Women, though, have no active role on the battlefield, with the notable exception of the Amazon Penthesilea. However, Athena can be found there supporting her favourite heroes and Thetis it was who gave Achilles back his weapons to enable him to resume fighting. After Penthesilea, the nearest we come to active participation is Hector's wife Andromache, who looks after his horses for him (*Iliad* 8, 185–90) and offers that sensible strategic advice before his final departure for the battlefield.

Homer's women do, nevertheless, have a vital role in narrating the tragedy that befalls Troy and, as we might expect, in funerals and in mourning dead heroes; for example, the *Iliad* 24, 723–46; 748–60; 761–776. With the exception of Helen and of Homer himself, the destruction of Troy is always described from the perspective of Trojan women; this gives them an important role as exclusive narrators of the Trojan catastrophe which is best illustrated when the women of Troy mob Hector at the Scaean Gate, desperate for news of their fathers, husbands, sons and friends: Hector is evasive and advises prayer. Homer, however, comes straight to the point when he interjects into the narrative the doom-laden pronouncement: 'grief – *kedea* – awaits many' (*Iliad* 6, 241). Hector's mother Hecuba takes control of the situation and advises Hector to sacrifice to Athena in order to enlist her protection of the Trojan wives and children from the marauding Diomedes.

Homer's women remain proud of their fighting men; Hecuba urges the Trojan women to remember Hector as god-like in their lamentations, the greatest glory (*Iliad* 22, 430). Despite their physical absence from the field of battle, Homer's female characters remain at the heart of the ten-year conflict.

Helen of Troy: casus belli

Helen became unwittingly embroiled in the Trojan War when Paris decided that Aphrodite (and not Hera or Athena) was the fairest goddess of them all, thus winning for himself the prize of the most beautiful woman in the world. Helen was no stranger to abduction and her role as *casus belli* goes back much further than the Judgement of Paris. Indeed, the true origins of the Trojan War can be found in her abduction by Theseus after which, as a young girl, she became the target for a number of suitors. Coincidentally, Helen's abduction here gave rise to a conflict when her brothers, Castor and Pollux, attacked Athens, captured Theseus' mother Aethra in retaliation, and returned their sister to Sparta.[7] The suitor who won the day was King Menelaus of Sparta who duly married Helen, beating off such peerless contenders as Odysseus, Menestheus, Ajax the Great, Patroclus and Idomeneus. The victory came after the drawing of straws and a deal in which Odysseus secured not just an agreement in which all the suitors swore a solemn oath to defend the successful husband in any future dispute – the Oath of Tyndareus – but also the hand of Penelope.

However, the Helen-Menelaus marriage was not a happy one: while Menelaus was out of town attending a funeral, Paris and Helen fled to Troy, despite brother Hector's protestations, causing the Oath of Tyndareus to be invoked and a fleet of 1,000 ships to be launched in retaliation. The Trojan War had begun.

Helen assumed a prominent role in the progress of the war when, at the Scaean Gate, the very epicentre of the battle, she discusses how things are going with Priam and some other wise elders. Priam absolves her of any blame for the conflict and asks her to provide military intelligence regarding some of her ex-kinsmen, notably Agamemnon. She obliges, but not before wishing herself dead for causing so much trouble. One of the elders, Antenor, attests to the accuracy of her information, so confirming her as a viable and reliable source of intelligence. Death, however, eluded her, so she spent her time 'pining away, weeping'. We deal with this in more detail in the section on teichoscopy.

During the war, Menelaus and Paris fought a duel which Menelaus won easily; however, Aphrodite spirited Paris away to the safety of Troy before he could be killed. Homer shows Helen's take on life as a military woman when he makes it clear that Helen, with Menelaus, had been trapped in a loveless marriage and that Paris presented an opportunity for her to live a more settled and happy married life. She explains to Paris that, while appreciative of Menelaus' prowess as a warrior, she had little interest in army life or in being an army wife; no more heroes for Helen. She wanted to grow old with Paris, and every day she spent with bellicose Menelaus made her want to walk into the sea and end it all. Moreover, she confides in Hector that 'I can't ask anyone to fight for me; I am no longer queen of Sparta', thus parading the loss of self-esteem and guilt she now felt for being the one person responsible for the bloody regional conflict that was the Trojan War.

Helen comes out of the fall of Troy very badly: both Homer, and Virgil after him, paint a picture of a woman now partnered with a Trojan warrior duplicitously and cruelly assisting the Greek military offensive. In the *Odyssey*, Homer describes how Helen circled the Trojan Horse three times, cruelly mimicking the voices of the Greek war wives left waiting anxiously at home and putting the men inside, which included Odysseus and Menelaus, through emotional agony as they envisaged their loved ones forlorn and far away. Helen effectively drove them to the brink of death: they had to be restrained by Odysseus from bursting out of the horse to certain massacre. In Virgil's *Aeneid*, a mutilated Deiphobus recounts Helen's treachery: he tells a shocked Aeneas how, when the Trojan Horse was admitted into the city, she was at the head of a chorus of Trojan women feigning Bacchic rites and brandishing a torch from the citadel, the signal the Greeks were waiting for to launch their deadly and cataclysmic attack.[8]

Paris died later in the war and Deiphobus, his younger brother, married Helen, only to be slain by Menelaus during the sack of Troy when Helen, again acting treacherously as a fifth columnist, hid his sword and rendered him easy prey.[9] Virgil's graphic description of Deiphobus' mutilation serves only to magnify the enormity of Helen's crime, both as wife to husband and as belligerent traitor to country:

> Priam's son, his body slashed to bits, can now be seen – his face mangled, his face and hands covered in blood, his head shockingly shorn of ears and nose. Aeneas could barely recognise this shivering shade as Deiphobus'; it struggled to hide its face and the scar of shame. (Virgil, *Aeneid* 6, 493ff.)

Indeed, Deiphobus is unequivocal about Helen's crime, in words replete with and redolent of deceit and dishonour:

> This was my fate (*fata*), and that Spartan woman's murderous crime (*scelus exitiale*) to mire me in this mess (*his mersere malis*) – these are the souvenirs she has left me with. We spent that final night in false (*falsa*) joy…when the deadly (*fatalis*) horse leaped into impregnable (*ardua*) Pergamon, pregnant with infantry armed to the teeth; she led the Phrygian women in choral dance and false (*simulans*) Bacchanalean song. (Virgil, *Aeneid* 6, 500ff.)

In the aftermath of the fall of Troy, the once double-dealing Helen is reduced to a cowering wreck, desperate to save her skin, deploying her most potent weapons: her beauty and sexuality. Sources differ on the exact details surrounding the reunion of Helen and Menelaus after the fall: one version has it that an angry Menelaus resolved to kill Helen himself, but when he finds her and raises his sword he takes pity on her as she weeps, begging for her life. Menelaus' fury evaporates and he takes her back as wife. Another has Menelaus, again intent on slaying her, captivated by her beauty and sparing her life; he takes her back to his ship 'to punish her at Sparta'.[10]

The *Bibliotheca* tells us that Menelaus raised his sword in front of the temple in Troy, but his anger subsided when she tore her clothes and revealed her breasts.[11] Stesichorus (ca.640–555 BCE), in his *The Sack of Troy*, reports that Menelaus gives her up to his soldiers so that they could stone her to death;[12] however, so stunned were they by her beauty when she tore open her clothes that the warriors dropped the stones from their hands, all agog.

Whatever happened to her, Helen remains for us a key player in the cause, progress and aftermath of the Trojan War. Indeed, things could have been much worse than events at Troy: she could have shared responsibility for igniting another much more serious war; literally the war to end all wars. As we noted at the very beginning of this chapter, according to Hesiod, Zeus planned to exterminate the race of men and heroes and was going to use the Trojan War – as triggered by the elopement of Helen – as the catalyst for this apocalyptic cataclysm.[13]

Briseis and Chryseis: never just spoils of war

Like Helen, both Briseis and Chryseis are compelling forces in the Trojan War; they form a basis for Homer's description of the military action at the gates of Troy and the eventual raising of the siege there. Briseis first encountered Achilles at the wrong end of his sword when he ruthlessly slaughtered her father, mother, three brothers and husband during a Greek assault on Troy.[14] A bereft Briseis was awarded to Achilles as war booty with a life of concubinage to look forward to; as such, she is one of the first female victims of war in classical literature.

Initially, all went well: the relationship between Briseis and Achilles blossomed into mutual love with the promise of marriage after the war assured by Patroclus. However, Apollo and Agamemnon spoiled the party when the king was required to give up his own concubine, Chryseis. A petulant and selfish Agamemnon then insisted that Achilles hand over Briseis in recompense. Achilles did not react well: he withdrew his troops from the Greek force with dramatic strategic consequences and retired to sulk at length and leisure in his tent, mortified and wounded by his loss. From Achilles' point of view, if the cuckolding of Menelaus could start a war, then how should he react to Agamemnon for stealing Briseis from him? Answer: by withdrawing and thereby compromising any successful outcome to the war for the massed Greek armies. It took the death of Patroclus and the return of Briseis – both of whom he loved in different ways – to spur Achilles back into action and save the Greek cause. Predictably, Agamemnon swore that he never laid a hand on Briseis. Well, he would, wouldn't he?[15]

Chryseis has the honour of participating in the opening scene of the *Iliad*. She, like Briseis, was war booty, given up to Agamemnon. He, with breathtaking insensitivity, tactlessly described her as better than his own wife Clytemnestra with, as we know, fatal consequences when he finally got home from Troy. Agamemnon stubbornly held onto Chryseis when her father Chryses, a priest of Apollo at Chryse, attempted to ransom her:

> I would not accept that marvellous ransom for the girl, the daughter of Chryses, since I much prefer to keep her in my home. For sure, I prefer her to Clytemnestra, my wedded wife, since she is just as good as her, in terms of beauty or in stature, or in mind, or in any handiwork.[16]

The priest's lack of success here and Agamemnon's oafish, hubristic disrespect towards him angered the gods to such an extent that they unleashed a 'loathsome pestilence' on the Greek armies.[17] If he wanted an army to command, Agamemnon had no choice but to renounce Chryseis and send Odysseus to return 'fair-cheeked' Chryseis back to her father. Agamemnon then followed one military disaster with another when he, with supreme military myopia, selfishly compensated himself by taking 'fair-cheeked' Briseis from a distraught Achilles, with menaces, should he refuse to relinquish her.[18]

Pawns as they were in the machinations of Agamemnon and Achilles, both Briseis and Chryseis, for all that, lie at the heart of the progress, or lack of progress, in the Greek war against Troy. It is the spat between Achilles and Agamemnon over whose bed Briseis warms which stalled the conflict and compromised the Greek war effort. Only with Briseis returned does Achilles marshal his armies again with renewed vigour; not because he had got Briseis back, but to avenge the death of Patroclus and win the war for the Greek alliance.

Andromache: devoted wife and military advisor
Andromache's fame lies not just in being the devoted wife of Hector and loving mother of their son, Astyanax. She shrewdly uses a lesson in military strategy in an attempt to protect Hector from the worst dangers of the war raging around them.

She, like Penelope, was one of the thousands of army wives who waited patiently for her returning hero, buoyed up by hope and by an enduring love. Tragically, Andromache was about to welcome her hero home, ensconced in domestic security, when she was floored by the dreaded news that he had just been killed:

> She was at work in an inner room of the lofty palace, weaving a double-width purple tapestry, with a multi-coloured pattern of flowers. Totally unaware [of Hector's fate] she had asked her ladies-in-waiting to set a great cauldron on the fire so that Hector would have hot water for a bath when he got back…

Andromache's tragic back story began when Thebes, her home city, was sacked by Achilles, and her father and seven brothers died in the ensuing carnage. Her mother then was ransomed (*Iliad* 6, 141ff) and Andromache became just another piece of collateral damage and one of the countless spoils of war. However, Hector had come along to provide renewed stability and love in a life rent asunder by trauma and conflict.[19] All the more bitter then is the tragedy when Andromache's life is ripped apart again by the Trojan War when Achilles kills Hector, leaving her once again bereft, rootless and alone in the world, a displaced person relegated to the margins of society and a pathetic emblem of the fate that so often awaits women on the losing side in warfare.[20] Hector had foreseen all of this; for him the writing was on the walls for Troy. He bewailed the certain fact that Andromache would be forced into slavery – weaving at another woman's whim, fetching the water as a slave and wailing in captivity – again.

Just before they part for the last time, the couple hold a conversation on the exposed and dangerous ramparts of Troy, 'the great wall of Ilios', a place generally inimical to a woman and certainly alien to a distraught Andromache. In contrast, though, to the martial environment, domestic harmony of a sort is conjured up as Hector describes a typical scene with women weaving and men warring: in real life this is a metaphor for the one partner protecting the *oikos* (the homestead), the other defending the *polis* (the city-state), both central and essential to the survival and continuation of normal Greek life. The pathos is palpable. Hector laid his child in his dear wife's arms, and she held him to her fragrant breast, smiling through her tears. Hector was moved with pity when he looked at her, and he caressed her with his hand, and said: 'My dear wife, do not be too upset…go home and busy yourself with your own tasks, the loom and the distaff, and tell your maids to get on with their work: war is for us men.'

Many have seen this as a sexist statement, and by our more enlightened standards it is, firmly putting women in their place and telling women bluntly to keep out of men's business. Yet it signifies much more than that in the context of the day it describes and in which it was written: if we go back to the protection that Andromache gives to the *oikos*, it surely is a confirmation of her invaluable role, and the role of all other married women and mothers, in preserving and extending the homestead as a safe and nurturing environment in which to raise new generations and new citizens and hoplites for the *polis*. Without a thriving *oikos* there was no *polis* and nothing for the Hectors of the world to defend. Women like Andromache, then, were performing an important, albeit indirect, military role by providing something worth defending and fighting for.

Homer reinforces this important message by repeating the phrase on two occasions in the *Odyssey*,[21] with slight variations. The first comes at the beginning of the poem where Odysseus' precocious son Telemachus asserts his authority in the Odyssean household: he dismisses the grieving Penelope, his mother, and tells her, and the slaves, to get on with the wool-working, making it abundantly clear, not least to his mother, that he is in charge and that he will do the talking to the suitors because talking and negotiation are man's work. The second echoes the first when Telemachus again rebukes Penelope, reminding her that, in his father's absence, he is now the master of the house and that the bows and arrows are his province. Penelope is again ordered to go back to the wool work; she, somewhat meekly, retires to grieve over ever-absent Odysseus. Just as Hector was fighting to save his city, so Telemachus is talking, and shooting arrows, to save his household, his *oikos* and his mother from the circling predatory suitors.

Much more unconventional and extraordinary is the gender role-reversal implicit when Andromache offers Hector military advice. On one level, this is a loving but astute wife's ploy to detain Hector with a lesson in military strategy, thus keeping him in the relative safety of the ramparts and out of the much more hazardous open fighting taking place down below;[22] on another level, it is nothing short of sound, calm-headed advice based on a woman's observation in a sea of male confusion and panic:

> Come on, show some pity, and stay here on the wall, in case you orphan your child and widow your wife. Post your army by that wild fig-tree, where the wall is most vulnerable to a scaled assault, and where the city is exposed.... [The Greeks] have tried to get in there three times already. (Homer, *Iliad*, 6, 429ff.)

Andromache is, like Penelope, the caring, loving mother and wife. She had woven a cloak for Hector in the domestic seclusion and safety of the interior rooms of the house and she runs that welcoming bath for him just before he is due home, sadly all to no avail. She is, though, at the same time, a wise and perceptive woman who has obviously observed the military activity raging around her and feels confident enough to offer a strategy based on her informed observations in the male world of war. Indeed, the reason she is out on the walls in the first place was because she heard that the Trojans were on the defensive, and that victory was in the grasp of the Achaeans. Most civilian Trojans would surely have fled in the opposite direction, but not so steadfast, military-minded, 'white-armed' Andromache.[23]

In the end Andromache was appropriated by Neoptolemus as a slave and concubine, just as Hector had predicted (*Little Iliad* fr. 20). After Neoptolemus' death she married her brother-in-law Helenus.

Andromache shares with her mother-in-law Hecuba, who detains her son in the relative safety within the walls of Troy, the distinction of being able to understand and expatiate on war and its consequences. Hecuba helps Hector – the warrior and son – in his prosecution of the battle: she facilitates his prayers to Zeus and his libation, and she has him drink a restorative cup of wine, an energy drink, before returning to the fray.

More generally, Homer's women in the *Iliad* are clearly shown as appreciating the fact that their men are obliged to fight, not least because of the inviolable treaty invoked at the snatching of Helen. The women never demand an end to hostilities, unpalatable as those hostilities are. Helen herself is never criticized by the Trojan women because by criticizing her the Trojan women would be calling into question the validity of the war. The best they can do is encourage their warrior husbands to adopt a less dangerous approach to the conflict…and pray to Athena.

Three heroic mortal women who deserve mention here are Epipole, Messene and Aglauros; the first for her exploits in the Trojan War. Although not mentioned by Homer, Epipole was a daughter of Trachion of Carystus in Euboea. She so much wanted to fight with the Greeks against Troy that she bravely dressed up as a man and inveigled her way into the massed armies; a very early case of classical cross-dressing. Unfortunately, when Palamedes discovered her true sex, she was stoned to death by the Greek army.[24] It is, of course, impossible to know how many Greek or Roman women ever dressed up as men in order to fight in the lines. Unlikely as this is in any great numbers, we should nevertheless remember Hua Mulan in China, Joan of Arc, the conquistador Catalina Erauso in sixteenth-century Mexico and Deborah Sampson wounded in the American Civil War, and one of a thousand or so women who fought in that war dressed as men.

Messene was the daughter of Triopas, king of Argos; she was married to Polycaon, son of King Lelex of Laconia. Messene was a very ambitious woman. After her father-in-law died, her husband's brother Myles assumed the throne of Laconia, thus sidelining Polycaon; however, it was not in Messene's script to be married to a nonentity, so she set about raising an army from Argos and Laconia and invaded and occupied nearby territory. This territory was then named Messenia in her honour. The couple then went on to found the city of Andania, where they built their palace.[25]

Aglauros was a brave virgin girl who stepped up to the plate when Athens, her city, needed someone to bring a protracted war to a successful conclusion. An oracle had pronounced that Athens would win the war if a citizen committed suicide for the sake of the city. Aglauros jumped off a cliff to her death; her reward was everlasting fame and a temple on the Acropolis built in her honour. It then became the custom for young Athenians, when they donned their first suit of armour, to swear an oath that they would always defend their country to the last.[26]

Teichoskopeia: the view from the walls

The *teichoskopeia* or teichoscopy is an epic device in which observers on the city walls describe the battle scenes raging below them; since the people watching from the walls are non-combatants, they are usually women and elderly men. Apart from providing commentary on the action unfolding below, the teichoscopy can also give us an insight into the effects of battle on women or on a particular woman, especially in relation to combatants who may well be husband, brother, father or son, or someone else close to them.

Probably the most famous and certainly one of the earliest teichoscopies is Helen's as described in the *Iliad*.[27] Helen is busy at her loom when approached in her bedchamber by Iris, the personification and goddess of the rainbow and messenger of the gods, disguised as her sister-in-law Laodice, the daughter of Priam. Iris takes Helen to the city walls where Priam asks her to point out the Achaean heroes she sees on the Trojan plain where the Greek and Trojan armies are preparing for the duel between Menelaus and Paris, past and present husbands of Helen. Helen thus becomes a vital source of military intelligence for the Trojans. In a parade of heroes, she points out Agamemnon, Odysseus, Telamonian Ajax and Idomeneus; she praises both the Greek and the Trojan armies: an indication perhaps of the paradoxical situation in which she finds herself. She, a Greek woman, is now firmly ensconced in and informing on the Trojan camp. The stakes are high, not only because whoever wins the duel will win Helen, but more crucially, he will also ultimately win the war for either Greece or Troy. Helen watches Menelaus defeat Paris, and then witnesses Aphrodite saving Paris; divine interference which serves to extend the war and results in many more casualties. What she sees of the duel turns Helen against arriviste Paris: she wishes him dead, praises the might of Menelaus and challenges Paris to resume the duel, sure that he will be slain. Paris is unimpressed and can think only of bedding Helen, while Menelaus desperately tries to find Paris in order to finish him off.

Hesiod's *Shield of Heracles* features a teichoscopy on the shield and is notable not just for the striking image of women wailing and tearing their cheeks – which must have been fairly typical female behaviour on the walls – but also for the fact that such a scene was depicted there on the shield in the first place, indicating that, for women, watching proceedings from the walls was by no means unusual behaviour.[28]

Chapter Eleven

Hell for the Heroes: Coming home, Domestic Crises, Murder, Incest and Infanticide

Homer's *Iliad* tells us all about the final days of the ten-year-long Trojan War. The fragmentary poems in the Epic Cycle, some of the non-extant works in the Theban Cycle and a number of the extant Greek tragedies continue the story by revealing the terrible things that happened to the Trojan heroes and women captives and to the Greeks when they got home. Both men and women, as in the *Iliad*, played a leading, and tragic, role in a number of these sequels, none of which, by definition, ended well.

The Theban Cycle is a collection of four lost epics which related the mythical history of Thebes. They were probably written down between 750 and 500 BCE. The most famous stories in the Cycle were those of Oedipus and of the Seven Against Thebes, both of which were heavily drawn on by later writers of Greek tragedy.

The epics of the Theban Cycle were as follows:

The *Oedipodea*, attributed to Cinaethon: this gives us the story of Oedipus' solving of the Sphinx's riddle, and presumably of his incestuous marriage to Jocasta.

The *Thebaid* told the story of the war between Oedipus' two sons Eteocles and Polynices, and of Polynices' unsuccessful expedition against Thebes with six other commanders: the 'Seven Against Thebes', in which both Eteocles and Polynices were killed.

The *Epigoni*, attributed to either Antimachus of Teos or Homer: a continuation of the *Thebaid*, which told the story of the next generation of heroes who attacked Thebes, this time successfully.

The *Alcmeonis*, of unknown authorship, told the story of Alcmaeon's murder of his mother Eriphyle for having arranged the death of his father Amphiaraus as told in the *Thebaid* and in Statius' first-century CE *Thebaid*.

We can yield much of the aftermath of the Trojan War through the women involved and their fates, as played out in the surviving tragedies. For our purposes, the three tragedies which are of interest are *Hecuba*, *Trojan Women* and *Iphigenia in Aulis* by Euripides.

Euripides: *Hecuba*

The action of the play (first performed in 424 BCE) takes place about the same time as events described in Euripides' *Trojan Women*: that is, after the fall of Troy and before the women's dispersal to various parts of Greece as slaves. The chorus is made up of Trojan women already consigned to a life of endless servitude; Hecuba's double tragedy is the sacrifice of her daughter Polyxena on the altar of the ghost of Achilles, and the treacherous slaying of her son Polydorus by the Thracian king Polymestor. The chorus of women, Polyxena and Hecuba all pay the heaviest price for their gender in the aftermath of the war. They graphically describe the fate that awaits them, dumb with grief, husband dead and city sacked. Prayers to Artemis, goddess of virginity, are prayed but go unanswered. Polyxena faces her fate bravely, proudly asserting that she would rather die than live a life of servitude and serial rape. Her fall from her regal status is profound as she finds herself reduced to slavery: 'it is that name of slave, so ugly, so foreign, that makes me want to die.' Her alternative is a life of abject misery and drudgery as described in lines (351–66), reminiscent of the fate Hector foresees for Andromache:

> Or should I live to be knocked down to the highest bidder, sold to a master man for cash? Sister of Hector…doing the work of a skivvy, kneading the bread and washing the floors, forced to drag out endless weary days. Me, the bride of kings compelled by some gutter slave to share his fetid bed.

Hecuba dutifully attends to the funeral rites due to her daughter and vows revenge for the slaughter of Polydorus; she enlists the support of Agamemnon, taking full advantage of the fact that Agamemnon is obsessed with Cassandra, his concubine and her other daughter. Hecuba lures Polymestor into a tent where she claims her treasures are hidden: Hecuba and women from the chorus slay Polymestor's two sons and put his eyes out; blinded and furious, he casts about for the women who have committed this 'vile act'. Polymestor is humiliated at having been blinded and made childless at the hands of slave women. However, justice is deemed to have been done but Polymestor, still raging, prophesies the deaths of Hecuba by drowning and of Agamemnon at the hands of his wife Clytemnestra. The Greeks set sail with the distressed women of the Chorus to their new lives as slaves.

Andromache may, on the face of it, seem comparatively fortunate given that she was handed over to be the wife of Achilles' son Neoptolemus. Not a bit of it: she too laments the loathsome fate that awaits her: 'A bed which from the word go I never wanted and now reject for good. God knows that that was a bed I never crept into willingly.' (Euripides, *Andromache* 36–38.)

Euripides: *Iphigenia in Aulis*

Iphigenia, eldest daughter of Agamemnon, is pivotal, like Helen, to the Trojan War. She is an essential pawn in the spat between Artemis and Agamemnon; he eventually decides to sacrifice his daughter on the altar of appeasement to the goddess and to sanction the sailing of his troops to Troy to do battle, thus preserving their honour and satisfying their lust for battle. Mysteriously becalmed at Aulis, the Greek troops become restless and hover on the brink of revolt: thus threatened, Agamemnon makes the invidious and terrible decision to sacrifice Iphigenia. He sends a deceptive message to his wife Clytemnestra, telling her to send Iphigenia to Aulis because she is to marry Achilles. Agamemnon vacillates to such an extent that he has a change of heart and sends a second message to his wife, cancelling the first. This second missive is intercepted by Menelaus, Agamemnon's brother, who is furious over the change of plan because the whole objective of the Trojan War was to regain Helen, his runaway wife. Menelaus eventually comes round, only to have Agamemnon change his mind yet again and prepare for the sacrifice of his daughter, anxious lest the army storms his palace at Argos and massacres all his family. Clytemnestra is by now on her way to Aulis with Iphigenia.

Iphigenia, Clytemnestra and Achilles soon discover Agamemnon's duplicity; Achilles is incandescent and vows to defend Iphigenia. His attempts to rally the Greeks, however, only result in the discovery that 'the whole of Greece' – including his own Myrmidon forces – demand that the fleet sails for Troy to do battle; Achilles narrowly escapes a stoning. Clytemnestra and Iphigenia fail to persuade Agamemnon to change his mind; Iphigenia implores Achilles not to waste his life over what she sees as a lost cause and bravely and heroically agrees to her sacrifice. She proclaims that she would rather die a hero, celebrated as the saviour of Greece, than be dragged kicking and screaming to the altar. She goes nobly to her death, leaving her mother Clytemnestra utterly distraught and presaging her murder of Agamemnon and Orestes' matricide.

Like Helen, Iphigenia has a leading role to play in the prosecution of the Trojan War. It is her life that is sacrificed to secure the war; without her death there would have been no conflict with Troy.

Euripides: *The Trojan Women*

Women also suffer horribly in *The Trojan Women*, first produced in 415 BCE; the play is a tragic commentary on the capture of the Aegean island of Melos and the subsequent slaughter and subjugation of its inhabitants by the Athenians. The play opens with Athena and Poseidon discussing ways to appropriately punish the Greek armies for condoning the rape by Ajax the Lesser of Cassandra, the eldest daughter of King Priam and Queen Hecuba, after he had sacrilegiously dragged her from a statue of Athena. Euripides shows how much the now destitute Trojan women suffer: more grief is piled on when the Greeks share out the women between them. The deposed queen Hecuba learns that she will be appropriated by Odysseus, while Cassandra is acquired by Agamemnon. Cassandra, though, had seen all this coming: she knows how Clytemnestra will slay both her and Agamemnon. Sadly, no one ever believes or listens to Cassandra when she offers sound counsel: 'Would ye be wise, ye Cities, fly from war! Yet if war come, there is a crown in death For her that striveth well and perisheth Unstained: to die in evil were the stain!'

Cassandra has already bewailed the lot of the Greek wives, denied the privilege of burying their dead husbands, languishing in widowhood while their men lie rotting in a foreign field.

Things get much worse when Andromache, widow of Hector, tells Hecuba that her youngest daughter Polyxena has been killed as a sacrifice at the tomb of Achilles. Not only is Andromache destined to be the concubine of Achilles' son Neoptolemus, but she is informed that her baby son Astyanax has been condemned to die because the Greeks are afraid lest the boy grows up to avenge his father Hector. The plan is to hurl Astyanax from the battlements of Troy to his death.

Helen of Troy does not escape the misery: cuckolded Menelaus arrives to take her back to Greece to face a death sentence. Helen begs for mercy and tries to seduce her husband into sparing her life but Menelaus is adamant, for now: he later relents and takes her back. The shattered body of little Astyanax is carried in on Hector's shield: Andromache naturally wished to bury her child herself with the proper rituals, but too late: her ship had already set sail. It is Hecuba who prepares the body of her grandson for burial before she is taken off in Odysseus' baggage train.

The play graphically highlights the fate of these women after a devastating ten-year-long war and the impact that war has on their later lives. They, along with countless others, are bereaved, homeless, deprived of their dignity and freedom and displaced; they are left with nothing apart from the prospect of lifelong slavery and the rape that comes with it. Hecuba, for whom Troy had been her lifelong home, has just seen Troy go up in flames, she has witnessed the deaths of her husband, children and grandchildren; the former queen and everything she ever had that was left was now the property of Odysseus. More generally, it reminds us that the horrors of war 3,000 years ago are of course just as bad today and women's suffering as victims is just as terrible. What Euripides showed has an eerie resemblance to the scenes we see daily of refugee camps and urban destruction in and around Syria and the Yemen. Euripides warns us that the more jubilant triumphant war is, the more wretched and miserable is the fallout for vanquished and victors like: beware the victors.

The women in the chorus sum up their desperate plight: these women can only foresee a life of dreaded nightly rape. They echo the words of

Polyxena in the *Hecuba*: 'Shall I be a skivvy, or forced into the bed of Greek masters? Night is a queen, but I curse her!' (202–204). Such profound thoughts and words must have been repeated by women victims of war through the ages down to this very day.

Chapter Twelve

Batrachomyomachia: of Mice and Frogs

The Batrachomyomachia translates as the battle between the mice and the frogs. It is a parody of the *Iliad*, of uncertain date but attributed to Homer by the Romans. Plutarch, though, thought differently and credited it to Pigres of Halicarnassus, the brother (or son) of Artemisia, Queen of Caria and ally of Xerxes.[1] The consensus now, however, is that it is by an anonymous poet of the time of Alexander the Great. The author prologues it as follows: 'That awful strife, that clamorous deed of war, and tell how the Mice proved their valour on the Frogs and rivalled the exploits of the Giants, those earth-born men, as the tale was told among mortals. Thus did the war begin.'[2] Here is the plot:

Psycharpax (Crumb snatcher, son of Bread nibbler and Quern licker), a thirsty mouse, is minding his own business drinking water from a lake; he has just escaped the clutches of a dangerous ferret when the Frog King, Physignathus (Puff Jaw) son of Mud-Man, approaches and invites him back to his house, giving him a lift on his back. The Frog King swims across the lake with the anxious Mouse clinging on his back when they come up against a terrifying water snake. The Frog panics and dives, completely forgetting about the Mouse; the Mouse drowns but not before he curses the cowardly Frog with a promise of retribution. Another Mouse (Lick platter), however, sees all of this from the bank and darts off to tell Bread Nibbler about it. The Mice arm themselves for battle with help from Ares to avenge the Frog King's treachery, and send a herald to the Frogs with a declaration of war. The Frogs blame their King, who denies any culpability. In the meantime, Zeus, seeing a war in the offing, proposes that the gods take sides, and specifically that Athena help the Mice. Athena refuses, saying that Mice have done her a lot of mischief in the past – spoiling her garlands and lamps to get to the oil and keeping her awake with their refrain after she's done a hard day's battling. Eventually the gods decide to remain spectators rather than get embroiled. A battle ensues heralded by gnats which the Mice win. Zeus calls up a force of paw-nipping crabs to prevent the annihilation of the Frogs. Powerless against the sideways-walking nut-cracker-jawed crustaceans, the Mice retreat, and the one-day war ends at sundown.

The *Batrachomyomachia* was one of a number of poems usually collected in what we call the Epic Cycle. Their themes extend from the formation of the world to the end of the Heroic Age. They were composed by a number of authors in the seventh and sixth centuries. Other works, all fragmentary, including a war theme or elements thereof, are as follows:

The *War of the Titans*: 'The Epic Cycle begins with the fabled union of Heaven and Earth, by which they make three hundred-handed sons and three Cyclopes to be born to him.'

The *Story of Oedipus*: '*The Story of Oedipus* by Cinaethon in six thousand six hundred verses.'

The *Thebaid*: 'Homer travelled about reciting his epics, first the *Thebaid*, in seven thousand verses.'

The *Epigoni*: 'Next (Homer composed) the *Epigoni* in seven thousand verses.'

The *Cypria*: 'This is continued by the epic called *Cypria* which is current in eleven books. Its contents are as follows. Zeus plans with Themis to bring about the Trojan War. Strife arrives while the gods are feasting at the marriage of Peleus and starts a dispute between Hera, Athena, and Aphrodite as to which of them is fairest. The three are led by Hermes at the command of Zeus to Alexandrus on Mount Ida for his decision, and Alexandrus, lured by his promised marriage with Helen, decides in favour of Aphrodite.'

The *Aethiopis*: 'The *Cypria*, described in the preceding book, has its sequel in the *Iliad* of Homer, which is followed in turn by the five books of the *Aethiopis*, the work of Arctinus of Miletus. Their contents are as follows. The Amazon Penthesilea, the daughter of Ares and of Thracian race, comes to aid the Trojans, and after showing great prowess, is killed by Achilles and buried by the Trojans. Achilles then slays Thersites for abusing and reviling him for his supposed love for Penthesilea. As a result a dispute arises amongst the Achaeans over the killing of Thersites, and Achilles sails to Lesbos and after sacrificing to Apollo, Artemis, and Leto, is purified by Odysseus from bloodshed.

Then Memnon, the son of Eos, wearing armour made by Hephaestus, comes to help the Trojans, and Thetis tells her son about Memnon. A battle takes place in which Antilochus is slain by Memnon and Memnon by Achilles. Eos then obtains of Zeus and bestows upon her son immortality; but Achilles routs the Trojans, and, rushing into the city with them, is killed by Paris and Apollo. A great struggle for the body then follows, Aias taking up the body and carrying it to the ships, while Odysseus drives off the Trojans behind. The Achaeans then bury Antilochus and lay out the body of Achilles, while Thetis, arriving with the Muses and her sisters, bewails her son, whom she afterwards catches away from the pyre and transports to the White Island. After this, the Achaeans pile him a cairn and hold games in his honour. Lastly a dispute arises between Odysseus and Aias over the arms of Achilles.'

The *Little Iliad*: Next comes the *Little Iliad* in four books by Lesches of Mitylene; its contents are as follows: 'The adjudging of the arms of Achilles takes place, and Odysseus, by the contriving of Athena, gains them. Aias then becomes mad and destroys the herd of the Achaeans and kills himself. Next Odysseus lies in wait and catches Helenus, who prophesies as to the taking of Troy, and Diomedes accordingly brings Philoctetes from Lemnos. Philoctetes is healed by Machaon, fights in single combat with Alexandrus and kills him: the dead body is outraged by Menelaus, but the Trojans recover and bury it. After this Deiphobus marries Helen, Odysseus brings Neoptolemus from Scyros and gives him his father's arms, and the ghost of Achilles appears to him.

'Eurypylus the son of Telephus arrives to aid the Trojans, shows his prowess and is killed by Neoptolemus. The Trojans are now closely besieged, and Epeius, by Athena's instruction, builds the wooden horse. Odysseus disfigures himself and goes in to Ilium as a spy, and there being recognized by Helen, plots with her for the taking of the city; after killing certain of the Trojans, he returns to the ships. Next he carries the Palladium out of Troy with the help of Diomedes. Then after putting their best men in the wooden horse and burning their huts, the main body of the Hellenes sail to Tenedos. The Trojans, supposing their troubles over, destroy a part of their city wall and take the wooden horse into their city and feast as though they had conquered the Hellenes.'

The *Sack of Ilium*: Next come two books of the *Sack of Ilium* by Arctinus of Miletus, with the following contents: 'The Trojans were suspicious of the wooden horse and standing round it debated what they ought to do. Some thought they ought to hurl it down from the rocks, others to burn it up, while others said they ought to dedicate it to Athena. At last this third opinion prevailed. Then they turned to mirth and feasting, believing the war was at an end. But at this very time two serpents appeared and destroyed Laocöon and one of his two sons, a portent which so alarmed the followers of Aeneas that they withdrew to Ida. Sinon then raised the fire-signal to the Achaeans, having previously got into the city by pretence. The Greeks then sailed in from Tenedos, and those in the wooden horse came out and fell upon their enemies, killing many and storming the city. Neoptolemus kills Priam who had fled to the altar of Zeus Herceius; Menelaus finds Helen and takes her to the ships, after killing Deiphobus; and Aias the son of Ileus, while trying to drag Cassandra away by force, tears away with her the image of Athena. At this the Greeks are so enraged that they determine to stone Aias, who only escapes from the danger threatening him by taking refuge at the altar of Athena. The Greeks, after burning the city, sacrifice Polyxena at the tomb of Achilles: Odysseus murders Astyanax; Neoptolemus takes Andromache as his prize, and the remaining spoils are divided. Demophon and Acamas find Aethra and take her with them. Lastly the Greeks sail away and Athena plans to destroy them on the high seas.'

The *Telegony*

The *Telegony* comprises two distinct episodes: Odysseus' voyage to Thesprotia, and the story of Telegonus. The poem opens after the events described in the *Odyssey*. According to Proclus' summary, the *Telegony* opens with the burial of Penelope's suitors. Odysseus sacrifices to the Nymphs. He makes a voyage to Elis, where he visits an otherwise unknown figure Polyxenos, who gives him a bowl depicting the story of Trophonius. Odysseus returns to Ithaca and then travels to Thesprotia, presumably to make the sacrifices commanded by Tiresias in *Odyssey* 11. There he weds the Thesprotian queen Kallidike, who bears him a son, Polypoites. Odysseus fights for the Thesprotians in a war against the neighbouring Brygoi; the gods participate in the war, Ares routing Odysseus and the Thesprotians, countered by Athena, ever Odysseus' patron; Apollo intervenes between the battling gods. However, Kallidike is killed in the war, Polypoetes succeeds to the kingdom and Odysseus returns to Ithaca.

Meanwhile, it transpires that Circe, with whom Odysseus had a year-long affair in the *Odyssey* (Books 10–12), has given birth to his son Telegonus. He grows up with Circe on the island of Aeaea. On Athena's advice, Circe tells him the name of his father. In a detail inserted into the account in the Epitome of Apollodorus' *Library* she gives him a supernatural spear to defend himself which is tipped with the venom of a poisonous stingray and was made by the god Hephaestus. A storm forces Telegonus onto Ithaca without him realizing where he is and unwittingly begins stealing Odysseus' cattle. Odysseus arrives on the scene: during the ensuing fight, Telegonus kills Odysseus with his toxic spear, thereby partially fulfilling Tiresias' prophecy in *Odyssey* 11 that death would come to Odysseus 'out of the sea' (the poison of the ray). However, in another respect, Odysseus' death here contradicts the prophecy of Tiresias, who predicted (*Odyssey* 11, 135) that a 'gentle death' would come to Odysseus 'in sleek old age'. As Odysseus lies dying, he and Telegonus recognize one another and Telegonus laments his grave mistake. Telegonus brings his father's corpse, Penelope and Odysseus' other son Telemachus back to Aeaea, where Odysseus is buried and Circe makes the others immortal. Telegonus marries Penelope, and Telemachus marries Circe.

Chapter Thirteen

Epilogue: Perpetuating Greek Myth in the Modern World

G reek mythology has, by virtue of its inherent qualities of excitement, adventure, fantasy, horror, universality and symbolism endured for more than 2,500 years. It continues to enthral, entertain, educate and evolve. It is vital that fresh and new ways and means are found to present Greek myths to successive generations in order to ensure their survival, especially in the digital age when there are more claims than ever on time in education and in leisure. We should allow it to be tested and invigorated with original and exciting new experimentation; we should make it push back the boundaries to discover new ways in which it is relevant, instructive and inspirational. Just as society and culture evolve constantly, so must our treatment of Greek myth.

Recently Leeds-born poet, translator and playwright Tony Harrison (b.1937), who studied Classics at Leeds University, demonstrated the universality and potential diversity of classical myth when he produced acclaimed translations of Aeschylus' *Oresteia* and Aristophanes' *Lysistrata*. Harrison's masked *Oresteia*, performed in a marathon session in 1981 at the National Theatre, has been called 'an epoch-making event', made all the more mesmerising by the directorship of Peter Hall. Tony Harrison's excellent translations inflected by Old English and his intertwined modern themes, also developed in his later *Medea*, *Trojan Women* and *Trackers of Oxyrhychus* (1988), have been described as an 'artistic reaction to the fall of the British working class at the end of the twentieth century ... the most important adaptation of classical myth for a radical political purpose for years', and Harrison's 'most brilliant artwork ... are all worthy of deep study'. Neither did *Herakles-Phrynicus* (1995), *Prometheus* (1998) in his film-poem or Iraq War in *Hecuba* (2005) escape the magical, unnerving Harrison touch. This body of work has been called 'the most striking and consistent engagement of classical themes and texts in contemporary poetry in the UK'.

The Trackers of Oxyrhynchus is based in part on the *Ichneutae*, a satyr play by Sophocles, which was found in fragments at the Egyptian city of Oxyrhynchus. Other works by Harrison include *The Gaze of the Gorgon*: a poem-film for television (1992) in which he examines the politics of conflict in the twentieth century using the Gorgon as a metaphor; and *The Labourers of Herakles* [*sic*] (1995) based on extant fragments of tragedies by Phrynichos, one of the earliest tragedians. Harrison's play tackles genocide and ethnic cleansing in the modern world head-on and uses Herakles' filicide as a metaphor for the odious horrors of war and man's inhumanity to man. Harrison portrays Herakles' 'furore' as 'racist rage' and the murder of his own children as 'part and parcel of genocide' and ethnic cleansing. Harrison also highlights Herakles' struggle with his own 'destructive impulses which led him to the unspeakable murder of his own children'.

Near the end of the play Labourer 1 gets stuck in cement and asks for his shirt to keep warm in the cold concrete. As soon as he gets his shirt he starts screaming as if his shirt just became the Shirt of Nessus, the poisoned shirt which killed Heracles. Harrison describes the scene as 'the shirt of modern Europe's agony.' Labourers 2 and 3 in unison then describe the shirt as having been made by the victims of the atrocities of the Bosnian War, describing the victims of the ethnic cleansing: 'Muslims that are mouldering in mass-execution trenches.... The fingers of the raped girl who wove herself a noose.... Sarajevo children his shells made amputees.... The mother of the mortared mosque's dismembered muezzin, assisted by the convoys of the cleansed of Knin.'

Tales from Ovid by Ted Hughes (1930–98) was published in 1997 and is a vivid retelling of twenty-four of Ovid's *Metamorphoses*. Its fame and universal mythic appeal led to a stage adaptation performed by the Royal Shakespeare Company in 1999 at Stratford-upon-Avon. In 2009, Fiona Shaw performed *Echo and Narcissus* as a prologue to Henry Purcell's *Dido and Aeneas*.

Professor James Shapiro, writing in the *New York Times* (14 December 1997) 'Sex and Violence in Latin Hexameter', said of the book:

In transforming Ovid, Hughes follows a well-traveled path. Even as Ovid himself pillaged Greek and Roman mythologies in composing his *Metamorphoses*, Chaucer, Milton, Dryden and especially Shakespeare (in whom, one contemporary noted, the sweet witty soul of Ovid lives) ransacked Ovid's stories to furnish their own artistic worlds. Hughes makes clear his admiration for the gift that Shakespeare shares with Ovid: insight into what a passion feels like to one possessed by it. Not just ordinary passion either, but human passion in extremis – passion where it combusts, or levitates, or mutates into an experience of the supernatural.

These works by Harrison and Hughes eloquently demonstrate the enduring relevance of Greek myth for today's world with all its supposedly modern problems and prove conclusively that, in the right hands, Greek myths can still be inspirational, important and engaging, sending out a compelling message, and maybe some solutions, to audiences some 3,000 years after they were first conceived.

Richard F. Thomas is the George Martin Lane Professor of the Classics at Harvard University. He has served as director of the American Philological Association and as trustee and director of the Vergilian Society of America, of which he has been president. Since 2001, he has been a trustee of the Loeb Classical Library, and has been editor of *Harvard Studies in Classical Philology*. He has written extensively on Dylan and his relationship with the classics, and details the debt Dylan owes to Ovid and Homer in his *Why Dylan Matters* (2017).

An article in 6 December's *Times Literary Supplement* by Richard F. Thomas tells us how 'on October 13, 2016, Sara Danius, Permanent Secretary of the Nobel Committee of the Swedish Academy, announced: "The Nobel Prize in Literature for 2016 is awarded to Bob Dylan for having created new poetic expressions within the great American song tradition." Speaking on behalf of the Committee, Danius invoked the poets of ancient Greece:

If you look back, far back, 2,500 years or so…you discover Homer and Sappho, and they wrote poetic texts that were meant to be listened to, they were meant to be performed, often together with instruments, and it's the same way with Bob Dylan. But we still read Homer and Sappho…and we enjoy it, and same thing with Bob Dylan. He can be read, and should be read.

That lecture, now published as a slim elegant book, is Dylan's account of where his art came from. The bulk of it focuses on three books out of many, read back in 'grammar school', from which Dylan acquired 'principles and sensibilities and an informed view of the world'. He names Herman Melville's *Moby-Dick* (1851), Erich Maria Remarque's *All Quiet on the Western Front* (1929) and Homer's *Odyssey*. Here we find Dylan's acknowledgement for the first time of what his fans have realized since 2012, when they Googled Dylan's new lyrics and got fragments of Robert Fagles' 1996 translation of the Homeric poem. The first paragraph, below, taken from the Nobel Lecture, is about Odysseus:

> He's always being warned of things to come. Touching things he's told not to. There's two roads to take, and they're both bad. Both hazardous. On one you could drown and on the other you could starve. He goes into the narrow straits with foaming whirlpools that swallow him. Meets six-headed monsters with sharp fangs. Thunderbolts strike at him. Overhanging branches that he makes a leap to reach for to save himself from a raging river. Goddesses and gods protect him, but some others want to kill him. He changes identities. He's exhausted. He falls asleep, and he's woken up by the sound of laughter. He tells his story to strangers. He's been gone twenty years. He was carried off somewhere and left there. Drugs have been dropped into his wine. It's been a hard road to travel.

For the full fascinating article see https://www.the-tls.co.uk/articles/public/metamorphosis-bob-dylan-ovid-homer

The following year Colm Tóibín published his highly-acclaimed *House of Names* which, according to his website, is 'a retelling of the story of Clytemnestra and her children…a powerful retelling of a classic Greek tragedy, a breathtaking story of a family at war with itself.' Tóibín is currently Irene and Sidney B. Silverman Professor of the Humanities at Columbia University and succeeded Martin Amis as Professor of

Creative Writing at the University of Manchester. More importantly, though, he has (re-)introduced Greek myth to his thousands of readers, and more still.

In 2018 Stephen Fry published two books: *Mythos: The Greek Myths Retold* and *Heroes: Mortals and Monsters, Quests and Adventures* which immediately became bestsellers. Some academics may sneer at this in a superior sort of way (just as some do at classics books written by non-academics), but surely the point is that Jackson, Dylan, Tóibín and Fry (as Melville, O'Neill, Joyce, Miller, Eliot, Harrison and Hughes before them) are doing the classics and classical mythology a huge service by massively opening up the audience for these wonderful stories to new generations of readers, including digital readers.

Recent years have seen an encouraging and much-needed upsurge in books narrating aspects of Greek mythology exclusively from a woman's point of view; in effect, re-writes of the familiar male-orientated stories from a uniquely female perspective. Those that spring immediately to mind include Natalie Haynes, *A Thousand Ships* (2019) in which she 'gives much-needed voice to the silenced women of the Trojan War', and *The Children of Jocasta* (2017); Madeline Miller, *The Song of Achilles* (2011) and *Circe* (2018); Pat Barker, *The Silence of the Girls* (2018) – the Achilles-Agamemnon spat from the perspectives of Briseis and Chryseis – and Margaret Atwood, *The Penelopiad: The Myth of Penelope and Odysseus* (2015). The point here is that while women and girls have always read the Greek myths, many more will be introduced to them as devotees of these inspirational authors. Women and men alike will be drawn to these books because of the fresh perspective they each take: after 2,000 years we have credible and feasible interpretations of the female side of things as pawns and victims in a traditionally man's game.

It is interesting to note just how much the issues raised by some of the Greek tragedies resonate even today. In her perceptive article regarding Euripides in the modern world, Lucy Jackson [https://www.kcl.ac.uk/people/lucy-jackson] points out that between the years 2000 and 2013 there have been 447 productions of classical plays staged by schools and amateur and professional companies in England. Every year in the last century saw a decade-on-decade increase in the productions of classical drama. Given the prominence of women and particularly of women in war in these Greek and Roman plays, it is reasonable to assume that the issues the Greeks and Romans faced and tried to resolve on their stage still have relevance and resonance today. There are obvious similarities between Euripides asking why go to war in *Iphigenia in Aulis* and the British parliament's debate over going to war against Iraq in 2003; both were agonizing over the same question. Just as interesting is the fact that the Greek tragedians, unlike the Greek historians, tackle the question of women as victims of war. The consequences of defeat for the Trojans are played out and agonized over time and time again: displacement, destitution, enslavement, homeland and household destruction, humiliation, ostracization and rape are constant and common themes throughout the plays discussed here.

Greek myths have valuable uses in today's world outside the purely literary and cultural. Since 2008, Professor Susan Deacy at Roehampton University (in collaboration with the ERC-funded project 'Our Mythical Childhood' (2016–21) based in Warsaw) has been working on a project to create resources for and 'trace the role of classics in children's and Young Adult culture', specifically exploring 'where classical myth might sit in autistic children's culture by producing three sets of activities'. Professor Deacy consulted dramatherapists and special needs teachers who confirmed that 'autistic children often engage with learning about classical myth'.

Professor Deacy takes up the story:

I completed the first set of activities in February 2018. This is based on a specific episode in the myth of Hercules: the point where he is tasked to choose between two contrasting paths in life. I opted for Hercules as a figure with what I consider to be particular appeal to autistic children. These reasons include the potential for Hercules – as the hero who repeatedly experiences hardships and who is ever needing to learn all over again how to respond to what life throws at him – to 'speak' to some of the challenges that autistic children encounter. More specifically, the activities concern Hercules when, on reaching a strange place, he is tasked with making a choice between what is on one side of the landscape and what's on the other side.

She continues:

> I designed the activities as a means to help autistic children deal,
> through an immersion in the experiences of a mythological figure,
> with some of the challenges they might encounter, including how
> to read body language or facial expressions, how to understand how
> the present can turn into the future, and how to deal with changes
> in routine. As well as seeking to respond to the challenges autistic
> children face, I was working on the premise that there is potential,
> via classical myth, to empower them and to draw on their strengths.

Professor Deacy was naturally keen to involve specialists in autism
and child development, or others who work with autistic children,
and, of course, autistic children. For the former she was able to call on
the pioneering autism specialist Rita Jordan, and Nicola Grove whose
adaptations of myths and other stories had long inspired her.

She goes on to explain just why Hercules in particular was of
significance and value in the therapy of autistic children:

> Why Hercules? Perhaps the most searching question that came up
> – indeed it's a question that goes to the heart of the project – is why
> I had opted for Hercules as a focal point. Would other sets of stories
> do just as well, the participants asked, for example Winnie the Pooh?
> I set out how I think Hercules bears on the resources. I described
> Hercules as one who is at home in the wilds – his own space – where
> he is capable of things that others cannot manage. He needs to learn
> the rules of each new scenario he experiences. Each time, he needs
> to find a new way to deal with a fresh situation. In the wilds, he
> invariably manages to overcome obstacles. Then, when he gets to
> civilization, something goes wrong, often terribly wrong. One of
> the participants from PARC [the Participatory Autism Research
> Collective] commented, 'that sounds like being autistic'. He said that
> what always interested him was fantasy, and Westerns, particularly
> outsiders and outlaws. He liked how Hercules could count both as
> a hero – the greatest of heroes no less – and as an outsider. The
> discussion turned to how Hercules is appealing because he performs

feats that others are unable to, which can also be the case for some autistic people. Hercules also experiences emotional overload and distress, and episodes from his myth might be a useful narrative in relation to acute perception.

The next stage was running a pilot study at a London primary school's autism base and involving members of the Early Childhood Studies Research Group at Roehampton. Susan Deacy's work and collaborations over the years have allowed her to hone her goals and objectives in this invaluable ongoing work. They are as follows:

- To present a series of activities for autistic children which fit current thinking around supporting autistic children which includes the exploration of individual interests and passions, one of which can be myth
- To show how classical myth can facilitate communication and engagement for autistic children, including by utilizing the potential for conceiving characters of myth as 'gateways' to understanding, identifying, contextualizing and conceptualizing oneself and others
- To empower autistic children by drawing on their strengths as well as addressing some of the sources of distress they may encounter, such as the sense that their actions are always beyond their control. Linked with this, the activities seek to offer an alternative model for articulating experience and for making sense of the world
- To utilize the potential appeal of Hercules for autistic children, including as a character who performs feats that others cannot and yet who experiences emotional overload and distress
- To demonstrate relevant aspects of the 'Choice of Hercules' myth, including reasons for choices and what choices mean in given contexts; the concept of causality, namely of assessing the consequences of such decisions in light of the past and future of the 'Choice' narrative.

Without successive generations enjoying and perpetuating the myths in all sorts of ways, the myths will surely die; so it matters little how this perpetuation is achieved, **so long as it is achieved on an ongoing, persistent basis**.

Appendix

War Deities in Greek Mythology

Alala: spirit of the war cry.

Alke: spirit of courage and battle strength.

Amphillogiai: goddesses of disputes.

Androktasiai: spirits of battlefield slaughter.

Ares: the main Greek god of war, despised by all the city-states except Sparta.

Athena: goddess of wisdom, war strategy and weaving, more beloved by ancient Greeks than Ares and tutelary deity of Athens, Sparta's rival.

Bia: spirit of force and compulsion.

Deimos: personification of terror.

Enyalius: god of war; in early periods apparently an epithet of Ares, they were differentiated later.

Enyo: goddess of war, sometimes appears to be identical to Eris.

Eris: goddess of discord and strife.

Hera: in the *Iliad* she has a martial character and fights (and wins) against Artemis; however, this warlike aspect of her appears nowhere else in the surviving corpus, suggesting it was dropped early on.

Homados: spirit of the din of battle.

Hysminai: female spirits of fighting and combat.

Ioke: spirit of onslaught, battle tumult and pursuit.

Keres: female spirits of violent or cruel death, including death in battle, by accident, murder or ravaging disease.

Kratos: personification of strength and power.

Kydoimos: spirit of the din of battle.

Makhai: male spirits of fighting and combat.

Nike: spirit of victory.

Palioxis: spirit of backrush, flight and retreat from battle.

Pallas: Titan god of war-craft and of the springtime campaign season.

Perses: the Titan of destruction.

Phobos: spirit of panic, fear, flight and battlefield rout.

Phonoi: spirits of murder, killing and slaughter.

Polemos: spirit of war.

Proioxis: spirit of onrush and battlefield pursuit.

Styx: goddess of the river Styx and a Naiad who was the first to aid Zeus
    in the Titan War.

Notes

Chapter One:
1. Honko, Lauri (1984), 'The Problem of Defining Myth', in Dundes, *Sacred Narrative: Readings in the Theory of Myth*, p.49. Dundes (1984), p.1.
2. Lincoln, Bruce (2006), 'An Early Moment in the Discourse of "Terrorism": Reflections on a Tale from Marco Polo'. *Comparative Studies in Society and History*, 48 (2): 242–259.
3. Kirk, G.S. (1974), *The Nature of Greek Myths*, pp.28–9. Kirk, G.S. (1984), 'On Defining Myths' in *Sacred Narrative: Readings in the Theory of Myth*, pp.53–61.
4. Kirk, G.S. (1984), 'On Defining Myths' in *Sacred Narrative: Readings in the Theory of Myth*, p.55.
5. Hawes, G., *Rationalizing Myth in Antiquity*, p.3.
6. Dowden (1992), p.161.
7. Wiles, David (2000), *'Myth', Greek Theatre Performance: An Introduction*, pp.5–6, 12.
8. Myth, n., 'mythos, n.', OED Online, Oxford University Press, July 2018. Accessed 12 March 2019.
9. Lydgate, John, *Troy Book*, Vol. II, ll, 2487 (in Middle English). Reprinted in Henry Bergen's *Lydgate's Troy Book*, Vol. I, p.216 (London), 1906. Accessed 3 March 2019.
10. Wiles, op. cit.
11. Morales, p.115.
12. Lincoln (1999), op. cit., pp.3–5.
13. Hanson-Heath, *Who Killed Homer?*, p.37.

Chapter Two:
1. Garlan, *War in the Ancient World*, p.17. Finley, *Ancient History*, p.67. Thucydides 1, 15, 3–5.
2. See Jameson, *Sacrifice Before Battle*.
3. Homer, *Iliad*, 4, 436f and 13, 299f; Hesiod's *Shield of Heracles* 191, 460; Quintus Smyrnaeus, *Fall of Troy*, 10, 51.
4. Hesiod, *Theogeny*, 934.
5. Apollodorus 2, 5, 11; 2, 7, 7. Pausanias, *Description of Greece*, 3, 19, 7–8.
6. *Iliad* 5, 798–891, 895–898.
7. Homer, *Odyssey*, 8, 361; for Ares/Mars and Thrace, see Ovid, *Ars Amatoria*, 2, 11, 585 which tells the same tale: 'Their captive bodies are, with difficulty, freed, at your plea, Neptune: Venus runs to Paphos: Mars heads for Thrace.' For Ares/Mars and Thrace, see also Statius, *Thebaid* 7, 42; Herodotus, 4, 59, 62.

8. Athens, NM 3851.

9. *Iliad* 889.

10. Ibid., 5, 830–834; 11, .410–414.

11. Ibid., 5, 711–769; 780–834; 855–864.

12. Ibid., 15, 110–128; 20, 20–29; 21, 391–408.

13. Ibid., 5, 385–391.

14. Nonnus, *Dionysiaca* 18, 274ff.

15. Quintus Smyrnaeus, 8, 424.

16. Eustathius on Homer, 944.

17. Pausanias, *Description of Greece* 4, 30, 5.

18. Homer, *Iliad* 5, 333, 592.

19. Nonnus, *Dionysiaca* 2, 358 and 2, 475ff.

20. Hesiod, *Theogony* 273.

21. Aeschylus, *Prometheus Bound* 788ff (trans. Weir Smyth).

22. Pausanias 1, 8, 5.

23. Pindar, *Dithyrambs*, Frag. 78.

24. Hesiod, *Theogony* 386–7; 389–94.

25. Quintus Smyrnaeus, *Fall of Troy* 5, 25ff.

26. *Shield of Heracles*, 248–57.

27. See Egeler, *Death, Wings and Divine Devouring*, pp.5–26.

28. Hesiod, *Theogony*, 226ff.

29. *Shield of Heracles*, 139ff.

Chapter Three:

1. Hesiod, *Theogeny* 176ff; 139–46; 501–506.

2. Theocritus, 11.

3. Callimachus, *Hymn to Artemis* 3, 46f. See also Virgil *Georgics* 4, 173 and *Aeneid* 8, 416ff.

4. Euripides, *Oresteia* 965.

Chapter Four:

1. Hesiod, *Theogony* 185. Hyginus, *Fabulae*, Praefatio gives Tartarus as the father of the Giants. Note also the birth of Aphrodite from the similarly fertilized sea.

2. Ovid, *Metamorphoses* 1.151–162. See also Horace, *Odes* 3.4.42ff and Servius ad *Aeneid* 8, 698, *Georgics* 166, 278; Hyginus (*Praef. Fab.* p.l). Plato had linked the Aloadae with the Giants, *Symposium* 190b–c.

3. Homer, *Odyssey* 7.56–63. Alcaeus and Acusilaus make the Phaiakians, like the Giants, offspring of the castration of Uranus. Homer, *Odyssey* 7.199–207. Homer, *Odyssey* 10.119–120. Pausanias, 8.29.1–4. Smith, William, 'Gigantes' and Hanfmann 1992, *The Oxford Classical Dictionary* s.v. 'Giants', following Pausanias, both assert that, for Homer, the Giants were a 'savage race of men'. For the mythographer Diodorus Siculus, the Giants were also a race of men; see 4.21.5.

4. Bacchylides, 15.63, *Brills New Pauly*; Crusius, p.93; *Batrachomyomachia* 7 (pp.542–543); Sophocles, *Women of Trachis* 1058; Euripides, *The Phoenician*

Women 1131; Lycophron, *Alexandra* 127 (pp.504–505), 1408 (pp.610–611). Hyginus, *Fabulae*, Preface.

5. Homer, *Odyssey* 7, 58–60.
6. Hesiod, *Theogeny* 50, 185.
7. Pindar, *Pythian Ode* 8, 12–18.
8. Bacchylides 15, 50f.
9. Alcman, fragment 1, *Poetarum melicorum Graecorum fragmenta*.
10. Apollodorus 1, 6, 1.
11. Ovid, *Metamorphoses* 1,182ff where Ovid seems to have conflated the Giants with the Hundred-Handers. Compare with *Fasti* 5, 35–42, where Ovid says 'Earth brought forth the Giants, a fierce brood, enormous monsters, who dared assault Jove's mansion; she gave them a thousand hands, and snakes for legs.'
12. Nonnus, *Dionysiaca* 1, 18.
13. Hesiod fragment 43a.65 MW; Hesiod fragment 195.28–29 MW.
14. Hesiod, *Theogeny* 50–52; Xenophon 121.
15. Pindar, *Nemean Ode* 7.90; *Pythian Ode* 8, 12, 18; 1, 67–9.
16. Euripides, *Heracles* 177–80; *Ion* 205–18.
17. Apollodorus 1, 6, 1–2.
18. Claudian, *Gigantomachia* 1–35 (pp.280–283).
19. Compare Hesiod, *Theogony* 185–186 which seems to have the Giants born, like Athena and the Spartoi, fully grown and armed for battle (Apollodorus, 1.3.6, 1.3.6). Also compare Plato, *Sophist* 246a, where comparing materialist philosophers with the Giants, says they 'drag down everything from heaven and the invisible to earth, actually grasping rocks and trees with their hands'.
20. Compare Pindar, *Nemean* 1, 67–69 where Teiresias prophesies that Heracles will aid the gods in their battle with the Giants.
21. Strabo, *Geography* 10, 5, 16.
22. Ovid, *Metamorphoses* 1, 151–162.
23. Ovid also refers to Giants piling up Pelion on top of Ossa in *Amores* 2,1,11–18 and *Fasti* 1,307–308, 3,437–442.
24. Ovid, *Metamorphoses* 1,182ff.
25. Ovid, *Amores* 2,1,11–18 has the Giants possess a 'thousand hands'. Hesiod, *Theogony* 617–736, 815–819. For the Hundred-Handers as opponents of Zeus, see for example Virgil, *Aeneid* 10.565–568.
26. Aeschylus, *Eumenides* 294; Euripides, *Heracles* 1192–1194; *Ion* 987–997; Aristophanes, *The Birds* 824; Apollonius of Rhodes, *Argonautica* 3, 232–234; 3, 1225–7. See also Hesiod fragment 43a.65 MW (Most 2007).
27. Strabo, 5.4.4, 5.4.6, 6.3.5; Diodorus Siculus, 4.21.5–7, 5.71.4. Lycophron, *Alexandra* 688–693 (pp.550–551). Servius, *Commentary on the Aeneid of Vergil* 3.578.
28. Plato, *Sophist* 246a-c.
29. Cicero, *De Senectute* 5.
30. Lucretius, *De Rerum Natura* 1, 62–79; 5, 110–125.
31. Horace, *Odes* 3, 4, 42ff.
32. Ovid, *Metamorphoses* 1.151–162.

33. Lucan, *Pharsalia* 9.654–658. For the use of Gigantomachy imagery in the *Argonautica* see Stover, pp.5–6, 71–73, 79–150.
34. Claudian, *Gigantomachia* 62–73.
35. It is not uncommon for cultures to attribute earthquakes and volcanoes to the movements of buried 'giants', see Andrews, 'Earthquakes' pp.62–63, 'Giants' p.81, 'Volcanoes' pp.218–219; Cook, n.5 pp.2–3; Frazer 1914, p.197: 'The people of Timor, in the East Indies, think that the earth rests on the shoulders of a mighty giant, and that when he is weary of bearing it on one shoulder he shifts it to the other and so causes the ground to quake'; pp.200–201: 'The Tongans think that the earth is supported on the prostrate form of the god Moooi. When he is tired of lying in one posture, he tries to turn himself about, and that causes an earthquake.'
36. Dio Cassius 66.22–23.
37. Vian and Moore 1988, pp.268–269.
38. Apollodorus, 1.6.2.
39. Apollodorus, 1.6.1.
40. Pindar, *Isthmian Ode* 6.30–35, *Nemean Ode* 4.24–30; 4, 44 with the Scholiast; *Isthmian* 6, 45.
41. Suda s.v. Ἀρισταῖος, Αἰτναῖος κάνθαρος.
42. Beazley Archive 310147; LIMC Gigantes 105: image 13/14.
43. Pausanias, 1.35.6 tells of Asterius, a son of Anax the 'son of Earth', buried on the island of Asterius, near the Island of Lade, off the coast of Miletus, having bones ten cubits in length; see also Pausanius 7.2.5.
44. For Heracles' expedition to Kos see Homer, *Iliad* 14.250–256; Pindar, *Isthmian* 6.31–35, *Nemean* 4.24–30; Apollodorus, 2.7.1. For the Meropes as Giants see Philostratus, *On Heroes* 8.14.
45. Apollodorus, 1.6.2; Euripides, *Ion* 987–997.
46. Apollodorus, 1.6.2.
47. Ptolemy *Hephaestion*, *New History Book* 6, 'Thetis burned in a secret place the children she had by Peleus; six were born; when she had Achilles, Peleus noticed and tore him from the flames with only a burnt foot and confided him to Chiron. The latter exhumed the body of the giant Damysos who was buried at Pallene – Damysos was the fastest of all the giants – removed the "astragale" and incorporated it into Achilles' foot using "ingredients". This "astragale" fell when Achilles was pursued by Apollo and it was thus that Achilles, fallen, was killed. It is said, on the other hand, that he was called Podarkes by the Poet, because, it is said, Thetis gave the newborn child the wings of Arce and Podarkes means that his feet had the wings of Arce.'
48. Beazley 14590, LIMC Gigantes 170, image 4/4.
49. Euripides, *Ion* 205–218.
50. Apollodorus, 1.6.2.
51. Virgil, *Aeneid* 3.578ff; Claudian, *Rape of Proserpine* 1.153–159 (pp.304–305), 2.151–162 (pp.328–331), 3.186–187 (pp.358–359).
52. Philostratus the Elder, *Imagines* 2.17.5.
53. Apollodorus, 1.6.2.

54. LIMC Gigantes 2. Beazley Archive 1409; Beazley Archive 220533; Beazley Archive 202916; LIMC Gigantes 361.
55. Homer, *Odyssey* 7.54ff.
56. Akropolis 2134 (Beazley Archive 9922, LIMC Gigantes 106).
57. Propertius, 3.9.47–48.
58. Apollodorus, 1.6.2.
59. Apollodorus, 1.6.2.
60. Akropolis 607; Beazley Archive 310147, LIMC Gigantes 105; Getty 81.AE.211 (Beazley Archive 10047, LIMC Gigantes 171).
61. Pausanias, 8.32.5, 8.36.2.
62. Apollodorus, 1.6.2.
63. Homer, *Iliad* 2.5.844ff; Hesiod, *Shield of Heracles* 226ff.
64. Apollodorus, 1.6.2.
65. Euripides, *Ion* 205–218.
66. Apollonius of Rhodes, *Argonautica* 3.1225–7 (pp.276–277); Claudian, *Gigantomachia* 85–91).
67. Silius Italicus, *Punica* 12.143–151 (II pp.156–159).
68. Apollodorus, 1.6.2.
69. Euripides, *Ion* 987–997.
70. Claudian, *Gigantomachia* 91–103.
71. Claudian, *Gigantomachia* 75–84.
72. Apollodorus, 1.6.2.
73. Getty 81.AE.211 (Moore 1985, pp.30–31, Beazley Archive 10047, LIMC Gigantes 171); Louvre E732 (Gantz, p.451, Beazley Archive 14590, LIMC Gigantes 170 image 4/4).
74. Apollodorus, 1.6.2. Compare Aristophanes, *The Birds* 1249ff: 'a single Porphyrion gave him [Zeus] enough to do.'
75. Pindar, *Pythian* 8.12–18.
76. Beazley Archive 220533: detail showing Zeus v. Porphyrion. Apollodorus 1, 6, 1; Pindar, *Pythian Ode* 8, 12; Horace, *Odes* 8,4,54; Claudian, *Gigantomachia* 114.
77. Apollodorus, 1.6.2.

Chapter Five:
1. *Homeric Hymn to Apollo* 306, 351–352; Pindar, *Pythian* 1.16, 8.16, *Olympian* 4.6–7; Pindar, fragment 93 apud. Strabo, 13.4.6; Aristophanes, *Clouds* 336; Hyginus, *Fabulae* 152, Oppian, *Halieutica* 3.15–25 (pp.344–347); Aeschylus, *Seven Against Thebes* 511. Nicander, apud. Antoninus Liberalis 28.
2. Nonnus, *Dionysiaca* 1.187; 2.30, 36; 1.173; 1.218; 1.508–509; 2.31–33; 2.141–142.
3. Nonnus, *Dionysiaca* 2.243; 1.154–162; 2.444–256; 2.381; also 2.244 ('many-armed Typhoeus'); Ovid, *Metamorphoses* 3.301; Nonnus, *Dionysiaca* 1.297, 2.343, 2.621.
4. Hesiod, *Theogony* 306–314. Compare with Lycophron, *Alexandra* 1351ff (pp.606–607), which refers to Echidna as Typhon's spouse (δάμαρ).
5. Apollodorus, *Library* 2.5.10 also has Orthrus as the offspring of Typhon and Echidna. Quintus Smyrnaeus, *Posthomerica* 6.249–262 (pp.272–273) has Cerberus as the offspring of Typhon and Echidna and Orthrus as his brother.

6. Acusilaus, fr. 13 Fowler (Fowler 2001, p.11; Freeman, p.15 fragment 6), Hyginus, *Fabulae* Preface, 151 and Quintus Smyrnaeus, loc. cit., also have Cerberus as the offspring of Typhon and Echidna. Bacchylides, *Ode* 5.62, Sophocles, *Women of Trachis* 1097–1099, Callimachus, fragment 515 Pfeiffer (Trypanis, pp.258–259), Ovid, *Metamorphoses* 4.500–501, 7.406–409, all have Cerberus as the offspring of Echidna, with no father named.

7. Hyginus, *Fabulae* Preface, 30 (only Typhon is mentioned), 151 also has the Hydra as the offspring of Echidna and Typhon.

8. Hesiod, *Theogony*, 319.

9. Pherecydes of Leros, fr. 7 Fowler (Fowler 2001, p.278); Fowler 2013, pp.21, 27–28.

10. Pherecydes of Leros, fr. 16b Fowler (Fowler 2001, p.286); Hesiod, *Theogony* 333–336; Fowler 2013, p.28; Ogden 2013a, p.149 n. 3; Hošek, p.678. The first to name the dragon Ladon is Apollonius of Rhodes, *Argonautica* 4.1396 (pp.388–389), which makes Ladon earthborn Tzetzes, *Chiliades* 2.36.360.

11. Lasus of Hermione, fragment 706A (Campbell, pp.310–311). Euripides, *The Phoenician Women* 1019–1020; Hesiod mentions the Sphinx (and the Nemean lion) as having been the offspring of Echidna's son Orthrus, by another ambiguous 'she' in line 326.

12. Apollodorus 2.5.10 (Orthrus), 2.3.1 (Chimera), 2.5.11 (Caucasian Eagle), 2.5.11 (Ladon), 3.5.8 (Sphinx), 2.5.1 (Nemean lion), Epitome 1.1 (Crommyonian Sow).

13. Hesiod, *Theogony* 836–838.

14. Ibid., 868.

15. Epimenides fr. 10 Fowler.

16. Pindar, fr. 91 SM apud. Porphyry, *On Abstinence From Animal Food* 3.16 (Taylor, p.111); m.Pindar, *Pythian* 1.15–16; Pindar, *Pythian* 8.16–17; Pindar, *Olympian* 4.6–7; Pindar, *Pythian* 1.15–28; Gantz, p.49.

17. Aeschylus, *Prometheus Bound* 356–364.

18. Pherecydes of Leros, fr. 54 Fowler (Fowler 2001, p.307).

19. Apollonius of Rhodes, *Argonautica* 2.1208–1215; cf. Herodotus 3.5.

20. Nicander, apud. Antoninus Liberalis 28.

21. Apollodorus, 1.6.3.

22. Oppian, *Halieutica* 3.15–25.

23. Nonnus, *Dionysiaca* 1.145–164; 1.164–257; 1.258–293; 1.294–320.

24. Nonnus, *Dionysiaca* 2, 1ff.

Chapter Six:

1. Nonnus, *Dionysiaca* 5, 611ff; 14, 193ff; 32, 65ff. Diodorus 4, 69.

2. Pliny, *Natural History* 7, 56, 3.

3. Homer, *Iliad* 11, 831.

4. Homer, *Iliad* 12, 128; Diodorus Siculus 4, 69; 5, 61.

5. Ovid, *Metamorphoses* 12, 210f.

6. Plutarch, *Theseus* 30; Ovid, *Metamorphoses* 12, 210.

7. Dumézil, G., *Le Problème des Centaures* (Paris 1929); Graves, R. (1960) *The Greek Myths*, 81.4; 102 'Centaurs'; 126.3.
8. Pausanias 5, 10, 8.

Chapter Seven:
1. *Naturalis Historia* 6, 3, 10.
2. Herodotus 6, 86; Walcot, *Greek Attitudes towards Women*, p.42.
3. Hippocrates, *Airs, Waters, Places* 17.
4. Herodotus 4, 110–17.
5. Lysias 2, 4. Strabo, *Geographia* 5, 50.
6. Hippocrates, *Airs, Waters, Places* 17.
7. Justinus, *Historiae Phillippicae ex Trogo Pompeio* 2, 4.
8. Strabo, *Geographia* 11, 503; Hellanicus fr. 17.
9. For details see Quintus of Smyrna, *Posthomerica* Books 1–4.
10. Virgil, *Aeneid* 1, 490–5. The twelve are Antibrote, Ainia, Clete, Alcibie, Antandre, Bremusa, Derimacheia, Derinoe, Harmothoe, Hippothoe, Polemusa and Thermodosa.
11. Diodorus Siculus *Library of History* 2, 46.
12. *Bibliotheca* 5, 1.
13. Propertius 3, 11.
14. Pausanias, *Description of Greece* 10, 31, 1 and 5, 11, 2.
15. Euripides, *Hercules Furens*, 408ff; Apollonius Rhodius, *Argonautica*, 2, 777ff and 966ff; Diodorus Siculus, *Bibliotheca Historica*, 4, 16; Ps. Apollodorus, *Bibliotheca*, 2, 5, 9; Pausanias 5, 10, 9; Quintus Smyrnaeus, *Posthomerica*, 6, 240ff; Hyginus, *Fabulae*, 30.
16. Plutarch, *Theseus*.
17. Pliny, *Naturalis Historia* 34, 75.
18. Statius, *Thebaid* 2, 635–8.
19. Homer, *Iliad* 2, 814; 2, 45–46; 3, 52–55; Diodorus Siculus 3, 54–56. See also Strabo, *Geography* 12, 8, 6 and Tzetzes on Lycophron, 243.
20. Stephanus of Byzantium, s.v. Myrina.
21. See also Strabo, *Geography* 11, 5, 5 = 12, 3, 22.
22. Herodotus, *Histories* 4, 110, 1–117, 1.
23. Homer *Iliad* 6, 186ff; scholiast *On Lycophron* 17.
24. *Iliad* 3, 189.
25. *Iliad* 3, 185–189; 6, 186.
26. Diodorus Siculus 2, 45; trans. Loeb Classical Library edition, 1935.
27. Justin 2, 4.

Chapter Eight:
1. John Tzetzes, *Chiliades*, 10, 32, 4.
2. See also Apollodorus 3, 5, 2 and Nonnus, *Dionysica* 2, 5, 9.
3. Ovid, *Metamorphoses* 3, 511–733.
4. Apollodorus 3, 5, 5.
5. Ibid., 3, 5, 5.

6. Pausanias 2, 6, 2.
7. Ibid., 9,5.
8. Ibid., 9, 5, 4.
9. Homer, *Iliad* 24, 603–610.
10. Apollodorus 3, 5, 7.
11. Sophocles, *Oedipus Rex*, 1191–1312.
12. Statius, *Thebaid* 11, 634–644.
13. Apollodorus 3, 6, 1.
14. Sophocles, *Oedipus at Colonus* 1350–1395.
15. Aeschylus, *Seven Against Thebes* 230–2.
16. Ibid., 99.
17. Ibid., 256–7.
18. Ibid., 268.
19. Ibid., 679–82.
20. *Cambridge Ancient History II* (1978), p.168.
21. Illustrated in Larissa Bonfante and Judith Swaddling, *Etruscan Myths* (Series 'The Legendary Past', University of Texas/British Museum) 2006, fig. 9, p.22.
22. Relief in the Museo Etrusco, Villa Giulia, Rome, illustrated in Bonfante and Swaddling, fig. 10 p. 23, and p.58.
23. Euripides, *Phoenissae* 535f.
24. Ibid., 160ff.
25. Ibid., 1490.
26. Ibid., 1577–9.
27. Apollodorus 3.7.3.
28. Pausanias 2,20,5; 7,3,1; 9,9.4; 9,5,13; 9,9,5; 9,5,14.
29. Apollodorus 3, 7, 3.
30. Ion of Chios in Sallustius' *argumentum* of Sophocles' *Antigone*.

Chapter Nine:
1. Homer, *Iliad* 7.451–453, 20.145–148, 21.442–457; Apollodorus 2, 5, 9.
2. Ovid, *Metamorphoses* 2, 689.
3. Apollodorus 2, 7, 3; Ovid, *Metamorphoses* 12, 555–572; Hyginus, *Fabulae* 10.
4. Mommsen, H., *Alternatives to Hitler: German Resistance Under the Third Reich*, p.7.
5. Hesiod, *Shield* 57–67.

Chapter Ten:
1. Dio Chrysostom: *The Eleventh Discourse Maintaining that Troy was not Captured.*
2. Wood, Preface to *In Search of the Trojan War* (2nd ed.).
3. See Rutter, 'Troy VII and the Historicity of the Trojan War', Dartmouth College http://www.dartmouth.edu/~prehistory/aegean/?page_id=630#L27Top
4. Latacz, *Evidence from Homer.*
5. Korfmann, *Was There a Trojan War?*
6. *The Times*, 20 August 2001.
7. *Shield of Heracles*, 248–57.

8. See Egeler, *Death, Wings, and Divine Devouring*, pp.5–26.
9. Hesiod, *Theogony* 226ff.
10. *Shield of Heracles*, 139ff.
11. See Apollodorus, *Bibliotheca*; Diodorus Siculus 4, 63, 1–3, and Plutarch, *Theseus* 31–34.
12. Stesichorus, fr. 201 PMG..
13. *Cypria*, fr. 1; Hesiod, *Catalogues of Women and Eoiae*, fr. 204.96–101.
14. Homer, *Iliad* 2, 688–94.
15. Ibid., 19, 261–3.
16. Ibid., 1, 110–14.
17. Ibid., 1, 10ff.
18. Ibid., 1, 320–325.
19. Ibid., 6, 425; 22, 470–72.
20. Ibid., 6, 450–465.
21. *Iliad* 6, 485ff; *Odyssey* 1, 356–9; 21, 350–3.
22. *Iliad* 6, 370–373; 6, 433–439.
23. Ibid., 6, 390.
24. Ptolemy, Hephaeston 5.
25. Pausanias 4, 1, 1–2.
26. Suda and Hesychius of Alexandria, s.v. Ἄγραυλος; Ulpian *ad Demosth. de fals. leg.*; Plutarch, *Alcibiades* 15; Philochorus, Fragm. p.18, ed. Siebelis.
27. Homer, *Iliad* 3, 121–244.
28. Hesiod, *Shield of Heracles* 242.

Chapter Twelve:
1. Plutarch, *De Herodoti Malignitate*, 43 = *Moralia*, 873f.
2. All translations from Hesiod: *The Homeric Hymns and Homerica* translated by Hugh G.. Evelyn-White (1914).

Further Reading

Abrantes, M.C., *Themes of the Trojan Cycle: Contribution to the Study of the Greek Mythological Tradition* (Coimbra, 2016).

Adie, K., *Corsets to Camouflage: Women and War* (London, 2003).

Afflerbach, H. (ed.), *How Fighting Ends: A History of Surrender* (Oxford, 2012).

Albersmeier, S. (ed.), *Heroes: Mortals and Myths in Ancient Greece* (Baltimore, 2009).

Andrews, T., *Dictionary of Nature Myths: Legends of the Earth, Sea and Sky* (Oxford, 2000).

Armstrong, C.B., *The Casualty Lists in the Trojan War, Greece & Rome* (1969) pp.16, 30–31.

Arthur, M.B., *Early Greece: The Origins of the Western Attitude Toward Women, Arethusa* (1973) pp.6, 7–58.

Baier, C., *Homer's Cultural Children: The Myth of Troy and European Identity, History & Memory* Vol. 29, 2017, 35–62.

Baur, P.V.C., *Centaurs in Ancient Art: The Archaic Period* (Berlin, 1912).

Bell, R.E., *Women of Classical Mythology: A Biographical Dictionary* (Oxford, 1993).

Bennett, F.M., *Religious Cults Associated with the Amazons* (1912).

Bergmann, F.G., *Les Amazones dans l'histoire et dans la fable* (1853).

Bergren, A., *Helen's Web: Time and Tableau in the Iliad. Helios* (1979) pp.7, 19–34.

Bisset, K.A., *Who Were the Amazons?* (G&R, 1971) pp.18, 150–1.

Blanshard, A.J.L., *Classics on Screen: Ancient Greece and Rome on Film* (London, 2011) .

Blok, J.H. (Peter Mason, tr.), *The Early Amazons: Modern and Ancient Perspectives on a Persistent Myth* (Leiden, 1995).

Blondel, R., *Helen of Troy: Beauty, Myth, Devastation* (Oxford, 2013).

Bluestone, N.H., *Women and the Ideal Society: Plato's Republic and Modern Myths of Gender* (Oxford, 1997).

Boitani, P., *The Shadow of Ulysses: Figures of a Myth* (Oxford, 1994).

Bonfante, B., *Etruscan Myths* (Series 'The Legendary Past', University of Texas/British Museum), 2006.

Bragg, M., *The Trojan War: In Our Time*, broadcast Thursday, 31 May 2012 21:30 BBC RADIO 4 http://www.bbc.co.uk/programmes/b01j6srl.

Bremmer, J., (ed.), *Interpretations of Greek Mythology* (London, 1987).

Brown, A.L., *The End of the Seven Against Thebes* (*The Classical Quarterly*, 1976) 26.2, pp.206–19.

Brown, F.S., ἐκτιλώσαντο: *A Reading of Herodotus' Amazons* (CJ 80, 1985) pp.297–302.

Burgess, J.S., *The Tradition of the Trojan War in Homer and the Epic Cycle* (Baltimore, 2001).

Burkert, P.F., *Structure and History in Greek Myth and Ritual* (Berkeley, 1979).

Burkert, P.F., 'Oriental and Greek Mythology: The Meeting of Parallels' in *Interpretations of Greek Mythology*, edited by Jan Bremmer (London, 1987).

Burkert, W., *Homo Necans: The Anthropology of Ancient Greek Sacrificial Ritual and Myth* (Berkeley, 1983).

Burkert, W., *Greek Religion* (Oxford, 1985).

Burkert, W., *Ancient Mystery Cults* (Cambridge, Mass., 1987).

Buxton, R., *Imaginary Greece* (Cambridge, 1994).

Caldwell, R.S., *The Origin of the Gods: A Psychoanalytic Study of Greek Theogonic Myth* (New York, 1989).

Campbell, B. (ed.), *Oxford Handbook of Warfare in the Classical World* (Oxford, 2013).

Carpenter, T.H., *Art and Myth in Ancient Greece* (London, 1991).

Cartledge, P., *Surrender in Ancient Greece in Afflerbach: How Fighting Ends* (2012) pp.15–28.

Cartledge, P., *Thebes: The Forgotten City of Ancient Greece* (London, 2020).

Chavalas, M.V., *Women in the Ancient Near East* (London, 2013).

Chrystal, P., *Women in Ancient Greece: Seclusion, Exclusion or Illusion?* (Stroud, 2016).

Chrystal, P., *Women at War in Ancient Greece & Rome* (Barnsley, 2017).

Chrystal, P., *Wars & Battles of Ancient Greece* (Stroud, 2018).

Chrystal, P., *War in Roman Myth and Legend* (Barnsley, 2020).

Clay, J.S., *Hesiod's Cosmos* (Cambridge, 2003).

Cloutier, G., *Andromache: Denial and Despair* The First-Year Papers (Trinity College Digital Repository, Hartford, CT., 2013) www.digitalrepository.trincoll.edu/fypapers/37.

Cohen, D., *The Imagery of Sophocles: A Study of Ajax's Suicide, Greece & Rome* (1978) pp.25, 24–36.

Cook, Arthur B., *Zeus: A Study in Ancient Religion. Volume III: Zeus: God of the Dark Sky* (Earthquakes, Clouds, Wind, Dew, Rain, Meteorites) Part I: Text and Notes (Cambridge University Press, 1940) Internet Archive.

Cook, B.A. (ed.), *Women and War: A Historical Encyclopedia from Antiquity to the Present*, 2 Vols (Oxford, 2006).

Cooper, H.M. (ed.), *Arms and the Woman: War, Gender and Literary Representation* (Chapel Hill, NC, 1989).

Darmon, J.-P. (ed.), *The Powers of War: Athena and Ares in Greek Mythology*, translated by Danielle Beauvais (Chicago, Illinois, 1992).

Davies, M., *Greek Epic Cycle* (London, 1989).

Dawson, D., *The Origins of Western Warfare: Militarism and Morality in the Ancient World* (Boulder, CO, 1997).

Deacy, S., *Athena in the Classical World* (Leiden, 2001).

Deacy, S. (ed.), *Rape in Antiquity: Sexual Violence in the Greek and Roman Worlds* (London, 2002).

Deacy, S., 'From "flowery tales" to "heroic rapes": virginal subjectivity in the mythological meadow', *Arethusa* (2013) 46.3, pp.395–413.

Delbrück, H., *Warfare in Antiquity: History of the Art of War*, Volume 1 (Lincoln, NE, 1920).

Dougherty, C., 'Sowing the Seeds of Violence: Rape, Women and the Land' in *Wyke: Parchments of Gender* (1988) pp.267–84.

Dowden, K., *The Uses of Greek Mythology* (London, 1992).

Dowden, K., *The Amazons: Development and Function* (1997) RhM 140, pp.97–128.

Downing, C., *The Goddess: Mythological Images of the Feminine* (London, 1996).

Du Bois, P., *Centaurs and Amazons: Women and the Pre-History of the Great Chain of Being* (Ann Arbor, 1982).

Ducrey, P., 'War in the Feminine in Ancient Greece' in Fabre-Serris, J., (ed.) *Women and War in Antiquity* (Baltimore, 2015), pp.181–199.

Dumézil, G., *Le Problème des Centaures* (Paris, 1929).

Dundes, A. (ed.), *Sacred Narrative: Readings in the History of Myth* (Berkeley, 1984).

Edmunds, L. (ed.), *Approaches to Greek Myth*, second edition (Baltimore, 2014).

Edmunds, L., *Stealing Helen: The Myth of the Abducted Wife in Comparative Perspective* (Oxford, 2015).

Edwards, A., 'Achilles in the Odyssey: Ideologies of Heroism in the Homeric Epic', Beiträge zur klassischen Philologie 171 (1985).

Edwards, R.B., *Kadmos, the Phoenician: A Study in Greek Legends and the Mycenaean Age* (Amsterdam, 1979).

Egeler, M., 'Death, wings, and divine devouring: possible Mediterranean affinities of Irish battlefield demons and Norse valkyries', *Studia Celtica Fennica 5* (2008), 3–24.

Fabre-Serris, J. (ed.), *Women and War in Antiquity* (Baltimore, 2015).

Fantham, E., *Women in the Classical World: Image and Text* (New York, 1994).

Farron, S., *The Portrayal of Women in the Iliad, Acta Classica: Proceedings of the Classical Association of South Africa* (1979) 22, pp.15–32.

Ferrill, A., *The Origins of War: From the Stone Age to Alexander the Great* (Boulder, CO, 1997).

Finglass, P., *The Glorious Water-Carrier: Stesichorus' Sack of Troy*, Omnibus 67 (2014), pp.1–3.

Finley, M., *The World of Odysseus* (London, 1956).

Finley, M., *Ancient History: Evidence and Models* (London, 1985).

Fletcher, K.F.B., 'Systematic Genealogies in Apollodorus' Bibliotheca and the Exclusion of Rome from Greek Myth', *Classical Antiquity* 27:59–91 (2008).

Fowler, R., *How the Lysistrata Works*, EMC 15, 245–59 (1996).

Fowler, R.L., *Early Greek Mythography*, Volume 1: Text and Introduction (Oxford, 2001).

Fowler, R.L., *Early Greek Mythography*, Volume 2: Commentary (Oxford University Press, 2013).

Fuhrer, T., 'Teichoskopia: Female Figures Looking on Battles' in Fabre-Serris, J. (ed.), *Women and War in Antiquity* (2015), pp.52–70.

Gabba, E., *True History and False History in Classical Antiquity*, JRS 61 (1981) pp.50–62.

Galinsky, G.K., *The Herakles Theme* (Oxford, 1972).

Gantz, T., *Early Greek Myth: A Guide to Literary and Artistic Sources* (Baltimore, 1996).

Garlan, Y., *War in the Ancient World: A Social History* (London, 1976).

Garlick, B. (ed.), *Stereotypes of Women in Power* (New York, 1992).

Georgiou, I.E., *Women in Herodotus' Histories* (Swansea, 2002).

Georgoudi, S., 'To Act, Not Submit: Women's Attitudes in Situations of War in Ancient Greece' in Fabre-Serris, J. (ed.), *Women and War in Antiquity* (2015), pp.200–213.

Gera, D.L., *Warrior Women: The Anonymous Tractatus De Mulieribus* (Leiden, 1997).

Gilaine, Jean, *The Origins of War: Violence in Prehistory* (Chichester, 2005).

Gill, C. (ed.), *Lies and Fiction in the Ancient World* (Liverpool, 1993).

Gossage, A.J., *Two Implications of the Trojan Legend: Greece & Rome* (1955), pp.23–30, 72–81.

Gould, J., *Women in Classical Athens*, JHS 100 (1980), pp.38–59.

Graf, F., *Women, War and Warlike Divinities*, ZPE 55 (1984), pp.245–54.

Grant, M., *Greek and Roman Historians: Information and Misinformation* (1995).

Grant de Pauw, L., *Battle Cries and Lullabies: Women in War from Prehistory to the Present* (Oklahoma, 2000).

Graves, R., *The Greek Myths* (London, 1955).

Green, F.J., *Homer's Helen: Greece & Rome 15* (1968), pp.32–39.

Green, M., *Celtic Goddesses: Warriors, Virgins and Mothers* (London, 1995).

Greensmith, E., 'The Elle-iad: Female Empowerment in the Iliad', *Omnibus* 66 (2013) pp.10–12.

Griffiths, J.G., 'The Flight of the Gods Before Typhon: An Unrecognized Myth', *Hermes* 88 (1960), pp.74–376.

Guthrie, W.K., *Greeks and Their Gods* (London, 1962).

Hallie, R.M., *Banging the Lyre: The Classical Plays of Tony Harrison* (pdf). Faculty of Graduate Studies (Comparative Literature) (University of British Columbia, Vancouver), p.151.

Hanson, V.D. and Heath, J., *Who Killed Homer?: The Demise of Classical Education and the Recovery of Greek Wisdom* (1998).

Hard, R., *Apollodorus: The Library of Greek Mythology* (Oxford, 1997).

Hard, R., *The Routledge Handbook of Greek Mythology* (London, 2004).

Hardwick, L., 'Ancient Amazon: Heroes, Outsiders or Women?' *Greece & Rome* 37 (1990), pp.14–36.

Harrison, T., 'Herodotus and the Ancient Greek Idea of Rape' in Deacy, *Rape in Antiquity* (1997), pp.185–208.

Harrison, Tony, *The Labourers of Heracles*, Arion, 4 (1) (1996), pp.115–154.

Hawes, G., *Rationalizing Myth in Antiquity* (Oxford, 2014).

Hawkes, C. (ed.), *Greeks, Celts and Romans: Studies in Venture and Resistance* (London, 1973).

Heath, E.G., *Archery: A Military History* (London, 1980).

Herzog, C., *Battles of the Bible* (London, 1978).

Higbie, Carolyn, 'Hellenistic Mythograpers' in *The Cambridge Companion to Greek Mythology* (ed.) Woodard, 237254 (Cambridge, 2007).

Hindley, C., *Eros and Military Command in Xenophon*, CQ 44 (1994), pp.347–66.

Hogg, O.F., *Clubs to Cannon: Warfare and Weapons Before the Introduction of Gunpowder* (London, 1968).

Holmes, R., *Acts of War: The Behaviour of Men in Battle* (London, 2004).

Honko, Lauri (1984), 'The Problem of Defining Myth', in Dundes, *Sacred Narrative: Readings in the Theory of Myth*, p.49. Dundes (1984), p.1.

Hosty, M., *Batrachomyomachia (Battle of the Frogs and Mice): Introduction, Text, Translation, and Commentary* (Oxford, 2019).

Huys, M., *Euripides and the Tales from Euripides: Sources of Apollodoros' Bibliotheca?*, Rheinisches Museum 140 (1997), pp.30–327.

Indick, William, 'Classical Heroes in Modern Movies: Mythological Patterns of the Superhero', *Journal of Media Psychology 9 (3)* (2004), pp.93–95.

James, S.L., *Companion to Women in the Ancient World* (Chichester, 2012).

Jameson, M., 'Sacrifice Before Battle' in Hanson, V. (ed.) *Hoplites* (1991), p.220.

Jestice, P.G., 'Greek Women and War in Antiquity' in Cook, *Women and War* (2006) pp.256–8.

Jones, D.E., *Women Warriors: A History* (Washington, 1997) .

Jones, H.P., 'Usages of Ancient Warfare', *Edinburgh Review* (January 1918).

Jones, P., *A Woman's Place in Homer* http://www.spectator.co.uk/2012/12/a-womans-place-in-homer (2012).

Keegan, J., *A History of Warfare* (London, 1993).

Keeley, L.H., *War Before Civilisation: The Myth of the Peaceful Savage* (Oxford, 1996).

Kelly, R.C., *Warless Societies and the Origin of War* (Ann Arbor, 2000).

Kenens, U., 'The Sources of Ps.-Apollodorus' Library: A Case Study', *Quaderni Urbinati di Cultura Classica* 97 (2011), pp.129–146.

Kenens, U., 'Text and Transmission of Ps.-Apollodorus' Bibliotheca: Avenues for Future Research' in *Writing Myth: Mythography in the Ancient World* (ed.) S.M. Trzaskoma (Leuven, 2013), pp.95–114.

Kerényi, K., *The Gods of the Greeks* (London, 1951).

Kerényi, K., *The Heroes of the Greeks* (revised edition) (London, 1978).

Kern, P.B., *Ancient Siege Warfare* (London, 1999).

Kirk, G.S., *Myth: Its Meaning and Functions in Ancient and Other Cultures* (London, 1973).

Kirk, G.S., *The Nature of Greek Myths* (London, 1974).

Knapp, B.L., *Women in Myth*, Chapter 6 (New York).

Korfmann, M., 'Was There a Trojan War?', *Archaeology* 57 (2004).

Lane Fox, R., *Travelling Heroes: In the Epic Age of Homer* (London, 2010).

Laqueur, W., *Guerrilla Warfare: A Historical & Critical Study* (London, 1977).

Larson, J., *Greek Heroine Cults* (Madison, WI, 1995).

Latacz, J., 'Evidence from Homer', *Archaeology* 57 (2004).

Latacz, J., *Troy and Homer: Towards a Solution of an Old Mystery* (Oxford, 2004).

Law, H., *Atrocities in Greek Warfare*, CJ 15 (1919) pp.132–47.

Lawrence, E.A., 'The Centaur: Its History and Meaning in Human Culture', *Journal of Popular Culture*, 27 (4): 58 (1994).

Lee, W.E., *Warfare and Culture in World History* (New York, 2011).

Leeming, D.A., 'Myth and Therapy', *Journal of Religion and Health* Vol. 40, (2001), pp.115–119.

Lefkowitz, M.R., 'Women in Greek Myth', *The American Scholar* Vol. 54, No. 2 (1985), pp.207–219.

Lefkowitz, M., *Women in Greek Myth* (London, 1986).

Leitao, D.D., 'Sexuality in Greek and Roman Military Contexts' in Hubbard, *Companion* (2014), pp.230–243.

Levithan, J., *Roman Siege Warfare* (Ann Arbor, 2013).

Lincoln, Bruce, 'An Early Moment in the Discourse of "Terrorism": Reflections on a Tale from Marco Polo'. *Comparative Studies in Society and History* (2006), 48 (2): 242–259.

Lissarrague, F., 'Women Arming Men: Armor and Jewelry' in Fabre-Serris, J. (ed.), *Women and War in Antiquity* (2015), pp.71–81.

Loman, P., *No Woman, No War: Women's Participation in Ancient Greek Warfare*, G&R (2004), pp.51, 31–54.

Louden, Bruce, 'Aeneas in the Iliad: The One Just Man', 102nd Annual Meeting of CAMWS, Classical Association of the Middle West and South (2006).

Lydgate, John, *Troy Book*, Vol. II, ll, 2487 (in Middle English). Reprinted in Henry Bergen's *Lydgate's Troy Book*, Vol. I, p.216 (London), 1906. Accessed 3 March 2019.

Lynn, J.A., *Battle: A History of Combat from Ancient Greece to Modern America* (Boulder, CO, 2003).

Mac Sweeny, N., *Troy: Myth, City, Icon* (London, 2018).

Man, J., 'Searching for the Amazons: The Real Warrior Women of the Ancient World'.

Mason, M.K., Annotated bibliography of *Women in Classical Mythology*, www. moyak.com/papers/women-classical-mythology.html.

Matyszak, P., *Hercules: The First Superhero* (Monashee Mountain Publishing, 2015).

Mayor, A., *The Amazons: Lives and Legends of Warrior Women across the Ancient World* (Princeton, 2014).

Meletinsky, E.M., *The Poetics of Myth* (London, 2014).

Michalopoulos, D., *Homer's Odyssey Beyond the Myths*, Piraeus: Institute of Hellenic Maritime History (2016).

Montagu, J.D., *Greek and Roman Warfare: Battles, Tactics and Trickery* (London, 2006).

Mommsen, H., *Alternatives to Hitler: German Resistance Under the Third Reich* (Princeton, 2003).

Montagu, J.D., *Battles of the Greek and Roman Worlds* (London, 2000).

Moore, M.B., 'Lydos and the Gigantomachy', *American Journal of Archaeology* (1979), pp.83, 79–99.

Moore, M.B., 'Giants at the Getty' in *Greek Vases*, J. Paul Getty Museum, Volume 2, (Getty Publications, 1985).

Moore, M.B., 'The Gigantomachy of the Siphnian Treasury: Reconstruction of the three Lacunae', *Bulletin de correspondance hellénique*, Suppl. 4, 1977, pp.305–335.

Murnaghan, S., 'Women in Greek Tragedy' in Bushnell, R. (ed.) *A Companion to Greek Tragedy* (Chichester, 2005), pp.234–250.

Murray, W., *Hybrid Warfare: Fighting Complex Opponents from the Ancient World to the Present* (Cambridge, 2012).

Myers, T., *Homer's Divine Audience: The Iliad's Reception on Mount Olympus* (Oxford, 2019).

Nagy, G., *The Best of the Achaeans: Concepts of the Hero in Archaic Greek Poetry* (Baltimore, 1999).

Nappi, M., 'Women and War in the Iliad: Rhetorical and Ethical Implications' in Fabre-Serris, J., (ed.) *Women and War in Antiquity* (2015), pp.34–51.

Nash, H., 'The Centaur's Origin: A Psychological Perspective', *Classical World* 77 (5) (1984), pp.273–291.

Neville, J.W., 'Herodotus on the Trojan War', *Greece & Rome* 24 (1977), pp.3–12.

Newark, T., *Women Warlords: An Illustrated History of Female Warriors* (London, 1989).

Nilsson, M.P., *The Mycenaean Origin of Greek Mythology* (Berkeley, 1931).

Northup, L., 'Myth-Placed Priorities: Religion and the Study of Myth', *Religious Studies Review 32 (1)* (2006), pp.5–10.

Ogden, D., *Drakon: Dragon Myth and Serpent Cult in the Greek and Roman Worlds* (Oxford, 2013).

Ogden, D., *Dragons, Serpents and Slayers in the Classical and Early Christian Worlds: A Sourcebook* (Oxford, 2013).

Olson, E.L., 'Great Expectations: The Role of Myth in 1980s Films with Child Heroes' (pdf), *Virginia Polytechnic Scholarly Library* (Virginia Polytechnic Institute and State University, 2011).

Otterbein, K.F., *How War Began* (College Station TX, 2004).

Pache, C. (ed), *The Cambridge Guide to Homer*, (Cambridge, 2020).

Padilla, M.W., *The Myths of Heracles in Ancient Greece: Survey and Profile* (Lanham, Maryland, 1998).

Padley, S., 'Hijacking Culture: Tony Harrison and the Greeks', *Cycnos 18 n°1 Le théâtre britannique au tournant du millénaire* .

Pantelia, M., *Helen and the Last Song for Hector*, TAPA 132 (2002), pp.21–27.

Parada, C., *Genealogical Guide to Greek Mythology*, Vol. 107 (Studies in Mediterranean Archaeology, 1993).

Parker, R.B., *Polytheism and Society at Athens* (Oxford, 2006).

Payen, P., 'Women's Wars, Censored Wars?' in Fabre-Serris, J. (ed.) *Women and War in Antiquity* (2015), pp.214–227.

Peel, M. (ed.), *Rape as a Method of Torture* (London, 2004).

Penglase, C., *Greek Myths and Mesopotamia: Parallels and Influence in the Homeric Hymns and Hesiod* (2005).

Pennington, R. (ed.), *Amazons to Fighter Pilots: A Biographical Dictionary of Military Women* (London, 2003).

Postlethwaite N., 'The Duel of Paris and Menelaos and the Teichoskopia' in *Iliad* 3 *Anthichthon* 19, (1985), pp.1–6.

Powers, D. (ed.), *Irregular Warfare in the Ancient World* (Chicago, 2013).

Pucci, P., 'Antiphonal Lament between Achilles and Briseis', *Colby Quarterly* 29 (1993), pp.258–72.

Renault, M., *The Bull from the Sea* (London, 2015).

Riley, K.R., *The Reception and Performance of Euripides' Heracles: Reasoning Madness* (Oxford, 2008), pp.340–341.

Robinson, V. (ed.), *Morals In Wartime* (New York, 1943).

Roisman, H., *Helen in the Iliad: Casus Belli and Victim of War*, AJP 127 (2006), pp.1–36.

Rosenmeyer, T., 'Seven Against Thebes. The Tragedy of War', *Arion: A Journal of Humanities and the Classics*, Vol. 1, No. 1 (1962), pp.48–78.

Rothman, J., 'The Real Amazons', *The New Yorker*, 17 October 2014.

Rousseau, P., 'War, Speech and the Bow are Not Women's Business' in Fabre-Serris, J. (ed.), *Women and War in Antiquity* (2015), pp.16–33.

Rutter, C.C., 'Harrison, Heracles and Wailing Women: "Labourers" at Delphi', *New Theatre Quarterly* (1997).

Rutter, J.B., 'Troy VII and the Historicity of the Trojan War', http://www.dartmouth.edu/~prehistory/aegean/?page_id=630#L27Top (2004).

Saggs, H.W.F., *Civilisation Before Greece and Rome* (London, 1989).

Salmonson, J.A., *The Encyclopedia of Amazons* (London, 1991).

Schaps, D., *The Women of Greece in Wartime*, CP 77 (1982), pp.193–213.

Schwab, Katherine A., 'Celebrations of victory: The Metopes of the Parthenon' in *The Parthenon: From Antiquity to the Present*, edited by Jenifer Neils (2005).

Scobie, A., *The Origins of 'Centaurs Folklore'*, 89.2 (1978), pp.142–147.

Scodel, R., 'Teichoscopia, Catalogue, and the Female Spectator' in Euripides, *Colby Quarterly* 33 (1997), pp.76–93.

Segal, C., *The Theme of the Mutilation of the Corpse in the Iliad* (Leiden, 1971).

Segal, R., *Myth: A Very Short Introduction* (Oxford, 2015).

Shapiro, H.A., *Amazons, Thracians and Scythians*, GRBS 24 (1983), pp.105–114.

Shapiro, H.A., *Myth into Art: Poet and Painter in Classical Greece* (London, 1994).

Sharrock, A., 'Warrior Women in Roman Epic' in Fabre-Serris, J. (ed.), *Women and War in Antiquity* (2015), pp.157–78.

Shear, I.M., 'Mycenaean Centaurs at Ugarit', *Journal of Hellenic Studies* (2002), pp.147–153.

Siefert, R., 'Rape in Wars: Analytical Approaches, Minerva', *Quarterly Report on Women and the Military* 11 (1992), pp.17–22.

Sobol, D., *The Amazons of Greek Mythology* (Cranbury, NJ, 1973).

Sowa, C.A., *Traditional Themes and the Homeric Hymns* (Chicago, 1984).

Spretnak, Charlene, *Lost Goddesses of Early Greece: A Collection of Pre-Hellenic Myths* (Boston, MA, 1984).

Suzuki, M., *Metamorphoses of Helen: Authority, Difference and the Epic* (Ithaca) (1989).

Swift, L., *The Character of Achilles*, Omnibus 58 (2009), pp.6–9.

Tyrrell, W.B., *Amazons: A Study in Athenian Myth-Making* (Baltimore, 1984).

Tyrrell, W.B., *Athenian Myths and Institutions: Words in Action* (New York, 1991).

University of Warsaw Faculty of 'Artes Liberales' Centre for Studies on the Classical Tradition (OBTA), Our Mythical Hope in Children's and Young Adults' Culture… The (In)efficacy of Ancient Myths in Overcoming the Hardships of Life Warsaw, May 15–21, 2017. Hercules the Hope-Bearer:

• Susan Deacy, Department of Humanities, University of Roehampton, Hercules and the Autistic Imagination: Introducing the 'Autism' Strand of Our Mythical Childhood

- Edoardo Pecchini, Faculty of 'Artes Liberales', University of Warsaw/Bolzano Hospital, Promoting Mental Health through Classics: Hercules as Trainer in Today's Labours of Children and Young People
- Markus Janka, Institute of Classical Philology, University of Munich, Hercules as Hero of Hopeful Culture in Ancient Poetry and Contemporary Media for Children and Young Adults http://omc.obta.al.uw.edu.pl/files/OMH_ Conference_Leaflet_9.5.2017.pdf.

Ussher, R.G., *The Cyclops of Euripides*, Greece & Rome 18, pp.166–178.

Van Creveld, M., *Men, Women and War: Do Women Belong on the Front Line?* (London, 2001).

Van Wees, H., *Greek Warfare: Myths and Realities* (London, 2004).

Vernant, J-P., *Myth and Society in Ancient Greece*, trans. Janet Lloyd (Brighton, 1980).

Veyne, Paul, 'Did the Greeks Believe in Their Myths?' An Essay on Constitutive Imagination *(translated by Paula Wissing)* (Chicago, 1988).

Vian, F., *Répertoire des gigantomachie figureées dans l'art grec et romain* (Paris, 1951).

Vian, F., *La guerre des Géants: Le mythe avant l'epoque hellenistique* (Paris, 1952).

Vian, F., *Les origines de Thébes: Cadmos et les Spartes* (Paris, 1963).

Vian, F., 'Gigantes' in *Lexicon Iconographicum Mythologiae Classicae* (LIMC) IV.1 (Zürich, 1988).

Vikman, E., *Ancient Origins: Sexual Violence in Warfare*, Part I, 'Anthropology & Medicine' 12 (1) (2005) pp.21–31.

Villing, A., *Troy: Myth and Reality* (London, 2019).

Vivante, B., *Daughters of Gaia: Women in the Ancient Mediterranean World* (Westport, CT, 2006).

Von Bothmer, D., *Amazons in Greek Art* (1957).

Walcot, P., *On Widows and their Reputation in Antiquity*, SO 66 (1991), pp.5–26.

Walcot, P., *Greek Attitudes towards Women: The Mythological Evidence*, G & R 31 (1984), pp.37–47.

Walcot, P., *Hesiod and the Near East* (1966).

Wasinski, V.M., *Women, War and Rape: The Hidden Casualties of Conflict*, Diss. (University of Leeds, 2004).

Webster, T.B.L., 'Homeric Hymns and Society' in *Le Monde Grec. Pensée, Littérature, Histoire, Documents. Hommages à Claire Préaux*, edited by Jean Bingen (Bruxelles, 1975), pp.86–93.

Wheelwright, J., *Amazons and Military Maids* (London, 1989).

Wiles, David, 'Myth', *Greek Theatre Performance: An Introduction* (Cambridge, 2000).

Willcock, M.M., *The Search for the Poet Homer*, Greece & Rome 37 (1990), pp.1–12.

Wood, M., *In Search of the Trojan War* (London, 1985).

Woodard, R.D. (ed.), *The Cambridge Companion to Greek Mythology* (Cambridge, 2007).

Yerkes, R.K., *Sacrifice in Greek and Roman Religions and Early Judaism* (London, 1953).

Zaidman, L.B., *Religion in the Ancient Greek City*, trans. Paul Cartledge (Cambridge, 1992).

Zaidman, L.B., 'Women and War: From the Theban Cycle to Greek Tragedy' in Fabre-Serris, J. (ed.), *Women and War in Antiquity* (2015), pp.82–99.

Index